By Donald Windham

NOVELS
The Dog Star
The Hero Continues
Two People
Tanaquil
Stone in the Hourglass (limited edition)

SHORT STORIES
The Warm Country

AUTOBIOGRAPHY
Emblems of Conduct
*Lost Friendships: A Memoir of Truman Capote,
Tennessee Williams, and Others*

DRAMA
You Touched Me (with Tennessee Williams)

EDITED BY DONALD WINDHAM
E. M. Forster's Letters to Donald Windham (limited edition)
Tennessee Williams' Letters to Donald Windham, 1940–1965

TENNESSEE WILLIAMS' LETTERS TO DONALD WINDHAM · 1940-1965

T. Williams
Am. Ex. Co.
Rome.

A/R//

Donald Windham, Esq.
747 Madison Ave.,
New York, N.Y.

TENNESSEE WILLIAMS' LETTERS TO DONALD WINDHAM 1940-1965

Edited and with comments
by
DONALD WINDHAM

Brown Thrasher Books
The University of Georgia Press
Athens and London

Published in 1996 as a Brown Thrasher Book
by the University of Georgia Press, Athens, Georgia 30602
© 1976, 1977 by Donald Windham
The letter to Kenneth Tynan © 1976 by Tennessee Williams
All other letters and comments © 1976, 1977
by Donald Windham

The paper in this book meets the guidelines for permanence
and durability of the Committe on Production Guidelines
for Book Longevity of the Council on Library Resources.

Printed in the United States of America

00 99 98 97 96   P 5 4 3 2

Library of Congress Cataloging in Publication Data
Williams, Tennessee, 1911–1983.
[Letters to Donald Windham, 1940–1965]
Tennessee Williams' letters to Donald Windham, 1940–1965 / edited and
with comments by Donald Windham.
p. cm.
Includes index.
ISBN 0-8203-1840-X (pbk. : alk. paper)
1. Williams, Tennessee, 1911–1983—Correspondence. 2. Dramatists,
American—20th century—Correspondence. 3. Windham, Donald—
Correspondence. I. Windham, Donald. II. Title.
PS3545.I5365Z49 1996
812'.54—dc20   95-26347

British Library Cataloging in Publication Data available
First published in a limited edition of 526 copies, Verona, Italy,
by Sandy Campbell, 1976.

PREFACE TO THE
BROWN THRASHER EDITION

For this new printing, the fourth since the original limited edition of 526 copies published in 1976, I have replaced a number of omitted names and phrases, the excision of which changed circumstances have made no longer necessary. And I note here that letter no. 49, with Tennessee's uncertain date, is, from internal evidence (Margo Jones still in Pasadena and Tennessee not yet on leave from MGM), slightly out of sequence. On page 99, the footnote to letter no. 51 stating that the University of Texas at Austin has none of my letters to Tennessee among his papers deposited there in the Humanities Research Center, as the University informed me, has turned out to be untrue. The autumn after Tennessee's death, a scholar researching at the University wrote me that he had read a number of my letters to Tennessee there. When I inquired of the University how this could be true in face of the information I had been given, it was explained that there had been no *cataloged* letters from me to Tennessee among his papers; he had deposited them in 1965 in a sealed envelope, contents unlisted, with the restriction that the envelope remain "sealed until the death of Tennessee Williams." An account of this and my letter answering Tennessee's letter no. 51, which was in the envelope, is given in *Lost Friendships*, pp. 188–90.

Finally, this new edition is dedicated to the memory of Sandy Campbell (1922–1988), whose enthusiasm and initiative shaped every detail of the first edition—printed by the Stamperia Valdonega in Verona, Italy, on which all subsequent editions are based—from the original idea of publishing the letters right through to the making of the index.

Donald Windham
New York, 1995

INTRODUCTION

I

In that happy period of the past when I met Tennessee Williams, I could not have created out of my imagination, as one does a character in fiction, a more perfect friend for myself. In my eyes, he combined the heroic fortitude of a Stephen Dedalus with the lovable ineptitude of a Wilkins Micawber; and for someone who liked him, as I did, he added the lagniappe of seeming almost childishly and humbly to need your liking. I have known some people who were indifferent to Tennessee, and some who disliked him, but I have never known anyone who liked him and did not feel the need to protect him. A great deal of the time in those unsuccessful days he was literally punch-drunk from writing. No one I have encountered any place, at any time, in any field of endeavor, labored as intently as he did; and the desire to prevent his walking straight into the wall when he got up from his typewriter, the longing to remind him of some of the meals he was forgetting, was irresistible. He asked no favors, except through his unresisting ineptitude; and his presence bestowed unexpected drama and richness on everyday events. For me at nineteen, his greatest gift was exemplary. His conviction that the best you could create out of yourself in the way of a work of art was a more important goal than any of the conventionally respected aims in life was daily visible in his improvident and dedicated existence. Added to this, he was made up of such an unlikely combination of traits that he possessed the most intriguing of qualities in a friend, an air of mystery.

The mystery came mainly from his contradictory unawareness and awareness. When playing cards with you, he would suddenly feel hungry, get up, open a can of sardines in oil, and begin to eat them with his fingers as he continued the game. Smoking a cigarette, he would smile into space and knock the ashes vaguely in the direction of your shirt pocket. As for being conscious of other people, he would claim never to have met, much less to have conversed with, the people you and he had spent hours talking to the night before. The only thing he apparently concentrated on was his work, and even his method of writing (described graphically if somewhat melo-dramatically in letter 47) exhibited aspects of unawareness. He paid no attention to where the typewritten pages he was tossing from his machine would land – on his table, the floor, the chairs, the bed, or on the piles of dirty clothing around the room.

But when I read the stories he put together from these scattered pages, they were accurately observed portraits of other sentient beings, in accurately observed milieux, per-forming a multiplicity of activities which he gave no hint of knowing anything about in his daily behavior. And from this contradiction, I had the strong impression, reinforced later when I saw him flee from the first tender involvement I knew him to be in, that his entire manner of behavior at that time was the result of his having such a backlog of emo-tional material stored inside him, so much accumulated "by-product of existence" pressing on his heart, that he dared not receive any more, only release the complex images and insights he was packed with, until the pressure of his obser-vations and involvements with the world was poured out in carefully dramatized works of art.

I do not mean to give the impression that he was monklike or grave. His attitude toward sex at the time was so enthu-siastic that he considered "tender" feelings to be involved when his partner was someone known rather than a total stranger. His manner was happy. He walked, if not exactly to the rhythm of "Managua, Nicaragua", as he later described sailors as doing, at least as though he were listening to some far-away tune. An impish smile lurked behind his eyes, one of which was covered by a milky cataract. In the face of everyday difficulties, his sense of humor came out in a wild whoop of laughter. The emotional material stored in him was concealed. I did not, for instance, know until after his success that he lied about his age. I still do not know which of the various explanations he has given for doing this is true. Or why, revealing so much to me, he included me in this deception. But as I grew familiar with him and his stories and plays that first year of our acquaintance, one thing from among the contradictions and mysteries became increasingly clear: his art sprang from his repressed self-knowledge and the resulting ingenuity his sense of self-preservation used in presenting these too-upsetting-to-face revelations to him in an acceptable way. This was corroborated as I gradually discovered that the emotions of the various characters he portrayed were always his own emotions. The completeness with which the characters retained their identities under the burden of the feelings he poured from himself into them only proved the skill of his transference and the individuality of his observations. There isn't a single character in Tennessee's work in the first ten years I knew him that is a simple self-portrait or symbol of himself, but each of them is a crucible in which he releases a part of his concealed self-knowledge.

II

But to get to the letters. In the 1940's, as now, Tennessee was mobile. I was stationary. And when we were in different places he wrote to me. I don't know if he wrote similar letters to other people. Certainly no other person wrote letters like his to me. They are as intimate as his presence was, and often more informative. To read them is to know why I liked him.

Alone with his typewriter, he talked to me almost as to an ideal listener, as though he knew that my faith in him was total. If he sometimes, to use his phrase, is "striking poses on paper", they are poses for himself, not for someone else. These early letters are a running account of what he was doing and thinking, frequently day by day – a gold mine of biographical information.

By the 1950's, our relationship and the letters have changed. Tennessee often says that he didn't change after his success. In an outward sense, and for what consistency is worth, that is true. But everything else changed. Hardly anyone succeeds as an artist in America without first devoting his whole being to the problems of obscurity and failure. Tennessee did this for ten years before 1945; then the tables were turned and overnight he was faced with a whole new set of problems. He combatted them remarkably well for the next five years. But a great deal of his strength must have gone into battles other than those of creation. When his emotional material began to run low, the priceless "by-product of existence" to be in need of replenishing, and he was forced to come out of his shell of unawareness, he found himself, both by design and by fate, in a totally different world from that which had enclosed him and nourished his heart before. I speak only as an observer. We were no longer in the same boat. But by 1955 I believe that both he and his work were suffering from the maneuvers he was making to protect himself and it; and his need for emotional material, combined with his way of life, made it difficult for anyone who did not fall into his plans and serve his particular needs for subject matter and psychic energy to be involved with him.

For my part, in our relationship, I had gone from wanting to protect him to wanting to protect myself. My affection for him as a person had not diminished. But I had discovered that in our encounters I was apt to get hurt. My necessity to have faith in him had gradually metamorphosed into a necessity to understand him. It is hard to be objective. Perhaps over the years I should have sacrificed more of life to work and he should have sacrificed less. In any case, we had different criteria; and I think that this is what he felt about himself. From a certain point on, I discovered that each time he questioned the ethical or aesthetic rightness of a decision he had made he looked toward me, seeking condemnation. I am under no illusion that I was the only person he made the object of this transference. Frank Merlo and Audrey Wood must have received more of it; and in the necessary circumstances practically anybody would serve his purpose. But that is peripheral to these letters. Early in the 1950's, without losing a bit of their emotion or entertainment, they tend to become self-justifying rather than self-dramatizing. The lode vein to be mined of facts, as opposed to insights, grows smaller.

Anyone who wants to get an idealized and simplified portrait of Tennessee isn't going to find it here. He is a complicated person, and it all comes out. His power of transference was, and is, as strong in his life as in his art. If, for example, he accuses you of having once tried to push him off a roof and you are sure you didn't, you may be almost equally sure that he once contemplated doing this to you. From the start, the reader will do well to keep in mind (as I learned to) that when Tennessee praises a piece of writing by someone else he is apt to be saying what he wants to hear about his own work rather than what he thinks of the work under discussion. And the reader will do still better to remember that when Tennessee complains of someone else's opinion of him, he is even more apt to be expressing his discontent with his opinion of himself. Nevertheless, for three-quarters of their length, these letters present the man

XIII

who was there, dramatizing the way things were, a far cry from his version of the same events a quarter of a century later.

III

Facts have a way of changing into fiction. I once read on a book jacket that I had written eighty-eight stories before I wrote one that was published, a once-removed version of my statement that I received eighty-eight rejections before an acceptance – of my first story. Much less innocent transformations take place. There is no need to list here the titles of books about Tennessee that contain made-up scenarios for the periods of his life the authors (even though relatives or friends) were not involved in. But it will be just as well to note that a good deal of this misinformation, however it got there, has ended up in Tennessee's "Memoirs". "Consistency, thy name is not Tennessee!" he says in this book; and "I have trouble with placing events in exact chronological order," in that one. Both statements are true. There is probably not an episode described in the "Memoirs" that did not happen at some time, to some one, in some way, but more likely than not to a different person, at a different time, with different details. Curtain after curtain of ambivalence has descended in his life. Self-portrait after self-portrait has intervened in his plays. And the same qualities that make Tennessee a good dramatist make him an impossible documenter. His stories grow better from morning to evening. After a quarter of a century . . .

Outside of one or two direct mentions, Tennessee's references to me in the "Memoirs" – that is, if it *was* me, to echo his letter about "The Hero Continues" – are all connected with violence or unpleasantness. And he has either forgotten, or someone has edited out, the first two years of

XIV

our friendship. For me it is otherwise. Two years is a long time when you are nineteen. My earlier and pleasanter memories are stronger. In this introduction and in my notes which follow I have avoided stating anything I could not corroborate from old correspondence or journals. But it is mainly in dealing with the later years that I have had to search out evidence of what was going on. I cannot deny the least pleasant things that have happened between us. That goes against the grain of my character. But the more pleasant things are the more important. A great deal of my life would have been different if Tennessee and I had not known each other. He remains the rarest, the most intoxicating, the most memorable flower that has blossomed in my garden of good and evil.

IV

A word about the editing. My aim has been to keep the letters as nearly as possible as written. I have, to the best of my ability, silently corrected mistakes in typing and spelling, but I have usually retained Tennessee's unorthodox use of hyphens, dashes, etc. Added words I have indicated by [ ], omitted names by [—], and cuts by [...]. In two cases, I have adopted the pseudonyms Tennessee gives his friends in his "Memoirs", Santo and Raffaello. In some letters the dates are supplied from the postmarks and may be days later than the actual writing. The majority of the letters are typewritten, or at least begin typewritten before turning to handwriting. Tennessee habitually uses dashes after his salutations when writing by hand and colons when typing; I have followed this and the interested reader can distinguish one from the other.

March, 1976

DONALD WINDHAM

TENNESSEE WILLIAMS' LETTERS
TO DONALD WINDHAM · 1940-1965

The loveliest thing that can occur to me in the Bicentennial year is our resumed contact – I needed it so badly – and the letters to bind it all back together.

Love,

TENNESSEE

January 9, 1976

Tennessee Williams and I met at the beginning of January, 1940. A mutual acquaintance brought him to the furnished room on West Fifty-second Street where Fred Melton and I were living in Manhattan, newly arrived from Atlanta and practically penniless. I was nineteen, Melton two years older. Tennessee, with his boyish good looks and high spirits, seemed to me our age, but he said that he was twenty-five and he was in fact twenty-eight.

I had worked for the previous year and a half as a laborer in a barrel factory in Georgia, Melton as a show-card letterer in a department store. We had come to New York to be with each other, and I think Tennessee was less impressed by our living the sort of improvident life that had been his own for the past few years than by our living it together. In his eyes our attachment was as romantic as his independence was heroic in mine.

Our growing friendship furnished a stable point for the three of us that winter. We went swimming at the West Side Y.M.C.A., where Tennessee was living. On St. Valentine's Day, we traveled downtown and walked through a snowstorm to the New School for Social Research to see Tennessee's one-act play, "The Long Goodbye", presented in the basement theatre – his first production in New York. Easter Sunday, like three proper sons of a Southern family, we attended the morning service at the Cathedral of St. John the Divine. The weather had turned warm. Tennessee was wearing a new straw hat. Compared to Melton and me, he was momentarily rich; he had come to New York on a Rockefeller Foundation fellowship of $1000, which was being given to him at the fabulous rate of one hundred dollars a month; and he had recently won a $100 prize from the Group Theatre for a trio of one-act plays;[1] but he was not yet adjusted to his affluence and his new hat

---

1. In a contest to encourage and discover writers under and up to the age of twenty-five. The main prize of $500 went to Ramon Naya for "Mexican Mural".

3

was lost that morning, a fate that had already overtaken the plaid topcoat he had arrived in town with.

The middle of April, we helped Tennessee to pack and saw him off on a train at Pennsylvania Station. His destination was St. Louis, then Mexico. The first of May, we welcomed him back. He had gotten as far as Mississippi, to call on his grandfather, when he had received a telegram from Lawrence Langner and Theresa Helburn informing him that the Theatre Guild was optioning "Battle of Angels", and thus adding another $100 a month to his income. By then, I had a job selling Coca-Cola at the World's Fair in Flushing. Melton was working in an architect's office. Tennessee went to Lake George to "check the swimming", then returned and the three of us sublet for the summer a duplex apartment on East Thirty-seventh Street. Soon after, Tennessee was off to "check the swimming" in Provincetown; and he shuttled back and forth between New York and the Cape until he left again for Mexico at the end of August, fleeing from his affair with Kip.

The self-mockery and quick-change gender in these early letters ("They have a light touch," Tennessee says, looking them over today) should not be misleading. They are a primitive form of dramatization and transference, a burlesque of the world we were supposed to live in and didn't – except in our senses of humor. As heterodox as our private lives were, our public demeanors were quiet. Tennessee lacked socially the characteristics he mimics verbally as "Auntie Froufrou". He was quite inadequately flamboyant, in his T-shirt and West Coast dungarees, even with his De-Nicotea cigarette holder, to qualify as a member of any "raffish and fantastic crew".

4

.1.

[*Postcard*]

[Lake George, N. Y.]

[*May 15, 1940*]

Got your letter. Let me know what man wants in advance –
if not more than $ 20 will instruct agent[1] to pay him that
amt. May leave here in a day or two tho, as it is too cold to
swim.

Yorestrewly

TENNESSEE

.2.

[*Postcard*]

[Provincetown, Mass.]

[*June 26, 1940*]

It is raining constantly and I left my glasses at home. Otherwise everything perfect. Met "our little group" last night.

10.

.3.

[30 Commercial St.] Provincetown, Mass.

[*June 28, 1940*] *Friday A. M.*

Dear boys –

Your old Auntie Froufrou is having herself a very gay time
at the Cape. Only trouble is the old bitch left her glasses at
home and wonders if you children would be good enough
to mail 'em to her special delivery – She'll send you something

1. Liebling-Wood: William Liebling and his wife Audrey Wood. The year
before, Miss Wood had begun to represent Tennessee and continued to do so
for more than thirty years.

real nice in return – and I don't mean something for a sick friend.[1]

The "crowd" here is dominated by a platinum blond Hollywood belle named Doug and a bull-dike named Wanda who is a well-known writer under a male pen-name. The most raffish and fantastic crew that I have met yet and even I – excessively broadminded as I am – feel somewhat shocked by the goings-on.

However the sun has come out and the lonely sand-dunes, sea-gulls and blue ocean is an excellent katharsis for a "sin-sick soul." All of this will go very nicely into a play some day.

I have rented a bike for $ 4.00 a week and a room for $ 5 right on the beach. John Dos Passos lives here – I will try to meet him. Also the artist Peter Hunt.

I decided to quit drinking and I bet my resolution lasted 24 hours longer than yours did, Butch.[2] I fell off the wagon last night with 3 rum collins and a carioca zombie. The Hollywood belle and I got in a fight over a piece of trade, a Yale freshman, the trade got away from us both and we went home together.

Eheu!

(An old Biblical expression.)

Don't forget the glasses. I don't know where I left 'em – looked for 'em every place but your room, Fred, as you were asleep. Let me know if they are lost as I'll have to buy new ones – lots of work on a new play to be done and can't start without them.

When I get back to New York I'm going to reform – get all this bitching out of my system and lead a new life. Maybe

1. Tag line of a queer joke I heard among the chauffeurs in the garages in the West Fifties.
2. My nickname for Melton.

enter a monastery – Can't say how long I'll be here – maybe a week, maybe two.

Write me and forward mail.

I love you both.

TENN.

·4·

[*Postcard*]

[Provincetown, Mass.]

[*July 4, 1940*]

Thanks for glasses. New address – ≠ 6 Capt. Jack's Wharf. Please forward mail. Swimming great now. Swell time.

10. WMS.

·5·

[*Note left in apartment, 151 East 37th Street, July, 1940*]

Dear Fred –

Stinky[1] phoned he'd be late – Sorry I didn't get back – lots of biznez – Solong –

10.

So long Stinky.

(over)

Been talking to myself for hours – love or schizophrenia or *both*!

Wish me luck.

.6.

[Captain Jack's Wharf, Provincetown, Mass.]

[*July 29 and 30, 1940*] *Monday P.M.*

Dear Donnie:

Your letter came at a very opportune moment as I was

---

1. Melton's nickname for me, to counter my sweet appearance.

7

feeling blue. My life is now full of emotional complications which make me write good verse – at least a lot of it – but make my mental chart a series of dizzy leaps up and down, ecstasy one moment – O dapple faun! – and consummate despair the next. Never thought I could go through something like this again. But never do you know!

Depression this morning occasioned by fact the ballet dancer stayed out all night. So far no explanation, though I suspect a nymph at the other end of the wharf and am moving to a single bed downstairs till suspicions confirmed or dispelled.

Shades of Gilbert Maxwell.[1] Isn't it hell?

But, oh, God, Stinkie, I wish you could see him in his blue tights!

Well –

It looks like I may stay here a week or so longer. Aside from the emotional business, life here is delightful. I am being courted by a musician and a dancing instructor and a language professor, one of them has a big new Buick and drives us all over the Cape. They all want Kip but hope to English off me or something since he is so apparently less accessible than me – an unmistakable bitch. – I think love has made me young again, or maybe it's the blue dungarees.

Full of quaint and curious people, this town, and the sand-dunes, sea-gulls and the clear, cool tranquil bay water is "Il Paradiso" sung by Enrico Caruso!

I even have a little female on the wharf who wants to be an actress and washes my sweat-shirts for me.

They had another announcement of my play in Sunday *Times*. Said the play cast first would be the first produced. But I have heard no definite statement from Langner.

If everything fizzles out I'll come home very quickly. But

1. One of whose memorable remarks was, "I am faithful to all three of them, and not a one of them is faithful to me!"

8

please don't hope to see me that soon. – Has Beatty[1] sent in? If she does keep the fifteen for rent. Otherwise I will send it. – Let me know. – You might write her personally – give her a goose in the conscience if she has one!

Love to you both, remember me in your orisons, sweet nymph –

TENNESSEE

Later: Everything is okay again and I didn't have to move downstairs after all. He slept alone on the beach because he needed some sleep. Doesn't get much with me. But that's his own fault for being so incredibly beautiful. We wake up two or three times in the night and start all over again like a pair of goats. The ceiling is very high like the loft of a barn and the tide is lapping under the wharf. The sky amazingly brilliant with stars. The wind blows the door wide open, the gulls are crying. Oh, Christ. I call him baby like you call Butch, though when I lie on top of him I feel like I was polishing the Statue of Liberty or something. He is so enormous. A great bronze statue of antique Greece come to life. But with a little boy's face. A funny up-turned nose, slanting eyes, and under-lip that sticks out and hair that comes to a point in the middle of his forehead. I lean over him in the night and memorize the geography of his body with my hands – he arches his throat and makes a soft, purring sound. His skin is steaming hot like the hide of a horse that's been galloping. It has a warm, rich odor. The odor of life. He lies very still for a while, then his breath comes fast and his body begins to lunge. Great rhythmic plunging motion with panting breath and his hands working over my body. Then sudden release –

1. Babs Beatty, an actress, in a room of whose apartment on West 121st Street Melton and I had lived briefly before we moved to Thirty-seventh Street. Tennessee had lent her fifteen dollars, a big event that year in his financial life.

and he moans like a little baby. I rest with my head on his stomach. Sometimes fall asleep that way. We doze for a while. And then I whisper "Turn over." He does. We use brilliantine. The first time I come in three seconds, as soon as I get inside. The next time is better, slower, the bed seems to be enormous. Pacific, Atlantic, the North American continent. – A wind has blown the door open, the sky's full of stars. High tide is in and water laps under the wharf. And now we're so tired we can't move. After a long while he whispers, "I like you, Tenny." – hoarse – embarrassed – ashamed of such intimate speech! – And I laugh for I know that he loves me! – That nobody ever loved me before so completely. I feel the truth in his body. I call him baby – and tell him to go to sleep. After a while he does, his breathing is deep and even, and his great deep chest is like a continent moving slowly, warmly beneath me. The world grows dim, the world grows warm and tremendous. Then everything's gone and when I wake up it is daylight, the bed is empty. – Kip is gone out. – He is dancing. – Or posing naked for artists. Nobody knows our secret but him and me. And now *you*, Donnie – because you can understand.

Please keep this letter and be very careful with it. It's only for people like us who have gone beyond shame![1]

10.

·7·
[Captain Jack's Wharf, Provincetown, Mass.]
[*August 6 and 8, 1940*] *Tuesday P. M.*

Dear kids:

I presume you received no remittance from that great but slightly overweight Bernhardt of Rhode Island,[2] so perforce

1. The first note of Tennessee's identifying me with his conscience.
2. Beatty, now working at a theatre in Rhode Island.

must delve into the perilously depleted sock for rent money. While in New York, Butch, I gave you ten dollars to cover some debts, personal and domestic, including, I thought, the telephone and electric light. If this is another bill that has come in subsequently, let me know and I will cogitate further. If you got two drinks out of Blondie,[1] by God, you shouldn't be discouraged about getting money from me!

Life here is very beautiful and serene, I am taking free conga lessons, working on a long, narrative poem, swimming every day, drinking every day, and fucking every night. What more could I reasonably ask for? Except to see you and Donnie.

Let me hear from you.

Love,

10.

Thursday.

Fred – Got your letter. Awfully glad you don't need complete payment all at once as I am in pretty tight spot at the moment. Here is ten bucks. Will send rest when my next cheque comes in the 16th.

Did you see the write-up I got under caption "New Playwright" in the *Herald Tribune* last Sunday, August 4?

Elevated my stock quite a bit on Capt. Jack's Wharf.

The belles are jingling gaily all over town and I am still in love.

But, oh, God, Fred, it's "competition in restraint of trade" – when you have to compete with a *woman*!

You are very lucky your little Stinkie is *completely* queer. Mine isn't, alas.

They had a "drag" at the "White Whale" night club last night. Most of the boys went as girls but Froufrou thought

1. A co-worker of mine at the Fair, whom Tennessee had bedded.

11

it would be more of a masquerade if she went as a *man*, so she *did*. Woo!

Your prodigal father

10.

P.S. Kip and I will probably stay out the month here. Return Sept. 1st. – *Don't* let the Saroyan actor[1] impose on you! It's *useless*.

.8.

[*Postcard*]
[Monterrey, N. L., Mexico]
[*August 29, 1940*]

Fabulous trip! Write in detail when finished. Address – General Delivery at Acapulco, Gro., Mexico, and *do* write, will you? Feel pretty good now. Adventures – ahoy.

TENN.

.9.[2]

[Acapulco, Mexico]
[*mid?-September, 1940*]

Dear Fred:

Awfully glad to hear from you. You must think me an awful bastard not having written sooner or sent money. The fact

1. An actor from "The Time of Your Life" who turned up for free meals.

2. Partly written, as the letters often are, on a draft of a poem. This one reads:

When will the sleeping tiger stir
among the jungles of the heart?
I seem to hear the sound of her
gentle breathing in the dark.

O you that are deceived by this
apparent innocence, take care!
You know that storms are presaged by
such trembling stillness in the air.

And all that breathe have in their breast
capacity for certain flame.

Domesticated cats are merely
beasts pretending to be tame.

Not for the pelt but for the passion
would I track that tiger down,
to dwell with her more dangerously
beyond the lighted streets of town!

TENNESSEE WILLIAMS
Acapulco, September, 1940

12

of the matter is I have been going through the most difficult period of my life so far and I must ask those who are my friends to bear with me for a while till things straighten out a bit. Breaking up with Kip was only an incident in a long cumulation of tensions and difficulties, actual and psychic, and the result was a sort of temporary obliteration of every-thing solid in me and all I thought of was my own immediate preservation through change, escape, travel, new scenes, new people. You don't realize quite what an awful state I was in or how hopeless I felt when I left New York. I actually hoped that my bad cough was tuberculosis or that some convenient accident would occur on the road and I would be relieved of the tedious problem of remaining alive.

Now I am glad to say that most of that is passed. I begin to feel fairly solid again and though the future is just as un-certain as when I left, I feel more ability to face things. I have been here in Acapulco about two weeks and the tranquil spirit of the tropics, hours of swimming and sun-bathing and a few sympathetic friends and a new lover have restored my faith in the possibility of going on with this strange business called life. Right now, my dear boy, I have about thirty centavos in my pocket which is such a negligible sum that it is barely translatable in terms of American money – something like four cents, I suppose. I sent a telegram to the folks last night for a twenty-dollar loan but haven't received an answer yet. Perhaps they are disgusted and decided to ignore my plea. My royalty check from the Guild has not arrived yet despite the fact that I asked them to send it early – it is now two days over-due. Wouldn't it be a beautiful kettle of fish if they had abruptly decided to drop the play and leave me stranded down here, where I couldn't get within shooting range of them? Well, I am convinced that I have stood enough in my life so far to be able to stand even that. Of course I don't actually believe that is going to happen, but

I must face the possibility. They are a goddam cold-blooded bunch [...]. I knew that when they sprung the phoney "reading option" check on me when we first began our negotiations. I am not looking for anything but self-interest in that direction so nothing would surprise me too much. – Perhaps I am being unjust. Time will tell.

So you see it is manifestly impossible for me to mail any money at this moment. I trust you are suitably grateful that I don't ask you all to send *me* any cash. – I don't!

We of the artistic world, my dear Alphonso – are the little gray foxes and all the rest are the hounds. We try to keep one jump ahead of the pack, and that is all, and that is the best we can do. The butcher, the baker, the candle-stick maker – also the typewriter rent man and the landlord, Etc. – are our natural enemies. We expect no quarter from them and are determined to give them none. It is a fight to the death, never mistake about that. I wish I could tell you how many houses I have sneaked out of in the middle of the night when rent was over-due, how many restaurant charge accounts I have neglected to pay, how many clothing, cleaning, pressing, Etc. bills I have permanently consigned to my capacious shirt-cuffs. The sum total would amaze not only you but me, too. Yet I don't feel that I am a fundamentally dishonest person, do you? Such tricks I was forced to resort to in the very beginning in order to survive. And on the other side of the ledger, I have generously shared whatever I had with people who needed it – for instance Babs.

Soooooo – All I can say is I will meet all my present New York obligations as soon as I can take the money out of funds necessary for my immediate survival.

Fuck the typewriter man. He has my old machine as rent till I can afford to pay him. – I will send Webster – at least part of the rent soon as – and if – the royalty check arrives. I appreciate his goodness to us and I really feel – *sincerely* – sorry about not paying him promptly.

But don't bear my sins upon your conscience, dear boy.

Right now I can't think of two people I like better than you and Donnie in all the world, so please don't criticize me too harshly for the next little while.

Love –

10.

.10.

[53 Arundel Place, Clayton, Mo.]
Oct. 11, 1940

Dear Don:

I've written Fred a letter so this one's for you. I'm back from Mexico and will probably soon be headed back to New York. I got a letter from Helburn the other day saying she was in long-distance communication with Hopkins, off and on, and that she was definitely interested and if she could arrange a recess from Hollywood, she would come East for the part in my play, so I should hold myself in readiness to return. This gives things a somewhat brighter appearance. She said Langner was absorbed in his own play now and that all of them were tied up with Helen Hayes, but my production *might* be the next in line.[1]

I am also supposed to return about a radio possibility. It seems that CBS is looking for someone to take over writing a weekly half-hour drama on Lincoln, at one hundred dollars

1. As an example of Tennessee's *continuing* dramatization, when he writes *The History of a Play* in 1944 for the publication of "Battle of Angels" this has become: ". . . shortly after we had again entered the States, I got hold of a copy of *The New York Times* and was startled to read in the dramatic columns that the Theatre Guild was doing 'Battle of Angels' as their initial play of the season and that Miss Miriam Hopkins had already flown from Hollywood to take the leading role. Well, I returned post-haste to New York . . ."

per script, and Liebling is negotiating to get me the job. It is now in the hands of E. P. Conkle, an old professor of mine, who recommended me for it.

Still more good news: I've finished a new comedy (long)[1] which looks pretty good and some of my one-acts are going to appear in two books, one by Dodd-Mead, "Best One-Acts of 1940"[2] and another, rather four others, in anthology called "American Scenes"[3] to be published in spring by John Day Co. Won't gross more than fifty dollars on these anthologies but getting the plays before public may result in amateur productions.

My last cheque came in after a considerable delay in the mail and I had nothing left over after I paid bills and transportation back here. But you can reassure my various creditors about future payments as it looks like I might be in the chips before so terribly long.

In Mexico no revolution, nothing but grease. The place was delightful but I simply couldn't take the food. We called it "frijole junction" – beans, beans, beans! The sleeping porch sounded like a shooting gallery at night. Finally my stomach just wouldn't take anymore so I had to leave – after one month. Had one brief, exciting affair with a native – Carlos from Vera Cruz! – and a long, dull, complicated one with a neurotic American writer from Tahiti who wants me to share an apt. with him in New Orleans this winter, or in Key West, Florida, but that appears to be out of the question now, if I wanted to, even. He was a football star at Michigan some yrs. ago and son of General Mgr. of [. . .] Co. – extremely wealthy – but always talking about suicide.

These and a change of scene accomplished their purpose and Kip is something that never enters my mind. Strange

1. "Stairs to the Roof".
2. "Moony's Kid Don't Cry".
3. Two were printed: "This Property Is Condemned" and "At Liberty".

how unreal an intense affair becomes in retrospect, much less actual-seeming than any number of small ones, and the personality of the one so intensely loved is more obscure, more indefinite, afterwards, than a casual friend's usually is. Probably because you never really got to know, you simply surrounded him with fiction, so when that fiction was shed by separation or loss, there was nothing left. Except a couple of letters, nice and affectionate, but from a person unknown.

So when you lose your baby – God forbid! – remember the world doesn't end as easily as that.

I feel very guilty running off from you all with debts unpaid and everything so unsettled. It was unavoidable, though. I always do instinctively what I know is necessary to save me, and that was necessary just then. I don't think it is right for me to take an apt. with people because I am so restless, so unstable, my intentions are good invariably, I want to do the right thing, but can never predict what will happen. Fundamentally selfish of course like everyone else.

I may leave here for N. Y. the eighteenth or twentieth and Mother is planning to come back there with me for a visit. I'll just stick her in a hotel and leave her mostly to her own devices – she is one of the nicest and most boring people on earth!

Have to play jam here and I'm getting horny as a jackrabbit, so line up some of that Forty-second Street trade for me when I get back. Even Blondie would do!

Was "Baby" faithful to you in Atlanta? Were you faithful to Baby? What are you going to do when the Fair closes? – Good luck!

If you write me, make it before the sixteenth so I'll be here to receive it. They open all my letters that come during my absence. – Marvelous espionage system!

So long –

10.

17

Hope you're doing some writing. *The Warm Country* – have you finished that? – We must find you some work that will give you time to write. I have some fine photographs for you, by Moctezuma.

Tennessee, wearing jodhpurs, returned to New York in November for the rehearsals of "Battle of Angels". Melton and I had moved to a cold-water flat in the East Seventies, and at the beginning of 1941 we took a larger apartment nearby with Jordan Massee and Paul Bigelow, whom we had known in Georgia. After the abrupt closing of "Battle" in Boston, Tennessee stopped in New York for the first of a series of cataract operations. He recuperated a few days at our Seventy-third Street apartment, then went on to Key West. In the spring he returned, via Atlanta, to St. Louis to touch home base once again.

.11.

The Trade Winds, Key West, Florida
[*February 13, 1941*]

Messrs. Paul, Jordan, Freddie, Donnie
Dear Kids:

I am situated in a tiny cabin in back of the 125-year-old mansion pictured above, my residence being what was formerly the slave-quarters. It is a beautiful old ante-bellum house, four stories and built entirely of mahogany – incredible as that may seem. It has a very romantic history. It seems that some old sea-captain promised his fiancée in New England that he would build her the biggest house in Key West if she would marry him and come to live with him here. Apparently she did.

It is now owned by a retired Episcopal clergyman's widow[1] – rather permanently retired, huh? – Jim[2] and I spent

1. Mrs Cora Black, the mother of Marion Vaccaro to whom Tennessee dedicated "Orpheus Descending".
2. Jim Parrott, an old traveling companion of Tennessee's.

19

our first night here in a sort of bridal suite that cost us five dollars for the one night. The widow and I were mutually charmed and I told her if I were rich I would remain indefinitely and she said, My dear, you don't have to be rich, I'll let you have the entire slave-quarters for eight dollars a week! Which is what I was paying for that little linen closet at the Y – everytime I entered it I used unconsciously to sniff for the cheese!

Jim is taking a flying course and could only stay a couple of days. He drove back yesterday so I am pretty much alone. I want you to know, however, that the town is literally swarming with men in uniform, mostly sailors in very tight white pants, but with a liberal dash of soldiers and marines. It seems there are maneuvers or something. Anyhow it is *extremely* interesting! The only trouble is the shore police who patrol the town like crazy. The poor sailors have to walk a chalk line. But I suppose they slip off it now and then. There are loads of bars, Sloppy Joe's being the main one with Ernest Hemingway's signature on one of the stools.

Today was the first bright day. I rented a bicycle for the week and went out to the beach. An English lady had invited me to her cabana where I met the famous philosopher John Dewey. He is 82 years old and spry as a monkey. Tomorrow I'm invited to meet the well-known poet Elizabeth Bishop and I have a dinner date with a wealthy old Auntie so I probably won't be lonesome very long even if the sailors are cagey. I would be pretty contented if it were not for an abominable ear-ache which has been plaguing me for the past five days. Some old veterinarian gave me a prescription for it which actually made it worse. Honestly if anything more happens to this old carcass of mine I'm going to sell it to the glue factory. Do you know there is a lot to be said for just the absence of pain, if you don't have anything else in life.

I also have a back tooth that is rotting to pieces and probably causing the ear-ache – I will have to have it extracted soon as my cheque comes in. Which reminds me I haven't paid you all for my board. Paul can deduct it from the five dollars he owes me.

I am not even trying to write till I get more rested. I seriously doubt that my ideas for revision will correspond with the Theatre Guild's so after these two months are up I may be in a very uncomfortable situation. Fortunately I am in a place where one can live on a string and a bent pin if necessary.

It seems that "Liberty Jones"[1] was pretty badly received.

Excuse me. I am being called to the phone. Write – all of you – when you have time.

Love,

10.

.12.

[*Postcard of "Battle of Atlanta", Cyclorama Building.*]
[Atlanta, Ga.]
[*April 26, 1941*]

This is how I feel after 2 weeks on the road! Just called yo' mothuh! She says you simply *must* come home! Surprise. Is well. Awful dull town. I *loved* Savannah. Now St. Louis, then N. Y.

Love,

10.

.13.

[53 Arundel Place, Clayton, Mo.]
[*May 1, 1941*]

Dear Fred:

At last you've written me, you infernal bitch! Letter followed my erratic course through Darien, Meridian, Savannah

1. A play by Philip Barry, with music by Paul Bowles, produced by the Theatre Guild.

21

and Atlanta and finally reached me here in St. Louis, too late for me to meet all those fascinating Atlanta people, except the ones on the street. I had a marvelous, marvelous time on the road, everybody who picked me up was so interesting, from millionaires to lovely young truck-drivers and not excluding a woman who told me five minutes after I got in the car that she'd just escaped from the hospital, having suffered a concussion of the brain the day before in an automobile accident. I couldn't get out of the car until she wrecked it. I came through all of this relatively unscathed and I am now resting up in the home-town before departing for New York, soon as Audrey sends my next cheque. I am still living off the Theatre Guild, though they have not seen the revised play yet nor renewed option. Saving fellowship money[1] till I get back East.

I have just about satisfied my traveling bug for a while and the idea of sharing your apartment this summer sounds heavenly to me. I am planning to buy a motorcycle when I get back to N. Y. and when the urge to move comes upon me, we can take little week-end trips to the summer colonies, as I will have a side-car on the cycle for you and Stinkie. If they are going to do the play at Westport as announced, I will probably spend some time up there, and Kenyon Nicholson has invited me to live as guest playwright at the Bucks County Playhouse, in New Hope, Pa., but I don't think I could take very much of that. But there will probably be plenty of opportunity for meeting interesting people which should make the summer pleasant. The new script looks pretty good, and if the T. G. likes it and renews option, I will have plenty of money to have a good time. I am becoming a more and more complete hedonist. As the world grows worse, it seems more necessary to grasp what pleasure you can, to be selfish and blind, except in your work,

1. A $500 renewal of the Rockefeller Foundation grant.

and live just as much as you have a chance to. Right now my nerves are exhausted from over-work, I have been at it without intermission since I left N. Y. – I will have to rest for a while.

My kid brother Dakin is directing and playing leading role in Ibsen's "Hedda Gabler" at the university – I am going over to assist the direction this afternoon. Aside from this, there is no activity here, I haven't called anybody and I will slip out of town without seeing anybody if I can manage it, as there is nothing deadlier than the old crowd I used to go around with here. There are just about five people in the world I care to see, two of them being you and Stinkie.

Love and best wishes.

P.S. Jordan and Paul make seven.

LETTER 14

Tennessee was in and out of New York between the last letter and this one, almost a year later. He arrived hopefully that May with the rewrite of "Battle of Angels", then went on, as the year before, to Provincetown. When he returned in August, the T. G. had rejected his rewrite and life in the Seventy-third Street apartment was in chaos. Melton had joined the Coast Guard. I was working at an unemployment-agency-found office job. Massee had gone south to Sea Island. Bigelow and I were not speaking. And the electricity had been cut off because no one would pay the bill. Tennessee stayed with Bigelow for a week while I went to Atlanta to see my mother. When I returned, Melton was stationed on Staten Island and we took an apartment in the Village on Leroy Street.

I do not remember the sequence of events that fall and winter; but Tennessee, both Guild and Rockefeller money gone, was in the Village part of the time. He stayed in the apartment of Fritz Bultman, a new friend from Provincetown. For a while, he worked at Valesca Gert's Beggar's Bar as a poetry-reciting waiter, wearing a black eyepatch after another cataract operation. Erwin Piscator, at the New School, had announced that he would put on "Battle of Angels"; but the production fell through when Tennessee discovered that the German director had "rewritten" the play with scissors, cutting up the speeches and giving them to different characters, and was planning to present it as a political document on life in the South. Before the year was out, he fled to New Orleans.

.14.
[53 Arundel Place, Clayton, Mo.]
2/24/42

Dear Donnie:

I meant to be in N. Y. by now – suddenly broke out with a dreadful itching rash. I thought sure I finally had the old

Joe so I rushed to the family doctor. He sent me to a skin specialist and it was pronounced to be The Seven Year Itch! There is an epidemic of it here among school-kids. And other undeveloped types. So I got it. I had to spend three days in long underwear and a coat of grease without bathing. Now I have graduated to lotions and ointments and bathing is permitted and the itch has subsided to where I can think of other things. If it has become non-infectious by this week-end I can leave town. But Gracious, what a mess! Me and the lower organisms have always had trouble. Fortunately they say you can [get] rid of it entirely in three weeks instead of the original long term with options. Have you heard of it in N. Y.? It is terribly prevalent here, even among us suburban bath-takers. But of course the family is outraged and appalled and I am told that gentlemen just don't have such things!

We've finally heard from Dakin after six scarey weeks of silence. He has arrived in India after "a long voyage with lots of nice officers".

I am reading "Moby Dick". Have you ever? It is lovely writing, and the tattooed cannibal in it would please you, as he apparently did the hero if I understand him correctly.

How is N. Y. now? But I will find out – won't I? Here it is really nice at last, smokey gold afternoons with plum-colored sunsets through the oaks on the campus – dogs and children chasing around the yards and nobody, nobody I know anymore but that old woman who writes me the letters – Alice! – she calls me twice a day. I will be ready for some society when I get to N. Y. – that is, if I've stopped itching.

TENN.

What a lot of itching
there is in life!   "The Life of a Sitting Target"
                                      (My Auto-biog.)

25

LETTERS 15-28

When Tennessee arrived in New York at the beginning of March, things were more chaotic than ever. I had quit my job. With Melton paying our rent from his subsistence allowance, I thought I could live on my savings and write. But Melton, visualizing himself as the center of a "Design for Living", and consulting no one, immediately married a friend of Massee's from Macon. I stayed at the apartment while she returned home to get her boxer dog, but the rug was pulled out from under my feet. My first project had been a play based on D. H. Lawrence's short story You Touched Me, *of which I had written an outline and several scenes. When Tennessee read them, he said that the play had greater commercial possibilities than I could realize alone and suggested that he collaborate with me. We worked furiously – hoping for at least such option money as he had received on "Battle" – first in the Leroy Street apartment, then in my room at the Sixty-third Street Y.M.C.A., where I moved when Melton's wife, Sara, returned. I was in a kind of daze, unable to believe what had happened. My money was disappearing fast. Tennessee, too broke to afford a room at the Y, was living in a nightmarish setup with an older song writer and his alcoholic friends.*

The first of June, Paul Cadmus, whom Melton and I had met the year before, and who looked on our attachment as romantically as Tennessee did, offered to help me. His studio, shared with Jared French, was in the next block to the Leroy Street apartment. Sara had a job, and Cadmus said that I could sleep at his place, when French had gone home, if I could work at Melton's in the daytime. The hours I was not supposed to be at either place, I spent in a diner on Christopher Street or walking by the river.

Soon after we finished the first version of the play and Tennessee left for Macon, French and his wife went away for the summer. Cadmus, who was in and out of the city, let me stay day and night at his studio, where the only person who now came to paint was his

26

sister, Fidelma. She had recently married Lincoln Kirstein, then away in South America, and she began to take me home with her for dinner. My situation was uncertain, from day to day; but the prospects of the play sustained me. I had almost no need for money. I worked on my writing. And I was on my own – as Tennessee had been for many years – for the first time in my life.

.15.

West Side Y. M. C. A., 5 West 63rd St. New York, N. Y.
[May 31, 1942] Sunday P. M.

Donnie –
Sorry missed you.
This card is all I have with me but can get you more or merely give my name at door if you want to take others.[1]
Today wrote new story *One Arm* about the 1-armed blond hustler in New Orleans – I want to show to you.[2]
I think I will leave for Macon next week-end.
Will call you tomorrow or call me.

10.

We have been having a dreadful time with the Baroness.[3] Last night she passed out three different places, Lindy's, The Monkey Bar and Savoy Plaza – interrupted the entertainment with wild out-cries about the glorious death of her imaginary brother at Pearl Harbor. This A. M. she phoned that she had run out of liquor in her apartment. Carley rushed over with a quart of Scotch and I am expected to join them in about an hour! *En* AVANT!

1. To see "This Property Is Condemned" at The New School for Social Research.

2. As an example of Tennessee's dramatization of everyday life, from my journal, Monday, June 1, 1942: "Tenn came by and showed me a new story, *One Arm*, and read my *The Hitchhiker*. He said there was no one literate who had led the lives we live."

3. An ex-actress friend of Carley Mills', with whom Tennessee was living.

[Note left at 119 Leroy Street apartment, June 3, 1942]

Dear Don –

I wanted to pick up my mss. as I leave tomorrow, probably late afternoon. If you will not be at home tomorrow about 2 P. M. could you leave the short stories with your (Fred's) apt. superintendent and I will pick them up. I have the play script and left the discard at Audrey's office. I told her you would pick it up. This will give you a good excuse to see her again. She hasn't heard yet from Collins (the Lawrence agent). She thinks the set should be simplified, possibly by eliminating the study. I don't think that is necessary though of course the daybed *could* be in alcove. I presume it is okay for me to keep our one copy a while to work on. I think Audrey will have it typed for us as soon as she is convinced we won't work on it any longer. She was very cheerful and laying a new plush carpet in her office – must be in the chips. If I don't see you, my best always –

TENN.

507 Georgia Ave., Macon, Ga.
[June 14, 1942]

Dear little brother:

In the few days I have been here so much has taken place it would require an epic work to give a full account. This letter is necessarily telegraphic and allusive rather than comprehensive. First of all, I like Macon and I think I will stay here, not merely because I haven't money to go anywhere else but because it seems as good a place to retire from the world as any. Bigelow is flourishing – like the root of all evil. He has gotten rather plump and while the jaw still troubles him I do not think it appears so serious as at times in the past. He read me the whole play of his at one sitting and I found it to be potentially a very powerful thing and I hope he will keep at it. It needs a little more "Ham", but has all the substance of a beautiful play. – I wish you would read a story called *The Fox* in a D. H. Lawrence volume of short novels called "The Captain's Doll". It is basically the same story as ours, the two women and man triangle – only these two women are not sisters but out and out "Lesbos" and the boy kills the rival one by chopping a tree down to fall on her. And the symbol of a fox is used very effectively – the boy is like a fox raiding a hen-coop. Bigelow says it is like me assaulting these little southern chickens – but that is beside the point. At any rate, it has some stuff in it we can use in the play, notably the fox – I don't know just how to use it yet but I think we can.

I have a job for next year. When I left you at the New School that last afternoon in New York Piscator offered me work starting in September as his publicity agent for the Studio Theatre and said I would receive money enough to live on. This is a great load off my mind as I don't think I could stand much more of this grubbing existence nor did I relish the prospect of returning to C.'s in the Fall. Then of course having a position in a theatre provides an out-let for plays and we could do worse than an experimental production of the comedy there. Incidentally there is a woman here, director of the Wesleyan drama dept., who wants to open their Fall season with the play and that might also be a good trial for us. A trial performance is better than half a year's revisions. Of course I gave her no promise and there is plenty of time about it.

I was interviewed by the newspaper – Bigelow called them immediately to tell them that "a distinguished young man of letters, collaterally descended from the Macon poet,

Sidney Lanier, was his guest" – a large article was printed –
It sounded rather like an account of a sporting-event as it
was written by the sports-editor, but it was amusing and has
resulted in the desired effect, a great many invitations to tea
and dinner. – Yes, I am rather like the fox in the hen-coop
down here, but I am not going to have my brush nailed on the
barn-door nor am I going to remain lean very long. – I was
received by Mme. Massee,[1] the great one, and I have met Andrew and found him to be a charming little creature – breast
of milkfed chicken!

The lake is wonderful for swimming and I also have a
membership at the "Y". – Harry[2] has received news from
Sara of Freddie going to sea and he says the family has accepted the news with admirable poise. He entertained us for
dinner last night at the best restaurant in town. Paul and I are
both to visit Sea Island later on.

I started writing yesterday – very slow so far as I am proceeding with caution. I don't want to risk changing more
than essential. I am doing most on the father right now.

All the soldiers in town are ugly – practically all, though
vast in number. – The "girls" are much more attractive.

I want to know how things are going at your end of the
line.

My regards to Fred, Paul, Sara, and French.

TENNESSEE

See Alan Ladd in "This Gun for Hire".

If you care to, write a scene in which Emmie or Matilda
mention a fox that has been raiding the chicken house and
ask Hadrian to kill it. – A wild thing in the tame place. –
Hadrian prefers the fox to the fowls. Though perhaps he
shoots it: – action.

1. Jordan's mother.
2. Sara's brother.

Later – "Jacked off" on a short scene this A. M. – The Mme.[1] is thrashing briskly about our 3-room suite with a duster – and I am singing to her as she works, which gives her no end of comfort.

.18.

[507 Georgia Ave., Macon, Ga.]
[*June 24, 1942*]

Dear Donnie:

The burning of the block of ware-houses and you wandering around with black eyes and cut lip[2] sounds like the "fin du monde": perhaps it can be used beautifully in a story, with drunkenness and smoke from the fire and sultry summer night heat and that peculiar desolation that the Village has in summer, but I don't like to think about it. I cannot imagine anybody striking you. It brings the ferocity of our times too close to home.

I continue to like it here, perhaps even better than I did New Orleans but in a totally different way and only because I was so fearfully tired and this was so exactly what my exacerbated nerves were in need of. It is funny how instinct draws me to what I need for survival at the last moment always. Andrew and Paul make it nice. Paul and I work and discuss our plays together and seem to help each other a lot. Andrew still has a crew hair-cut and I regard him as being extraordinarily beautiful and after a long string of purely objective relations it's good for me to exercise a capacity for tender feelings.

Then there is H[–]. I wonder if you know him? He is my connection with the gay-mad world. He has the most fantastic house, decorated by himself. It is the maddest

1. Bigelow.
2. I had been beaten up in the Village.

31

Victorian decoration with yellow silk parasols for lamps and gilt and scarlet framed mirrors for tables – that sort of thing – he calls it "Club Rococo". Tyner[1] is coming to see him and also Walter Neblett, probably this week-end, and there will be a big party. And H[—] has promised to take me up to Atlanta to visit the crowd there. Paul is not on good terms with H[—] so that is a sort of double life I lead here.

I have written the fox into the play. His first attack comes the night of the touching and it is Emmie's wild shots that bring Matilda downstairs, in negligee – after that she enters the study and touches Hadrian. Emmie always misses the fox and kills a rooster. The second attack comes while they are waiting for the police in the parlor. While Emmie's out to shoot the fox, Hadrian wins over Matilda with an embrace – once again Emmie misses the fox and at the close of the scene the father enters with the dead rooster, the pride of the hen-yard, and announces that all the hens are now widows. – I read Paul the first few scenes and he thought the play "excellent" and we laughed our heads off at the tea-scene which now contains a passage in which the Minister obliquely suggests a purely sexless marriage to Emmie, just before the father bursts out. – Let us hope this play will put an end to our impecuniosity. Oh, yes, Audrey wrote that Lawrence's estate had agreed to a 60-40 basis – she thought it should be 70-30 and said if I thought so I should write her a strong letter to that effect. I felt, however, that 60-40 was good enough to accept rather than possibly anger Mrs. Lawrence into refusing the release. What do you think? You might talk to Audrey about it. – It was a big relief to me to know we could use the story.

I also got a letter from Robert Lewis the director confirming his determination to produce the one-acts. He is

1. Don Tyner, mentioned in the "Memoirs" as "a young man of Cherokee or Choctaw extraction".

talking to financiers and may try them out first in Hollywood where he is going to spend the summer.[1] – No money from him, though.

Carley sent me ten dollars and I get a little from home. Just enough to scrape through. Two meals a day cost only sixty cents here – we eat at [a] boarding-house next door.

Oh, my dear, there is a red-headed grocer's boy come to live here! Paul has a room on one side and I on the other and the grocer's boy sleeps on a couch in the hall. Who are you betting on? I'll let you know how it comes out. The Madam is quick as a fox but her self-imposed reputation for chastity works a hardship on her in this situation as she must profess to find the grocer's boy totally unattractive.[2] It is an amusing game for these hot summer nights and the stake is worth the play. You can imagine the Madam and I crouched behind half-closed doors, breathing heavily as we map out tactical maneuvers and watch the innocent quarry in a flood of moonlight, sleeping.

The Madam's play is doing fine and she works like a trooper!

Keep me posted and take care of yourself.

Love,

10.

.19.

[507 Georgia Ave., Macon, Ga.]
[*July 20, 1942*]

Dear Donnie:

The play is finished. I will send it to New York as soon as I can get it typed. We have tried two typists, business school students, one typed two pages in three hours, and the other did the same number in the course of an afternoon. Another

1. Nothing came of this.
2. With the darkening of time, Tennessee professes the same thing in the "Memoirs".

33

applicant will be tried tomorrow. I would send it to New York to be typed but you can imagine the state of the script when I tell you that the one I left New York with was relatively in apple-pie order, and I hate to send the single copy of anything involving such labor through the mails. I think it has turned out as well as we originally thought it might be: it is certainly as good a play as you and Lawrence and I are capable of knocking out among us. Maybe Lawrence would be a little confused by all that has happened to his little story but that old goat, luckily, is beyond all confusion. Naturally I have no money to pay for the typing and I have written to inquire of Audrey if there is not some fund that will advance five dollars for it. Yes, money is a dull problem. Maybe dull isn't exactly the word, but problem *is*. I am about two weeks back on my board-bill and every time I slip unobtrusively up to the dining-room table the land-lady looks at me with a perceptibly reduced cordiality and of course I imagine that everybody at the table knows exactly what I owe her and I am afraid to lift my eyes from the plate or to ask for anything that isn't in my immediate reach – I have the arms of an Octopus, however! – Paul eats there, too. He is less bashful than I am and when he enters he heartily announces, "My dear Mrs. Griffin, I haven't the slightest intention of paying you for my dinner!" and laughs as though he had made some brilliant witticism. The poor woman is rather dull-witted but I think she is slowly evolving some plan of action that will probably take care of us both. Paul does get money, and so do I on even rarer occasions, but Paul must, of course, buy endless birthday presents and rare old first editions for rare old opera-singers and things like that. I was not born an adventuress and becoming one is not simple – but some have greatness thrust upon them, as the fellow says. I only regret that it isn't on a grander scale, like murdering someone for the Maltese Falcon.

I am worn out. Even tireder than when I left New York, as I have been working even harder, every day without letup. In addition to the play I have finished three long one-acts about the Deep South which I give the composite title of "Dragon Country". Bobbie Lewis writes that Libby Holman is interested ("Thrilled") by the one-acts and wanted me to write one for her to sing in. Which I did. They hope to do something about it in the Fall but have taken no option. David Merrick, the Shumlin man, has written me twice and we are sure of a very sympathetic reading there. He is awfully sweet and said some lovely things about "Stairs to the Roof" which he said would not make any money during these times. Saroyan is in New York now. Why don't you go to see him? *New Yorker* says he is staying at "Hampsted House" – No – correction! "Hampshire House", a suite on the 28th floor. It seems that he swindled Mr. Mayer (Hollywood) out of $ 60,000 on some kind of legal fraud. We must find out how he did it. There is no trick too low for my present nature. Or yours, I hope. – Kid him along about his genius and our sufferings. Both of us starving, selling our souls and trying to sell our asses. And all that. – He may have some good will in him, though there is so much in his plays that I suspect he must have the heart of a crocodile in actuality. – Tell him that I am living (this is quite true) in an attic with one window the size of a transom in the hottest town in America! – And that I was recently picked up on Cherry Street (this is also quite true) as a suspicious character because of my dark glasses and cigarette holder and detained at the Chief of Detectives office for some time because I did not have my draft card with me. – Tell him also, that he is making a fool of himself, writing letters for the Sunday *Times*. And declaring himself to be the only living playwright. Tell him he soon *will* be – unless we are given some help!

35

I think you should go to Atlanta, and do it soon. You may not like the prospect but it will freshen you up and coming back to New York will be sort of a fresh start for you. Then you may find it better working on the novel[1] down here where your material is. – I am glad that I got away from New York.

Carley writes that his new piece "If I Cared Etc."[2] is being introduced by the Ink Spots, Guy Lombardo and Danny Kaye. He sounds dreadfully puffed up – I am afraid he would be unbearable after this.

Read Katherine Anne Porter's *Pale Horse, Pale Rider* and never mind the *Fox* – It's all taken care of, what could be used of it.

I like to hear of you and things in New York so keep on writing me.

Love,

10.

Wrote this a week ago and forgot to mail it. The play is being typed now. Audrey sent money. 5 copies. Got your letter about situation on Leroy.[3] Come home for a while. Better for you, better for Cadmus, better for Fred. You get what I mean? – 10.

I *loved* that "greedy bore" epithet for St. Ang.[4]

1. I had started "The Dog Star".

2. "If I Cared a Little Bit Less and You Cared a Little Bit More", a song he had written to Tennessee.

3. I had been classified 4F in the draft. Sara had been expecting me to disappear into the Army. I, apparently, had been expecting her to disappear into thin air. And we were left facing each other.

4. St. Angelica was our name for a boy we had known at the West Side Y.M.C.A.

20

[507 Georgia Ave., Macon, Ga.]
[*July 23, 1942*]

Dear Donnie:

I think for a good summer fuck you should cover the bed with a large white piece of oil-cloth. The bodies of the sexual partners ought to be thoroughly, even superfluously rubbed over with mineral oil or cold cream. It should be in the afternoon, preferably soon after lunch when the brain is dull. It should be a bright, hot day, not far from the railroad depot and the scene of the fornication should be a Victorian bedroom at the top of the house with a skylight letting the sun directly down on the bed. On a table beside the bed should be a pitcher of ice-water and a bottle of sherry wine and plenty of cigarettes and a portable radio. If the sexual partner is a southern belle with intellectual pretensions and a beautiful ass, it must be plainly told where the charm is concentrated and urged to keep the loftier cerebral processes out of the picture at least till after the first ejaculation.

This little item is from my Mother's Recipe Book, on the page for meat dishes. Hope you can use some of it.

About the play: it is finished and looks very good. Audrey has sent five dollars to pay the typist. The typist is Paul. He starts on it tomorrow, will make 5 copies and thinks he can get it finished in two days. I will mail all the copies to Audrey and you can get one from her.

Advice: leave New York for a while and let Freddie keep house for himself. These links with the past should not be left to break of their own fatigue but snapped off cleanly. Then you have more energy for new things and the past is less painful to look back on. I always wait to be thrown out of a place, but I find it creates a coolness. I think it is best to move out just five minutes before the person extending the hospitality to you begins to even subconsciously wonder when you will. After Atlanta, the job is a good idea. Now that you're one of us 4F boys you ought to find something pleasant and not too exacting like Gilbert's job.[1] – I wish you'd described his appearance with that crew hair-cut! – To me it is unimaginable. His hair was the one part about him that I thought justified some measure of vanity. Paul has just received a letter from him saying that lechery was a thing of the past, that he was now completely pure of heart. Paul remarked at the time, "This is the sort of thing Miss Maxwell always writes just before dashing off to the Turkish bath."

Henrietta Callaway is here and we have been going to parties at the rate of two or three a day. Sara was over this morning, she and Harry took us out for a drink. She said that Freddie was not going to sea, but they were moving to White Plains. How charming! And she was planning to quit her job and you were planning to get one and the dog was going to be shipped home. Jesus, little brother, how can you stand all that shitting around over nothing? I see no reason why you should let yourself be mixed up in it at all.

Don't think first love is the only love and after that you're a bitch – It ain't necessarily so! What was so wonderful mostly came out of yourself and that's still there as good as it ever was and probably better.

If you come to Atlanta I will see you. Paul is leaving here the end of next week for North Carolina, without seeing Jordan once since I have been here. I can leave anytime and only need to go home for about a week before I return to New York at the end of the summer. – Hope some money comes in from the play before then.

With love to you and my kindest regard to Paul.

10.

1. Working in a hotel. Tennessee's characterization of it changed when he tried it a year later.

[*Postcard*]
[Macon, Ga.]
[*August 5, 1942*]

Don – Mailed play copies last week. Please write me what
you think about it, if anything, right away.

10.

[507 Georgia Ave., Macon, Ga.]
[*August 11, 1942*]

Dear Donnie:

It has been over a week since I mailed the plays to Audrey
so when I got your letter this morning I assumed you would
write about it. No reference. Paul says he thinks you have
decided to preserve a merciful silence as you feel I have done
some unspeakable outrage to the intention of the divine Mr.
Lawrence. Is this so? Or have you not been to Audrey's or
has the play failed to arrive from the railway express? I
have not heard from her office and naturally I am acutely
concerned as this job is sort of a last, desperate throw of the
literary dice in the direction of Broadway. If you aren't
pleased with the changes I've made, for God's sake tell me,
don't be bashful about it. I myself am only partially satisfied.
Paul, on the other hand, thinks the play is very good. I think
it is still rather tenuous and a little contrived, especially
in the ending. That ending can be improved by a little more
finagling, however, and certainly it has more dramatic punch
than the other one did. The problem is to obscure the denoue-
ment till the very moment that Matilda appears in her bridal
dress. This is not yet done as well as it might be. I personally

39

think the play has the elements of a good commercial success, and so does Paul.

I put H[—] on the train for New York. He was wearing sort of a picture-hat, amber transparent straw with an enormous brim, a bottle-green sport coat and pale yellow trousers. He intends to see you in New York. Treat him gently. He is a sweet person, likely to be pretty knocked around by the crowd he'll get in with. Vain, a little silly, but fundamentally decent. I am sorry to see him headed for Bar 13. – Try to steer him away. He has offered me a room in his house and I may move there when Paul has left. He is going to New York in about a week, I believe, as his jaw has become troublesome and needs treatment. My friendship with H[—] annoyed Paul and made Andrew furious. Andrew said, If you must have affairs, why don't you have them with interesting people? – My answer to that created a definite coolness. So now I am infra dig. Ah, well, the summer is nearly over. New York? No sooner than I have to. I have a dreadful cold, hung on for a month, and the only thing that will help is salt-water swimming. I must manage to get away to one of the beach towns.

I finally went to Atlanta, to see Sally off on the train. The only thing I liked there was the view across those open spaces to the sun on the distant buildings that you get from Neblett's front window. Neblett himself was dead drunk, stretched out on the floor, and being urged by a female follower to get up and go to the Chinaman's for supper. I am now heartily in accord with your decision to spend your "Return to Atlanta" fund on more or less riotous living in New York.

I loved the quotations: can it be that I am a hold-over from the Palatine era? – the sentiments, especially about the boys with the purple-edged robes, have an almost autobiographical familiarity to me, though I have certainly never read them before.

I want you to take the play to John C. Wilson, but more of that later.

Love –

TENNESSEE

Don – Yesterday I got a long letter from Audrey. She has the play, and although she says she has not finished reading it yet, the general tone of her letter indicated at least a mild sort of approbation, which I found very comforting as it is not her custom to commit herself. I suspect she is pleased with it and is going to make a real effort to effect a sale. I am reasonably sure that this will eventually be done. She spoke of Lillian Gish for the role of Matilda and said if the play was not copyrighted, she would take care of that, and that she would sign contracts with Curtis Brown this week for the rights. She seems to have plenty of steam up, for a change, so if I were you, I would not press her about anything. If one does, she gets cagey. Of course if she is to handle the play she will have to represent us both, and no doubt she will suggest some agreement or contract with you, which you would do well to sign. She wanted to know what the agreement was between you and me and I told her it was a fifty-fifty agreement.[1] We may be required to make out a formal contract to that effect. Keep the play under your hat until Audrey has completed all these negotiations. All my trouble with the Theatre Guild came of trying to operate independently, while Audrey was in California.

Paul has made up his mind that I shall go to Chapel Hill, North Carolina. Four letters were dispatched this afternoon to pave the way for this migration. One to Audrey, informing her that I was threatened with consumption and must have an immediate change of air and altitude and one to Paul Green informing him that I was coming. I know Green

1. See page 100, footnote 1.

slightly, and that was what gave Paul the idea. Two more to raise funds, from the family and Carley respectively. I, of course, wrote the letters, dictated by Bigelow. The fact is I can't stand it here any longer, my cold gets constantly worse and I am barely able to get out of bed in the mornings.

Today was a rainy day and we spent practically the whole time talking about Lady Beatty. I had never heard that preposterous story about her staying at the Astor and having to work off that enormous bill in various smaller hotels. I am sorry I did not know what a character she was – I never really appreciated her till Paul gave me her complete history, as only he could, this afternoon . . . while washing out a couple of polo shirts which he told me cost him $ 8.50 and $ 5.00 respectively. Do you remember that old sarong he made me to exchange for my genuine one I got in Acapulco? He had given it to Andrew, telling him he got it on the Riviera. In Bigelow's play there is a character, the heroine, who at one dramatic point exclaims, "Oh, my pearls, my pearls! They are worth a hundred thousand!" When he got to that point I grinned – Bigelow asked why – I said, "My dear, that woman's pearls are probably worth a dollar and ninety-nine cents!" I hope you will hear that play sometime – it is autobiographical, in a sense.

I have felt very peaceful lately – sad and serene. Just to have a bed of my own and a few cigarettes is enough. Your letters sound peaceful, too. Isn't it much better when there is not much to lose?

.23.
[*Postcard*]
[St. Augustine, Fla.]
[*August 17, 1942*]

My dear Donald – Your roving collaborator, of bad character and worse fame, is now on the beach at St. Augustine

Florida – lonely, penniless, and *exalted*! Write me care of S. E. Worley, 246 Charlotte St. Every pt. of me except the most private and least important is scorched and peeling!

Ever –

10.

.24.

[246 Charlotte St., St. Augustine, Fla.]
Friday, Aug. 21, 1942

Dear Donnie –

I hope you will keep me posted on what Audrey is doing about our play. I've only had the one letter from her which I wrote you about. I was greatly relieved you liked the final draft. Of course it was impossible for me to judge clearly anymore. I don't think I've ever so desperately wanted *anything* to succeed, as I have just about lived as long as I *can* under these dreadful circumstances of dependence.

I am staying here with a character who makes "character dolls". I shall have to leave soon for St. Louis as my Grandmother is in very bad condition, only 83 pounds, and there is really no other place for me to go. I have never dreaded any trip so much but it appears unavoidable. I can't bear illness in those I love. To *see* it.

My face and body are covered with a fantastic pattern of new pink and old brown skin as result of a terrific sunburn. I am leaving tomorrow on a short bike trip along the coast, up to Jacksonville and back.

I see Saroyan's plays were panned by critics. Hope you will see them and report.[1] I would like to get back to N. Y. now but afraid I can't for several weeks. Horrible interim

1. See page 52, footnote 2.

in prospect! Write me c/o S. E. Worley, 246 Charlotte St.,
St. Augustine, Fla.

Love –

10.

.25.

[*Postcard*]
230 E. Forsythe, Jacksonville, Fla.
[*August 31, 1942*]

Don – Hope you haven't written me at home as I am not
going there. *I have a job.* In the U. S. Engineers office (War
Dept.) operating teletype machine at $120.00 a month,
working night shift, from 11 P. M. to 7 A. M. At last moment couldn't endure prospect of St. Louis, so I abandoned
my ivory tower which never was much anyhow. Let me hear
from you.

TENN.

.26.

United States Engineer Office, Jacksonville, Fla.
Sept. 12, 1942

Dear Don:

I am glad you are having a little change of scene at Fire
Island. Beaches are nice for a while and it must be nice to be
with Fidelma. She struck me as being unusually charming.

Well, Audrey finally sent me the Frieda Lawrence contract
papers which I have signed and returned for you to append
your signature. She has also sent [a] copy of the play to Gassner of the Theatre Guild and will hear from him probably
next week. Have you seen the criticism written by Alan
Collins of Curtis Brown, Lawrence's agent? Audrey mailed
me a copy of it and said you would receive one, too. He

44

ended by saying he thought the play was "Damned good" but took exception to Matilda's character. Felt her "fear of the world" was unexplained and not understandable and should be related to something more tangible. I don't agree about that, do you? These successful Broadway people think everybody is as brave as *they* are. He also was dissatisfied with the "symbols" in end of play. I agree that the last scene is still the weakest and we may have to do more work on it, but I don't think we should plunge into any changes before a producer has taken an option on it.

Bigelow is in New York. He and Audrey both wrote me about each other. Audrey said she "liked him enormously" which usually means that she finds something amusing. And Bigelow said she is very pleased with "You Touched Me" and is, in his opinion, going to work hard with it. Poor Paul has been suffering a good deal with his jaw and he says the situation is "not encouraging" and he doesn't want to see anybody, so I won't urge you to look him up. I am afraid Audrey could not give him much encouragement about his play, either. It is distinctly non-commercial – that is between us, however. Don't mention it to other people.

I am getting along well with the new job. In fact, too well. I have been offered a permanent civil service appointment, the only one on the night shift that received this offer, and promoted to work on the day shift which I didn't want. But the hours are good, from noon to eight in the evening. I have rented a bicycle and discovered a marvelous dive on Ocean Street where I spend my evening hours mostly. It is like the Silver Front, only younger, rowdier, and more dangerous: fights and cuttings every half hour, the sailors dance with each other, and there is a group of tough queens who are out of the world – I will probably meet my end there. I am living at the "Y". It is operated by a sanctimonious couple, like a pair of missionaries. The woman looks' like

45

Elsa Lanchester with her legs sawed off and more pop-eyed and sinister-looking. I pass through the lobby whistling a church hymn but the piety disappears at the turn of the stairs. I have a room-mate not quite sixteen, a blond moron who works as a theatre usher, wakes me up every few minutes when I am trying to get my day sleep in to ask me how I like the new wave in his hair or some such interesting detail. Today he came in with a wrist watch he'd just bought for thirty dollars at the "Tricks and Novelties Store". He took it off to show me and it fell into three pieces, case, crystal, and works. It was named "Lorna": we had it appraised and it was a three-dollar watch.

I don't like working but it is good to have plenty of money again, to eat all I want when and where I want it, and to see all the movies and buy all the drinks I care for. If we make any money on the play, I have a better plan than Texas. Texas would drive us both crazy – I would prefer Mexico City – in a motor-cycle with a side-car. No, Texas is too heart-breaking. It is the most heart-breaking state in America, or in the whole world I imagine. One is always bumping into it other places without going there and being annihilated by it. Of course you go through it on the way to Mexico and coming back – that is enough. It is wonderful coming back. But it is nearly all visual – that's how it was for me, anyhow. See Texas and die of it. It looks to me like they've got most of it in the navy now. Which makes it worse. You can't put Texas in a pair of tight white pants and create anything but disaster. Ocean Street is full of it and sometimes I go home at night with a belly full of burning saw-dust. One needs a peacefully fiery Latin after being consumed in all that cyclonic blond repose. I am for *Mexico*! – Love,

TENN.

27

United States Engineer Office, Jacksonville, Fla.
Oct. 3, 1942

Wrote this one *first*

Dear Donnie:

What's cooking at your end of the line?

Have you made any spectacular changes in your mode of existence since I last heard from you? I guess by this time you have run out of money and have either gotten a job or a profitable clientele. These beautiful Norwegians won't do. I think you should have some pictures made like the one you sent me. And drop them coyly behind you as you go about town. Or slip them up people's sleeves as you shake hands with them or leave them on saucers in restaurants with Cadmus's address on the back for appointments. I am sure Paul would be glad to handle the phone calls while you were out distributing.

I hope this does not sound callous. I do worry about you a little, in spite of the fact I know you are capable of doing better than I am.

Bigelow writes that I should return immediately to New York but I am not in such a rush to. The reckless caprice which became me so well in my green salad days is wisely tempered now with occasional pauses for reflection, and when I go back to New York I should prefer to have something more comfortable and dependable than Bigelow's trunk bottom to sleep in. Also there exists a certain tenderness between me and the approximate imbecile I room with. A sudden cold snap and only one blanket in the bedroom resulted in a friendlier understanding between us which has continued in spite of more moderate weather. Also I have obtained permission to swim at the USO which is very lovely. The

47

Jacksonville period has taken flower. It is not any Paradise, or anything like it, but I feel that I should allow it to go on a while. But in the meantime, let me know what employment conditions are in N. Y. If I go there – living costs being what they are – I would presumably have to get some kind of work. I grant you that life is hardly acceptable on such terms – having to work, I mean – however since we do have the prospect, or hope, of selling our play to buck us up morally, I guess we can stand it a while. I ought to be saving some money but I'm not. I seem to be hungry all the time, maybe because I stinted on food for such a long time, especially just lately, and I go in and out of restaurants all the time, everything seems so delicious and it is so wonderful being able to pay for it. Also when I go in a bar it is three cuba libres instead of one beer. Consequently I don't even make my money go around.

As I told you the town is over-run with sailors, worse than New York, and their conduct is ridiculous and pitiable, there is so little for them to do.

Last night I was sitting out on the porch of the "Y", it was my night off and about three o'clock. A huge drunk sailor was staggering along the street and making belligerent gestures at the lamp-posts. He came up to the steps of the "Y" and stopped and looked up at me, sitting alone smoking a cigarette. "What is wrong here?" he asked me. "Nothing I know of," I said meekly. He came on up the steps and stood over me. "What is wrong here?" he repeated. I could see that he was dead set on having a fight and I was equally anxious to keep out of one. So I started looking around as if to discover if anything was wrong. "There is something going on in this place and I don't like it," he said. "Yes," I said, "I think it is that woman who lives downstairs." I knew that only a reference to a woman could possibly divert him. "What's she up to?" he asked me. "Oh," I said, "she's a bitch!" "Is that right?" "Yeah." "Where is she at?" "Down-stairs." "How do I get down there?" I directed him to the basement door, which opens on the stairs to the disagreeable couple's apartment, the ones who operate the "Y", and a few minutes later, having gone quickly upstairs, I heard the three of them all shouting at once. They had to call the police to get him out, and as he was being dragged to the wagon I heard him shouting, "By God, I knew there was something wrong in this fucking place!"

I am beginning to be rather quick-witted in situations like this, they come up so frequently here. So far I have not been injured. Knock on wood.

Have you heard anything of Fritzi? I wonder what he is doing this season. I guess speaking of sailors made me think of him.

Carley's piece "If I Cared Etc." has begun to appear on some of the juke-boxes here in town and sounds like it might be a hit.

Bigelow is blue, at least he is writing blue letters, maybe because he knows I have a job and mistakenly supposes I have some money. I take that back, a very unkind remark and not at all warranted. As a matter of fact, I owe poor Bigelow some money for typing and he is undoubtedly hav-ing a pretty hard time of it with his jaw treatments and long separation from Jordan. Jordan did not come to Macon once last summer.

I look forward to reading your novel when I get to N. Y. Such things always go through very bad stages, especially if they are going to be very good.

Write me all the news. Love –

10.

49

"Stinky Darling"

Just got your letter. Apparently you have not been apprised of the latest development on our professional front. Prepare yourself for a shock. It appears that we shall have to go back to work on "You Touched Me". I got a letter from Audrey just the other day saying that she had had lunch with John Gassner and that he felt, as she did, that what the play needed was connection with some "definite period or locale" and that Gassner thought it should be 1942, that Hadrian should be coming home on leave from the battle, the war should still be in progress, and the village one that had escaped bombardment. This to give it "contemporary significance". Audrey is apparently of the same mind, and from the tone of her letter our capitulation to these plans is virtually demanded. The letter was sort of an ultimatum. Evidently she envisages a much quicker sale and a more popular reception if this change is made. She says Gassner feels that it would then interest the Theatre Guild as a vehicle for the Gish sisters, that he admires the structure of the play and thinks a contemporary setting would greatly enhance its present values. All of this is distressing, my dear, especially as I worked so hard on the script all summer and had felt it was finally off my hands and I could go on with other work somewhat more appealing to me. However I see no way out. There is only one clear space in this jungle, and that is after we have scored a commercial success – therefore we shall have to satisfy the commercial demands of the moment.

Audrey thinks I should come back to N. Y. if "I can afford to" and get started on this work at once. She says Bigelow tells her that he has a friend who will "give me a place to stay". I do not believe that I will live through another period without money in New York. I say that in all seriousness. I do not think that I *will* live through it. But I will probably try. I've just been hanging on in the hope of an early influx of money from this play, feeling that when that happened, and it would soon, I could stop and rest and let my dreadfully torn up nerves have a chance to recover.

As for the proposed change, I feel we can make it. I shall not try to change the body of the play and I'm sure you won't either. We will only make such changes as are absolutely necessary to put it where they want it on the calendar. It is certainly not going to be converted into another sickening "Mrs. Miniver" or "Morning Star" business – only over both our dead bodies.

Your instinct is right in working on the Matilda-Hadrian scene in the last scene of the play. That scene is definitely the weak point and I think what the audience is waiting for at that point is a scene between the romantic protagonists. The one you suggest – over the drapes – sounds a little too homely, something a little more dramatic will have to be worked out. The last scene should pack more of a wallop.

Well, darling – remember how many times I had to write over "Battle of Angels" and be comforted. The script was pretty near "over the hump" and more work will be on the right side. I do not question the fact that a contemporary play laid in England will have more commercial promise, and maybe we will actually find some good new material in the present set-up. If we are in good form, the work shouldn't take more than a week or two.

When it is over, you can give me a "third class funeral" and move slowly across the stage with a 2 × 4 coffin containing my dismembered body – making big eyes like Libby

Holman! Describing yourself as a heap of old fish-heads and rotten bananas.[1]

Isn't that amazing about the Saroyan one-act?[2] As I remember, it was so silly and phoney that we nearly died laughing at it.

We are trying to communicate with emotional imbeciles.

Why don't you see Audrey and see what you can learn from her? It will take me several days to make up my mind what to do. I may leave for N. Y. on or shortly after the sixteenth when I get my pay-check. What is the employment situation there? I will just have money enough to last about a week when I get there.

Courage and love –

.28.

[United States Engineer Office, Jacksonville, Fla.]
[October 29, 1942] Thursday

STINKIE DARLING:

I wrote you right after I got your last letter but know I haven't mailed it yet. I'll look it up and try to get them both off together. Although I will probably land in New York almost the same time. Yes, the fatal step has been taken, and I have asked for a "release without prejudice" from my job here, and whether I get it or not, will blow town about the first. It was hard to do as for once in my life I appeared to be a vital industry. The draft had winnowed the night shift down to only two of us and apparently no replacements can

1. As Libby Holman did in "Mexican Mural" by Ramon Naya.

2. From my journal, Saturday, October 10, 1942: "I walked to Times Square and saw Saroyan's 'Hello Out There' and Chesterton's 'Magic'. The production of the Saroyan was amazing. I had read the play with Tenn and Butch when it came out in the 'Best One-Act Plays of 1941' and thought very little of it. Dowling's performance was excellent. When I finish my carnival story I want to send a copy of it to Julie Haydon."

be had. However working all night and writing during the day has just about finished me off. Browned me off, as they say so picturesquely in the British air force! My nerves are all shot. However a good deal of the work on the play is done, I believe. We can discuss that when I get there. It's damn sweet of you to offer to put me up but I never stay with my best friends if I can avoid it. How my friendship with Bigelow managed to survive a summer in one attic is a little miracle, attributable to Bigelow's self-control and my impunity to insult. It is all worked out, apparently, that I am to live in a studio apartment with some person, an artist, named Karl Free, at least until he goes into the army. And I will have money enough to live on till the job is finished on the play. I don't think it will take more than two or three weeks. Then either we sell it or I go back to work for the government if they'll take me. I think I've made a pretty good go of it here, and the boss has promised to give me his personal recommendation for future employment. I suggest you read up a little on the R AF. I now have Hadrian a flyer home on leave. And there is a new character, a sort of literary bull-diker named Dame Edwina de Capet[1] who appears in the tea-scene as the guest of honor and gives all her attention to Hadrian, leading him into his speech about the war. This incenses Emmie and touches off the fireworks. I don't think it is necessary to let the war change things much. However a number of things in the play could stand more work. Let's bat it out as fast as possible and turn our delicate attention to more delightful matters! I've been rather repressed here lately. By circumstances. The room-mate's older brother appeared on the scene and there began a battle of wills between us. He wanted to take the rabbit back north with him, to work in a defense plant, and I was determined he

1. This character, and several others written into the play in Macon to my dismay, eventually came out.

wouldn't go. I lay on my bed and smoked like Frieda Lawrence, and glowered at the ceiling, while the controversy raged, and in the end the brother went off without the rabbit. The rabbit remains a bell-hop. But something is dead inside me! The older brother has wrecked the innocent aura that surrounded our idyl. All that incredibly sensitive balance of centrifugal and centripetal forces which make up a good relationship has been destroyed! I hope there'll be plenty of hell to raise in New York when I get there. Here I have been very good, very quiet and restrained. *Basta*!

Bigelow writes that Jordan is there and they are apartment-hunting. Bigelow has a wonderful gift for editing and I think he will help putting the mended pieces together in our script. It's the exacting sort of business you and I are least suited for, so the more we can get out of him in the way of assistance the better. I have promised to help him with his Bergner script, which I think is all he expects in the way of return. He has been almost *ominously* noble lately.

I'm afraid you won't have time to write me before I leave. Probably Sunday night. But as soon as I get settled in New York I will call you at the Maestro's office,[1] as I haven't any idea where you're located.

Salud y Pesadas!

10.

---

1. Earlier that month Lincoln Kirstein had given me a $25-a-week job to help him get out *Dance Index* while his secretary was having a baby.

The place Bigelow had arranged for Tennessee to stay was a disaster. He lasted one night and moved to a furnished room. Also, Bigelow delayed in typing the play once it was in his possession, and Massee refused to reveal the whereabouts of the manuscripts Tennessee had left that summer in Massee's house in Macon. This cooled Tennessee's friendship with the two of them almost to the point of mine. After ten days, while Melton and his wife were in Georgia, I moved Tennessee to the Leroy Street apartment.[1] Later, because every time he got on the subway he ended up in Brooklyn, he stayed a week at the Hotel St. George. The typescript of "You Touched Me" was finally ready in January. The producers who we thought were going to option it turned it down flat.

Tennessee had a chest cold and a cough that hung on. His appearance reached the nadir I describe as Denis Freeman's in the opening chapter of "The Hero Continues". Horton Foote helped him get a short-lived job as an elevator operator. Then he worked as an usher at the Strand Theatre. Day after day, he typed in the Dance Index *office, making copies of his poems for me to give to Kirstein, who had promised to submit them to James Laughlin of New Directions. I felt responsible for Tennessee and worried if he disappeared for a day;[2] and I believe that he felt responsible for me. But neither of us was the best of protectors. One night two sailors beat us up in the Claridge Hotel. Finally, Tennessee fled. Even St. Louis was better than this.*

1. From my journal, Wednesday, November 18, 1942: "After I got off work I came and moved Tenn downtown to Butch's. His room was desolate confusion, clothes and folded typewritten mss. piled intermixed between each other, suitcases full and overflowing onto the floor, cigarette ashes and butts, empty wadded cigarette packages, old magazines, shoes, underwear, dirty unwritten-on paper. A most complete lack of order."
2. From my journal, Saturday, November 7, 1942: "Tenn is capable of going off in so many directions that I should not worry that I haven't heard from him for two days, but I do. His heart is faint and his eyesight weak and his constitution worn from much abuse."

.29.

53 Arundel Place, Clayton, Mo.
April 1943

Dear Donnie:

So you see I really did go. Things are even worse here than I had expected. It has come to such a pass now that the family cannot even sit at the same table with each other. Father eats first, separately. He evidently opposed my coming here and has ordered me to do all sorts of absurd things such as transferring the woodpile from one corner of the yard to another and washing windows in the garage. Dear Grand was actually at death's door last week, Mother tells me, and the old devil chose that occasion to give a party in the rathskeller. They made so much noise that Mother had to appeal to the guests to leave. Just for my benefit, Grand has gotten up out of bed, pretending to be well, and goes tottering around the house, holding onto things for support, like a tipsy old crane in her pale blue kimono and pink cap and giggling apologetically when she nearly falls. It is so heartbreaking that I have a lump in my throat the whole time, it is almost impossible to speak. It is like a Chekhov play, only much wilder and sadder.

They showed me the letter from Rose[1] which they regard as so encouraging, but in it she remarks that I am lucky to be still in the penitentiary as "hordes of hungry people are clamoring at the gates of the city". Dakin finishes his military training in five weeks and will probably be sent abroad. He has insured his life for ten thousand naming me as the beneficiary, and is making the payments out of his army pay. He would have been a commissioned officer but Father refused to pay his board at Harvard so he had to give it up and

1. His sister.

56

go through the basic training. What a dark and bewildering thing it is, this family group. I can only feel one thing, the necessity for strength and the pettiness of all other considerations. I guess that is what I came home for. Because I can't give them any help.

This afternoon I had to get out for a while so I went downtown and took a long walk along the river-front which is very old and beautiful. Faded old river packets are tied up along the levee and across the river in Illinois are power plants and red and orange box-cars in a cloud of smokey sunlight. It made me think of Hart Crane. Then I came home and sat upstairs with my Grandmother. She has an extraordinary beauty. Her face is very gaunt and beautifully chiselled and ivory colored. Her hair pure white and silky and her eyes a deep brown, still sparkling. She lacks so entirely the harshness of reality that it is hard to believe she is anything but a dream, or at least something out of a dream that has been helplessly and inappropriately attached to life. Those two things, the experience of the intense and compassionate vision of Hart Crane and the gentleness of my Grandmother seem like a dual blessing from which to distill some higher conception of life. And there is an heroic lesson, I think, in the fact that both of them were set in such surrounding horror. The disintegration of Crane's life and my Grandmother's projection into this haunted household.

I haven't yet begun to try to make up my mind what to do. In any case, you will take good care of the scripts I left in your office and if I decide to avoid the further destruction in New York, I rely upon you to send them to me safely when I can give you an address.

I have just finished a long letter to McClintic about our play and the theatre in general. But I have a superstitious feeling that success of this kind is blocked by concentrating on it and planning for it. One must create and then put aside and create again. Then it happens, the success side of it, but not until then – not until it is looked away from. That is why it is so bad to be in New York and listening for telephones and watching for letters and notices. Success is like a shy mouse – he won't come out while you're watching. And you must remember that he is only a mouse – not a god. That he is fortuitous and not the whole show.

Give Fidelma my love and let me hear from you very soon.

Always,

10.

.30.

[53 Arundel Place, Clayton, Mo.]
[*April, 1943*]

Donnie my dear:

I'm afraid my letter didn't cheer you at all. I am not unlike my Aunt Belle, the religious one that died of an infected wisdom tooth. She was always ascending to some high spiritual level and writing people about it and the letters were intolerable.

Well, the old man has just now left the house on his long anticipated trip to the West Coast. We hope he never comes back, but nothing returns more certainly than evil. His last act was a bellowing accusation that Mother had hidden his poker chips in the attic.

The situation here is pure fantasy. I am trying to figure something out to improve things. The only thing I could do is make money, the very thing which I am least likely to do.

So you, too, have decided on the necessity for strength? Bueno, chiquito!

For a while I was planning to head West, but that would only remove me further from the only place where money can be made. I will probably return to New York. I have been working several hours daily on "The Gentleman Caller".[1] It is developed into a long play and may be finished when I get back. I might also call it the "Not so Beautiful People" or "The Human Tragedy", as it is taking on the atmosphere of 53 Arundel Place.

How is the traumatized libido and how is the novel? They ought to be good for each other. Why don't you complete the part in the reform school first, it seems complete in itself, and market it as a novella? A limited canvas gives one more courage, and to have one part done perfectly is encouraging, too.

My libido is lost in pure and general sorrow. In New York I feel a little importance, that is the insidious thing about New York. You play a little game of importance and begin to believe it, because it is nurtured by others playing their little games of importance, too. It is all an artificial aura, created by New York. As soon as you get away, it is gone and you are the least significant little microcosm. There is nothing to distinguish you from your grandmother, coughing her life away, or your younger brother in the army, except they both have more sand in their craws than you have, or better dispositions. You are an artist? So what! You are not coughing your life away and you are not in the army? So what! You will die and the army will do you no good whether you're in it or not. You say, well, I have my friends. They carry tales to your enemies and they devise little methods of giving you annoyance and messing up your little game of importance. What do you have finally to fall back on?

ENDURANCE! – Much love,

10.

1. "The Glass Menagerie".

59

[53 Arundel Place, Clayton, Mo.]
[*April 22, 1943*]

Dear Donnie:

I am out of cigarettes and very nervous so I can not write much of a letter. I have been writing with tigerish intensity on "The Gentleman Caller" every day, and today I felt like I was going to just blow up, so I quit. What I am doing to that quiet little play I don't know.

I haven't written sooner because I wanted to be able to tell you definitely what I am going to do. I still can't say definitely but in all probability I will come back to New York. For a while I was all set to head for New Mexico. Then I became to think of Audrey and Mr. Gering and all my manuscripts scattered to the four corners of the world and figured I had better come back and not burn anymore bridges behind me. If I keep doing that I will ultimately be in the northern tip of Tunisia with the fox of the desert, as they call him.

Still – who knows what I will do! Neither you nor I! Perhaps you can advise me. I have to make up my mind and do it in less than a week now as the old man will be returning from his trip.

I haven't heard from anyone but Mary Hunter and Horton Foote. Horton is investigating a farm for the two of us this summer. Could I bear it? Or could Horton? They are re-organizing their company[1] for next year, hope to get a larger theatre and call it a "Playwrights Company". I think they have their eyes on "You Touched Me". It might not be a bad thing if Mary directed – she would have to. I haven't heard anything from Audrey, not a word. I expect she is a

1. The American Actors Company, directed by Mary Hunter who earned her living playing Marge on the "Easy Aces" radio program.

little baffled and discouraged as I am, and possibly angry with me for extorting that bus-fare from Gering through her. He still has "Stairs to the Roof" and I wonder if I will ever see it again or any of the poems I gave to Laughlin. If those two things weren't on my mind, I'd feel free to head West and just forget New York and the theatre. If I don't come back to New York, will you take a brotherly interest in my scripts and other properties? I intend to make a will before I leave here and will probably appoint you as my literary executor – unofficially regard yourself in that capacity now. I once told Audrey I wanted Bigelow and Clark Mills to look after my scripts if I died, but that arrangement would no longer be suitable – that is, the Bigelow part. This does not mean that my health is unusually bad at the moment. Just usually! And if I run off to New Mexico I would undoubtedly get into some hazardous situations.

What a dispiriting prospect New York again is! That is, for another whole season. Some arrangement must be made to get away this summer, to be on the water somewhere. I hope that you, too, can work out something, for I feel that you will find it tedious to continue this exactly same life much longer. One must know when the juice is gone from something, and throw it away. Or put it aside for a while till it gets juicy again. – Dear me, what a vulgar image!

Well, I must go out and get me some cigarettes and take a swim. I have been as good as gold and the old traumatized department has been lost in a pure and general sorrow. But I wonder what you are up to and how it is in Central Park these spring evenings.

Give Fidelma my love – and yourself.

[*At top*] If you write me, be sure it reaches me before next Wed. Letters arriving here during my absence usually opened.

Tennessee returned to New York only briefly. Audrey Wood had sold him to Metro-Goldwyn-Mayer. He departed again in a few days, seated in a compartment of the Twentieth-Century Limited, holding a copy of "The Sun Is My Undoing", which he had been hired to adapt.

I had been made editor of Dance Index *in March, when Kirstein went into the Army. There was no other staff. But I felt far from secure. One week Kirstein wrote that I was a miracle, the next, when I misspelled a Russian name, a miracle of incompetence. In the midst of this uncertainty, my friendship with Sandy Campbell began.*

.32.

[*Written on flyleaf of the catalogue* Twentieth Century French Paintings from the Chester Dale Collection, The Art Institute of Chicago.]

[Chicago, Ill.]
[*May 8, 1943*] *Saturday, A. M.*

Dear Don –
Spent A. M. in Chicago at this exhibition, much finer than any I've seen in N. Y., in fact anywhere except possibly the World's Fair one in San Francisco.

Karl Hofer, *Girls Throwing Flowers*, and the best Gauguins and van Goghs and lovely Georges Braques. The Picassos barely hold their own.

Trip so far very restful.

I continue at 5:30 aboard the Super Chieftain.

Love –

10.

[*In the catalogue, over the first plate,* Braque*'s* Full-Length Figure of a Nude Woman with Fruit: *"They lose almost everything in these black and whites." Over de* Chirico*'s* Conversation among the Ruins: *"This was my favorite – lovely colors." And over* Léger*'s* Woman with Mirror: *"Gorgeous in color."*]

·33·
[1647 Ocean Ave., Santa Monica, Calif.]
[*May 12, 1943*] *Wednesday*

Dear Don –

I am just getting settled, it is sunset of my third day here which seems like the third month at least. I have taken a little 2-room apt. in Santa Monica, nothing at all grand, in fact a very honky-tonk air about it with stained wallpaper and a plaster model of Mae West on the dresser and very gaudy curtains. It took me 2 days to find any place at all, due to the terrific overcrowding with defense workers. But I am in view of the ocean and I have a little cookstove and icebox and the place seems almost sentimentally home-like, it re-minds me of the dreadful little flat we lived in when we first came to St. Louis, except for Mae West.

I have my own little office at the studio but no secretary. And I am, at present, re-writing a vehicle for Lana Turner which she will appear in as soon as she is finished with her pregnancy.

More about the studio another time – I am sleepy.

I met Christopher[1] today. I invited him to lunch at the Brown Derby. I recognized him at once, just by instinct, and he does look just the way I imagine myself to look – it was funny.

I like him awfully, and I think he must have thought me rather school-girlish about his writing which I place with

1. Christopher Isherwood, to whom I had written introducing Tennessee.

Chekhov's. After lunch we went shopping for a motor scooter, which is necessary for me as the ride to the studio on buses is interminable. I haven't gotten a pay check yet and Christopher wanted to pay for the scooter but I wouldn't, of course, let him. I will buy it tomorrow with an advance on salary.

We talked a great deal about you, and I know you will be pleased to hear that Ch. admires your stories as much as I do. He also loves Lincoln's book about Pete[1] – according to him it is quite extraordinary. I am surprised a little, as I did not suppose Lincoln would be sufficiently integrated to pull off a fine novel, but I think we must take C's word for it. Anyhow, I am glad to hear it.

We discussed whether or not you ought to give up the mag. and come West. There were many pros and cons, such as how Lincoln would feel about it and how the glittering desolation of the West Coast with its curious emphasis on the animal in one would affect you.

Well, my dear, you are not a child and the decision is up to you. That is how Ch. put it, too. I will try to write more fully about things in general here. You *might* like it and you *might* be miserable. At any rate, there is room in the apt., really 3 beds, and plenty of food and the scooter can carry 2 passengers.

Keep it in mind but don't act hastily.

Even I feel sad when I look at the weird scenery from my window, and I have seen it before.

There is no sex in my life now. I don't even think about it. Later on I probably will again.

I literally have no friends here, as yet.

Love –

10.

1. "For My Brother": A true story by José Martínez Berlanga as told to Lincoln Kirstein.

64

Metro-Goldwyn-Mayer Pictures, Culver City, Calif.
May 17, 1943

Dear Sandy:

How nice of you to write me! It is the first letter I have received since I got here, and though I can scarcely credit your statement that everybody misses me, nevertheless I appreciate your good will in telling me so.

As a matter of fact, it will be doing myself a favor to call somebody, even though it is another victim of the film industry, for I have been very lonely since I got here. Everyone has been lovely to me, but I feel strange and sort of adrift. I made the mistake of taking an apartment on the Palisades at Santa Monica. There is nothing worse for loneliness than a view of the ocean, especially the Pacific, and crowds of happy beach-people only make you feel more dissociated unless you have a genius for mixing and a lot of adaptability.

My first assignment here is a vehicle for Lana Turner to appear in as soon as she is finished having a baby. It is a relief to stop work on it a few minutes to write this letter. It is not the sort of thing I would choose to do, but I am not getting paid to exercise any choice. "The Sun Is My Undoing" is waiting on Gable.

Well, I will call your friend right away and add a postscript if I reach him.

Write me again.

Best,

TENNESSEE

P.S. Just called Paramount and they say they do not have a Lionel Wiggam there.

Find out where he is and I will contact him for you. I don't much care for his verse, but I understand he has a great deal of charm.

[1647 Ocean Ave., Santa Monica, Calif.]
[*May 21 ?, 1943*]

Donnie dear –

Why do I always wait till I come home and have neither typewriter nor paper to write you? Probably because the setting sun on the Pacific through my white lace curtains makes me sad and lonely and I must talk to someone friendly as I presume you to be!

I am up to my neck in Lana Turner and it is madness and agony. I could *almost* hope she will die in childbirth. Jane Loring (producer) and I became hysterical this afternoon, trying to invent new sexy situations that would pass the Hays office. It seems that is what they really *want* me for – *sex*! What a world!

Lemuel Ayers arrived this P. M. He will be a terrific success here. He is appalled by nothing and has unlimited self-assurance. But he is very sweet, fundamentally, and he says Audrey has appointed him to look out for me. He said Audrey told me I was totally irresponsible and had friends who *beat* me.

[*The letter ends here, unfinished.*]

.36.

Metro-Goldwyn-Mayer Pictures, Culver City, Calif.
May 22, 1943

Dear Donnie:

The Venetian blind is down and my office door is locked. The walls refract a soft pearly glow and my sister's face in the picture stares gently and sadly into space. Down the corridor Mr. Berman and Miss Loring are basking in the complacent idea that I am hammering relentlessly at Lana Turner's next picture, and only I know I am not, so there is a feeling of sanctuary here, the same that you must experience when you are alone with *Dance Index*, no Lincoln, no Levine,[1] no me.

Your exploits with Sandy are the sort of plum that one occasionally snatches from the lean crust of life when that austere mystery is not looking right at you. I applaud the success, and let us not pull long faces before the mirror to convince ourselves that we regret the betrayal. It seems, however brutal, to be peculiarly appropriate because of the care that [—] took to rub it in continually about his glorious romance. I can sense your complete satisfaction in what has happened, aside from the living dream which you don't have to tell me took place in bed.

The first letter I got here was from Sandy, wanting me to contact Lionel Wiggam at Paramount, but they did not have him there, poor things.

Lem Ayers arrived yesterday and breezed in to see me. Says Audrey has appointed him my guardian, but I don't think he will have much time for me as I see him sweeping grandly about the lot with a whole retinue of the maddest element here, the ones that put on technicolrmusicals – that word is technicolor musicals.

He tells me also that Margo Jones – Texas Margo, you know – is going to be the summer director at the Pasadena Playhouse and has written him she plans to do "Battle of Angels" and wants him to design it. This happy bit of news was probably in the letter that Bigelow intercepted in New York. He alluded to the letter, and having opened it, but said nothing about what was in it. I hope this goes through. Poor unhappy Myra Torrance would be good company for me this summer. The ocean fills me with sorrow and the

1. Doris Levine, Kirstein's secretary.

67

bright flatness of the California landscape needs a dark, vaulted interior and some goatish cries from the soul.

I have gotten the nicest and friendliest letter from James Laughlin. He wants to use both of the prefaces[1] and me to visit him at his ski lodge as he says he is fed up with ski-ers, they are too one-sided. He assures me the Mss. are safe.

I talk only of letters for they are all that happens right now.

Audrey says her whole office rocked with laughter when they heard I was writing for Lana Turner. I replied that it was an ill wind which blows no good, and I could be grateful for their merriment at least.

I am glad that you made a "wonderful impression" on McClintic. So did I. Perhaps if we had both made horrible impressions he would have bought the play. I knew before I left that he was a dead issue for "You Touched Me" but saw no reason to deepen the sorrow of departure by telling you this. I feel unshakably that that play and Sandy's ass remain the two most valuable properties on Broadway (or hanging over it) and the fact that you have already profited from the one is a hopeful augury for the other. I am convinced that it would sell to the movies for a really handsome price.

I think we should give Mary Hunter every encouragement to go ahead with it.

My salary is temporarily tied up by the Wage Stabilization Board. It seems one is not supposed to get more money now than he was making on or before Oct. 7, 1941. In my case it is only a technicality, but in the meantime I am living on small advances. As soon as this is settled, I will start paying you back the debt incurred when I returned to New York. Suggest you save for the trip out here.

Right now I don't know anybody, hardly, and the life

1. To "The Summer Belvedere", his poems which Laughlin had accepted for "Five Young American Poets: Third Series, 1944".

is rather drab. By the time you are ready to leave New York, things will be more in the groove.

I had a rather bad accident on the scooter when the rear tire blew out on Wilshire Blvd. I was thrown off it and knocked unconscious. The people who picked me up said they thought I was dead as I did not appear to be breathing, but only my glasses were broken. Two days later the front tire also blew out and the scooter is back at the dealer's. I don't know whether to buy new tires or just forget it.

Love,

Tenn.

·37·
Metro-Goldwyn-Mayer Pictures, Culver City, Calif.
[May 27, 1943] Thursday

Donnie

I am terribly, terribly busy, my dear, what with my own writing and Berman's out-fit crouching like hungry dogs outside my office door for scraps of scenes I toss out to them now and again for Lana Turner's new celluloid brassiere!

But I must take time out to quote a little from a letter I have just received from Margo Jones, as the news affects us both. Only let yourself remain fairly skeptical until we see it is not one of those Texas dust-storms.

I quote from Margo as follows:

"Audrey Wood let me read 'You Touched Me' and I've gone completely off my nut about it. That is the one I want to do at Pasadena because I'm sure that it can be worked into the schedule this summer. Gilmore Brown has assured me as much. I honestly think something pretty terrific can be done about it. I told Lem Ayers that I'd give anything he would do the sets for me and he sounded as if he would. I feel something can really be accomplished in a hurry. A really fine production of it should and I believe *will* call the attention of every important person on the Coast – perhaps (and I know a way to manage this) Metro or some other Studio would be interested in backing a production of it in New York (after they see how wonderful it is at the Playhouse – that's the place 'Angel Street' got its start). A movie studio might do this if they felt that after the Broadway production the play would have great movie value and I think 'You Touched Me' might. Honestly, I've not been so excited about anything in a long time."

That is the Margo statement, just as she wrote it, the interpolations all her own. You will see that she is in a lather and I trust you will make suitable reservations in your own mind as I have made in mine, knowing the charm of the lady and her southern effervescence. However it does sound very promising, I think, and I felt you would like to hear about it even at this very tentative moment.

If it goes through – I mean if she actually gets to working on it out here – I think it would justify your coming West. I will do what I can to help you make the trip, for I feel it would be a worthwhile experience for you regardless of how it turned out. And in such an event, Lincoln would no doubt understand and pardon your leaving – and you could probably get back on the magazine in case show fizzles.

I think the entirely genuine and spontaneous enthusiasm for the play of people like Mary Hunter and Margo and Audrey really means something, and it confirms my own brave conviction that it is a solid piece of work that has a future.

Margo says she also plans to do "Angel" but apparently "You Touched Me" has the inside track.

I want you to feel happy about it but not set hopes. And even if for some reason you can't or don't want to come out, you know you can depend upon me to protect our mutual interests.

Margo says she will get here about the middle of June –
I don't suppose she would start work on the play till sometime considerably later in the summer. We have plenty of
time to correspond about it.

Love,

TENNESSEE

.38.

Metro-Goldwyn-Mayer Pictures, Culver City, Calif.
[*May 29, 1943*]

Dear Sandy:

I am glad that our correspondence is going on, and I hope
the army won't terminate it.

As for loneliness, very few people ever understand it, and
I doubt that you are one of the elect. It requires moodiness
and inability to get along with most people – and lack of
social charm always helps. (To acquire it.) I feel that you
would fall short of the last requirement. From what I hear,
boys in the army are not necessarily lonely – unless they
want to be. There are many situations in which loneliness is a
good thing, but in Hollywood it can result in embarrassment.
For instance, yesterday I saw a friend of New York whom
I used to make strenuous efforts to avoid. But because I was
lonely I ran up to him and greeted him effusively. Result –
he invited himself out to my place for the week-end and I
half expect to see him arrive with his luggage. Which would
be most disturbing. Donnie will tell you why. We won't say
his name, but he is a terrifying Prussian! – Could Toby
[Wiggam] be worse?

Last night I visited Herr Issyvoo in his seraglio. I say
seraglio because it is much more like that than a monastery
as there were present about eight women and three men,
sitting on cushions in a semi-circle and preserving the most

absolute expressionless silence. I made a terrible fool of myself, trying to make conversation – because the silence was appalling. I turned to one of them and said, "Why is it that the word Krishnamurti comes into my mind?" You see, the monastery is designed to resemble a little Taj Mahal and the walls are covered with pictures of Hindus. This was a dreadful thing to say, it turned out, as Krishnamurti – I had no idea who or what he was – was a follower of Annie Besant, a notorious crack-pot. This was explained to me very acidly, and I felt like abasing myself to very dust. Herr Issyvoo came to my rescue by suggesting a walk – and I had a feeling that he was nearly as relieved as I was to escape the overpowering atmosphere of outraged sanctity which my entrance had evoked. Herr Issyvoo is not one to speak very frankly all that he is thinking or feeling but I am wondering a little if he is not going to write a wonderful story of what is going on there. No one could do it so well.

Herr Issyvoo is charming. I would say that he and Katherine Anne Porter and of course Donnie are the only charming writers I know.

The studio is very well pleased with my work which is making a sort of celluloid brassiere for Lana Turner to appear in. It is derived from a Harper's Prize novel called "Marriage Is a Private Affair" but we are using practically nothing but the title and a general air of "just got out of bed, let's get back in!"

I visited the producer just now and she looked at me with a dreamy sigh and said, "Oh, Tennessee, you get the sex-values so clearly!" I said, "Jane, if you lived right across from muscle-beach you'd get them, too!" Muscle-beach is where weight-lifters take their girls on week-ends to toss them around for exercise of a most comprehensive nature. There is a big platform and sand-pit across from my apartment reserved for this practice.

Good luck to you, Sandy, and let me hear from you as often as you can.

TENNESSEE

·39·

Metro-Goldwyn-Mayer Pictures, Culver City, Calif.

[June 2, 1943]

Dear Donnie:

I had just inserted a yellow sheet in this machine to write a little bedroom scene for Lana Turner in which her husband discovers she had spent the night in another man's apartment. Nothing happened, by virtue of the Hays office, but of course he does not understand.

Then the mail-boy delivered your letter and poem and the scene must temporarily hold its breath.

The poem is by no means "goo" nor do I find it unoriginal nor imitative.[1] On the contrary, I think it is the best thing in poetic form you have shown me and the last line is very lovely indeed, in fact it has that lift and exultation which is pure poetry which is pure light. It comes closer than you usually come in verse to having form as well as content and I think it will bear sculpturing a little more and the elimination of one or two easy statements such as "singing to the stars" could be lifted right out with improvement. The images are lovely and I think you could dispense with the quotation and still have the whole meaning there.

I will finish this after my work.

Later – next day:

I had a sudden, acute attack of sinus trouble, terrific sledge-hammer blows in the forehead, and had to rush to a special-

---

1. A poem I had written on a quotation from Dostoevsky.

ist. Have you ever had your sinus drained, dearie? It sure is fun! All the space in the cranium not occupied by the brain is squirted full of a liquid. Cotton wadding is stuffed way up between the eye-brows on long steel poles. Then you are left to strangle for a while. Then you are hung head down from the ceiling and horrible suction tubes are inserted and you feel as though your thamatosis[1] (rear section of brain) were being sucked out of your nostrils! I haven't had such a good time since our evening at the Claridge!

All of this had only a temporary effect. This morning the sledge-hammers were at it again, worse than ever. I ran to Pandro Berman's office, incoherent with anguish, and he said, "Come along, we're going to the barber's". We went out to the studio barber-shop. The barber slapped a steaming hot towel on my forehead! Presto! My head was clear as a whistle!

It cost me twenty cents and the nose specialist charged me ten dollars!

But I can tell by the worried looks that the studio thinks they've bought a dead horse to run in the derby. They are pleased with my work, but doubt that I'll live to finish it.

If only the damned sun would stay out, but there are continual fogs, and now I can't swim till this damned thing clears up.

I ran into [—] last week and he came out for the week-end. I entertained him in the grand-manner with quarts of Myers rum and dinners at the beach-club, I was so happy with human companionship, even with thick glasses and a Prussian hair-cut. Well, we did have fun, doing the Palisades together. I called him Chichonya and he called me Babushka, meaning Little Grandmother, and we intrigued the sailors no end with remarks like "Stay out of the lamp-light, Babushka. Romance ends where visibility begins!" It was decided

1. Thalamus?

that I should appear at noon sharp, every day, along the Palisades, singing "Un bel dì" in a Madame Butterfly costume – until results are noticeable.

The week-end netted a relative of Ramon Novarro's, a first cousin who looks rather like him, the right age for you, not me, with my passion for chicken. He has written me some mad letters which I will save for you.

I must read the Shapiro shit.[1] Then we must both write vigorous letters on our official stationery to *Harper's*. Attacks on Crane or Lawrence, the only pure light in modern letters, are not to be tolerated.

I wish you could interest Lincoln in starting another *Hound & Horn* with us as the editors. I feel that I could be daemonic in such a capacity, and I am sure the two of us would constitute a new school. Of some kind.

Pray for my sinus condition and cheer me with letters.

10.

.40.
[Metro-Goldwyn-Mayer Pictures, Culver City, Calif.]
[*June 12, 1943*]

My dear little Brother:

I don't know whether to feel very joyful or terribly scared at the prospect of receiving both you and the *enfant terrible* of New Jersey into my quiet little household. I am wondering just what kind of design for living the two of you have in mind, and how much responsibility I will have to assume? It wouldn't be fair not to warn you that my feeling of responsibility is limited and that after three weeks of adjustment I would expect you both to be fairly self-sufficient,

1. A derogatory poem, "D. H. L.", by Karl Shapiro in the June, 1943, *Harper's*.

because I know that friends can only stay friends by preserving a mutual independence.

Do not misinterpret this warning, which I make only to clear my conscience in case of unhappy developments when you get here. I love you dearly, within such limits as a selfish creature like myself is capable of loving anyone he is not in love with, and as for Sandy, he is too delectable an article to be exorcised as evil.

Margo has arrived and I spent the entire evening with her the day she got here. She did the mad scene from "Lear" as only she can do it, raving and raving. Obviously "You Touched Me" is a script for the ladies, as Audrey and Mary Hunter and Margo are the only ones who have gone mad about it. Margo has incredible ideas. She thinks everybody at Metro will come to see it and fall in love with it and put it right on Broadway. Unfortunately the only person here who has looked at the script only read two scenes and received the painful reminder of the Barrie who wrote "Peter Pan". Being a man, his reaction is unimportant, but most of the potentates at MGM are men.

So far Gilmore Brown at Pasadena has not read the play. He has consented to have Margo do it, unconditionally, in the small auditorium which only seats 100 people. Margo hopes that when he reads the script he will re-arrange his schedule to allow its presentation on the main stage. And she has ideas of getting some movie actors to act the main parts – strictly ideas at this stage. And we called on Lemuel Ayers to try and interest him in designing a set. He was very interested till he heard about the small stage. Lem is living here in a place that is more elaborate than any set he has probably ever designed and his wife has taken on the airs of a Chinese nightingale. There was, however, a mysterious third party present in their ménage, who was too homely and uninteresting to be a friend so he must be a paramour, and I don't think the wife's. Also Eugene Loring stays with them. He and Lem and Aaron Copland and I are going to do a movie short of "Billy the Kid" and I am to write the ballad for it. Loring is so cute, only five feet three inches.

As for Christopher, I haven't seen him since the strange night at the monastery which I described in a letter to Sandy. Yesterday, however, I got a long letter from him, and we are to meet again, at which time he will explain Vedanta to me. J. Laughlin wants me to write an article about Isherwood and Vedanta for New Directions. I have gotten the advance royalties on the book of poems and Laughlin is coming here the end of the month to arrange the poems with me.

L. A. is seething with violence. The zoot-suiters are rioting with the service-men and the service-men are out for blood – indiscriminately. I am told by those who should know that all the local girls have gone underground for the duration, speaking in whispers and dropping never a pin in public places.

The building is so quiet I guess it must be Saturday. I never really know what day of the week it is, for I write all the time and rarely on Lana Turner, which keeps me a bit hazy about other things.

I wrote Bigelow just how baffling I thought he was and he replies, "My dear Tennessee, I am just as blandly innocuous as a glass of water!" I replied to that, "I have seen very bland and innocuous-looking glasses of water that turned five different colors when poured by a stage magician!" I will let you know his counter-retort when it comes.

I may lose all my friends by excessive honesty with them, but as it's my only reliable virtue – honesty – I have to display it. Now, Bigelow, on the other hand, has a warm and generous nature such as you and I could not equal if we tried. Compared to him most of us are regular Englishmen, but the lack of straight-forwardness, the drug-like addiction to misrepresentation, has made him seem right down sinister.

I have three separate bank-accounts, the one that Audrey keeps in New York, which takes most of each pay-check, a joint one with Mother in St. Louis which is to provide my grandmother with proper medical care, and my own checking account in Culver City. I am enclosing a small check from the latter, which I will go on doing each week so you'll have something to come out here on. Will mail you another on Wednesday. This is money I owe you, not an endowment.

Love,

TENNESSEE

.41.

Metro-Goldwyn-Mayer Pictures, Culver City, Calif.
[*June 16, 1943*]

Dear Donnie:

Adding just a note and another installment of what we won't call an endowment.

You haven't told me anything about the situation at *Dance Index*. I think that makes a lot of difference in the plans for you. I can't get it off my mind, or conscience, that when you give that job up, if you have to do it, you will be back where you were before you got it. Now in California there are naturally loads of jobs but nearly all are the kind that you have had in the past and I am wondering – in fact I *know* – how you would like them. Nevertheless you would have to get some kind of job, as two unquestionably live twice as expensively as one and I am just keeping within the limits of my living allowance as it is. I worry about it a good deal, naturally. Now if you could just get a leave of absence from *Dance Index* and only take something not *too* difficult or tiresome out here for a while – that would be okay. But I hate to think of you just leaving that phenome-

78

nally pleasant and easy job cold and depending on what you can get out here for an indefinite period. You have *all* of your career as a writer before you and if I remember even vaguely how things go, it will be a long, long time before you can make a living out of it. Bless you, my dear, I don't mean you are not a damn fine and pure artist now, but that that isn't going to be money in your pockets maybe for quite some time. There is of course "You Touched Me". But you must remember what a sorry mess depending on the quick sale of that script got me into last winter. I very barely – nobody knows how barely – avoided something really disastrous. By luck and Audrey. I couldn't feel impervious to your unhappiness, no matter how I tried, so I want you to be very careful and don't do anything rash, even if it doesn't involve me.

This is the last reference I shall make to the negative side of your leaving the job in N. Y. and if I have seemed excessively conscientious – Well, I do have a conscience!

Love,

Tom

P.S. Tell Sandy I don't know any actors nor go to any parties – really none.

.42.

Metro-Goldwyn-Mayer Pictures, Culver City, Calif.
June 25, 1943

Dear Sandy:

I am glad to hear from Donnie that you are thinking of coming out here. You didn't mention it in your last letter so I wonder how actual the plans are, and also how you have managed to remain out of the army.[1]

I have been talking to Donnie like a Dutch uncle (through

1. He was a freshman at Princeton on the college student deferment plan.

79

the mail) about his own plan of coming out here. Naturally I want him out here, but also I worry a great deal about the consequences for him. Maybe you – since you now appear to know each other reasonably well – can give me a clearer picture of Donnie's situation in general at the present time and how the trip would affect it than I am able to gather at this distance and from Donnie's own letters. You see, I feel that Donnie has achieved something very remarkable in New York, at his age and with his lack of experience, to be the editor of a magazine as distinguished as *Dance Index*, and the fact that he would not find any occupation out here with nearly the dignity, prestige or even pleasantness, causes me more and more concern, as I cannot free my conscience of the knowledge that were it not for my presence here, the idea of giving up his position in N. Y. would not have occurred to him.

As you have presumably discussed the trip out here together, wish you would tell me what you gather from Donnie about his hopes or intentions, so that I can judge their practicality. I am not in a position to be of much help to Donnie as all my money goes through my agent who is allowing me a very minor allowance to live on and salting the rest away in a savings account so I can quit the films when my six-months term is up and devote myself to creative work.

I shall make no further reference to either you or Donnie to the dangers involved in the excursion but expect you both to evaluate them for yourselves and plan accordingly. Of course I regard your plans as being entirely your own business, but Donnie's are also mine as we are sort of brothers under the skin.

I don't see how a trip out here could possible hurt you as you have no position to give up, and there may be more opportunities for you out here than in N. Y. I can't say. Anyhow I hope you both work out some feasible plan, something that will permit you both to do what you *want* to do and at the same time not sacrifice too much to make it worth while.

Best always,

TENN.

·43·
Metro-Goldwyn-Mayer Pictures, Culver City, Calif.
[*June 25, 1943*]

Dear Donnie:

I liked your letter and the calm and pragmatic tone of it. Perhaps I expected you to be a little annoyed at the frankness of mine. Sometimes I think I am being nicest when I am being naturally but superficially sweet. However all in all I am at my best, where other people are concerned, when I talk or write straight from a rather boney (as distinct from bonny) shoulder!

So – Let us plunge into news.

Margo is still going full-steam ahead and the script is typed up even better than Bigelow typed it for less money and copies are being shown to Gilmore Brown and Thomas Mitchell – you know, the Academy Award character actor – whom Margo thought of with real inspiration as Cornelius Rockley. Reports should be coming in this week. Lem Ayers has also got a copy and Margo still hopes he may do the set. As for the main stage, Margo discourages me in any hopes for it due to the adamant fixation on a drama festival of Tarkington plays – Holy Cats!

Also – Audrey sends a letter from McConnell, director of the famous Cleveland Play House which stacks up with Pasadena as the two leading national little theatres. He asks permission to do the play next season at his theatre. It may soon be a problem to keep our potential producers at peace with each other, as I dare say Mary Hunter is still in the running, with or without Carley Wharton's financial support.

Where I am concerned there has been a big shake-up at MGM. I am removed bodily and spiritually from the Lana Turner script, it being decided that my character was "too fay" for Lana to deal with. I will probably be passed over to another producer, the one who dealt with Saroyan and whom Lem Ayers is working with. In the meantime I am happily writing my own stuff and caring not a fig nor a thistle what goes on in the offices of my mentors.

The sinus condition has cleared up and the season has become rather brilliant in Santa Monica, with the shrine of Mae West taking on an aspect which only Mae could fully appreciate.

Horton Foote arrives on the coast this Saturday in some obscure connection with "Only the Heart". Don't ask me what about.

Oh, how I loved the picture of K. A. P.![1] It goes on my study wall with Hart Crane and Chekhov, all three nicely framed.

Thank you so much for it!

I will write you again next week when Margo gets in some reports on the script.

Love,

10.

P.S. Please *do* see that K.A.P. gets this note. I think it would please her, and she is someone I would love to please.

(Note enclosed)

---

1. Katherine Anne Porter, a photograph of her by Cadmus that I had sent him.

Metro-Goldwyn-Mayer Pictures, Culver City, Calif.
July 1, 1943

Dear Donnie:

I am certainly happy to learn how intelligently you are arranging matters in N. Y., about the magazine, Etc. I had the idea you were intending to just give it up and the more I thought of it the more inadvisable it seemed. Now it appears to me that you should be able to simply get a leave of absence, or better still, combine the trip out here with some project for the magazine, such as getting material on the dance in the movies. Such people as Eugene Loring and Agnes de Mille being now out here to do picture work, there must be some material of that kind obtainable on the coast. At any rate, if you provide for the issues that would come out during the absence, Lincoln should certainly continue your pay. I would make it very clear to him that this is expected, as well as justifiable, as it would make all the difference in the world. Fidelma should be useful at this, if Lincoln is difficult about it.

Horton Foote has arrived out here and was on my hands the last 24 hours. I was bathed in sweetness and light which has such a withering effect on my spirit. But I bore up bravely, realizing he probably believes in his sentiments more than I do. One cannot fail to recognize his "niceness" however little one is capable of responding inwardly. He has gotten hold of a producer-actor, Jacques Thery, who is going to back "Only the Heart" on Broadway next season with Mary Hunter and the Actors Company as co-producers. A $500 advance and expenses on the coast while working on it. He claims that he is "home-sick" and as soon as he entered my apartment he sighed, "Tennessee, this is home!" but I pretended not to get the point. I just couldn't bear it more than one night.

Horton says the Company (N. Y.) definitely want to produce "You Touched Me", even would like to open the season
with it. With Mary Hunter's direction and Perry Wilson
probably available for the role of Matilda, I think that is the
best bet of the three production offers. However Margo
would die if she knew anyone else had the inside track on a
N. Y. production, as she is still blissfully expecting her
Pasadena showing to be removed intact to Broadway. So as
long as she is doing it in Pasadena, no final commitments can
be made with anyone else – that is, honorably. Not till she
gives up the notion of making Broadway with it. So you
see what the game is, sort of a juggler's trick, keeping two
balls in the air at once. The Cleveland deal makes no difference
as it would be strictly Cleveland, but Margo and Mary are
sort of running neck-and-neck it would seem, and the idea
is to keep them both running. Now Mary is my choice of the
two, in spite of the fact that I dearly love Margo, for I think
that Mary is the most intelligent woman I have ever met and
would do the play better than McClintic, for instance. About
Margo I can only say she has the energy of Niagara Falls and
an enthusiasm which is either irresistible or overwhelming.
She directed plays for seven years in Houston, all the way
from Chekhov's "Uncle Vanya" to the plays of Theodore
Apstein, so she is no amateur in experience. Both look too
good to discourage. I think I will write Mary that in my
private opinion (which is true) the Margo deal will be just
laboratory, and while I can't make any promise until after
that production pans or peters out, there is no reason to
hesitate much in her own plans for putting it on. Incidentally,
it seems that Perry Wilson is now free of the Barrymore show
and might be available for Matilda.

The Pasadena production would be for an invited audience
only, no charge of admission and no author's royalties – simply a show-case. From Cleveland the usual amateur royalties,

not amounting to much, would be forthcoming I presume. Mary's company would be the same in royalties as any Broadway production; that is, percentage. It is worth observing, however, that Mr. Foote never apparently made much money out of them.

The question of which stage at Pasadena delays crystallization of plans. I will let you know soon as a starting date is scheduled.

Just received a note asking me if I had a story idea for Margaret O'Brien? If you are very lucky, you haven't seen her. She is a smaller and more loathsome edition of Shirley Temple before *that* one retired from the screen. I do indeed have a story idea for her, but it is unprintable. Must return to work.

Love,

10.

·45·

Metro-Goldwyn-Mayer Pictures, Culver City, Calif.
[*July 12, 1943*] *Monday*

Dear Donnie:

Just got your letter with the printed enclosure. It has had a shattering effect on my nerves.[1]

Later – I had gotten just so far when a sailor friend of yours and Lincoln's appeared on the lot, a Mr. Romney,[2] to whom I have devoted the last three hours, conducting him about the lot and giving him lunch and providing him

1. I have no memory of this, but I believe his remark is meant facetiously.

2. Richard Romney reportedly entered the N. Y. art world by lying down on the floor in front of a Tchelitchew painting in the Museum of Modern Art and not getting up until he met the artist. He was a great success. Three days after Tennessee's letter, Isherwood wrote that his introduction to Romney was one which worked out, in contrast to his to Tennessee, one which didn't.

with a picture of Garbo whom he will return to Greenland as his pin-up girl. He would make a good pin-up girl himself. Or even better, pinned down. I did not succeed in accomplishing this. I really must have a sofa put in my office for occasions like these. Nearly everyone else on the lot has one. All I have is my over-stuffed chair and a couple of straight ones in far corners of the room that cannot be used for a very subtle approach.

I wish I could give you some definite news about the Pasadena situation. I may be able to by the end of the week. Wednesday evening Margo is having Lem Ayers and Gilmore Brown and I over for dinner and on that occasion we may be able to get some definite commitment out of Gilmore. He has told Margo she can put the play on, but the question of when and which stage is still suspended. If it's done on the main stage, it won't be till after the Tarkington festival has run its horrible course, which would delay the production probably till early Fall. If it's done on the Playbox stage it might get started a good deal sooner. I ought to know after Wednesday night. I know that Lem disapproves of the Playbox. I haven't seen it yet, but I think he's right. Margo says she is willing to give up her $300 a month job in Texas to stay over for a production on the main stage if that is decided on.

Horton Foote has been on my hands almost continually the past week or two. He is doing Hollywood in the big way with his producer friend, and they have introduced me to all kinds of film people. Simone Simon and Geraldine Fitzgerald were the two that I liked. However I got my fill of them all and finally left word at Horton's house that I had left town and would call him when I returned. Most people's lives here are a round of meeting people and having drinks with them, and as they are still more tiresome than corresponding groups in New York, you must do something

86

like this to extricate yourself after a while. Horton is more like a pineapple ice-cream soda than ever.

I have been having an affair with a famous dancer. This is *entre nous*, so if you guess who it is, don't tell as the character is terribly afraid of such publicity, as well he may be with my transcontinental reputation to think of.

I got the most amusing letter from my sister a few days ago, the first she has written me since her retirement. She wrote quite normally and lucidly except for the remark toward the end of the letter that she had been hearing me on the radio lately. She is spending the summer at a rest-home in North Carolina and Grand and I are paying her expenses there. It is the first time I have ever been able to do anything for my family which is naturally a satisfaction.

In spite of everything I manage to live a very quiet and simple life here, the sort I could never have in New York. I have a little wind-up victrola and am collecting some records. I got the wind-up type so I could use it if I retire to the New Mexican ranch after my term here. That is still my favorite dream. I think you might enjoy and approve of this sort of life as it contains all the elements which we both desire in our peculiar fashion.

I got such a sweet letter from Katherine Anne Porter in response to my note. Which reminds me I must write her and ask for the pictures of Hart Crane she has.

I will enclose another small check. I would like to send you a big sum of money all at once, as you are the one person I know could use it to the best advantage. However I just barely break even every week with all the places money has to go. Margo simply wallows in Scotch, Horton invariably forgets his pocket-book, and poor David Gregory spends every week-end with me and the house we run, modest as it is, has a terrific overhead on Saturdays and Sundays. I remind myself more and more of a character I am writing

87

about in a story called *The Rich and Eventful Death of Isabel Holly.*[1]

Please send me a copy of the *Carnival*[2] when you get it in final draft. I want you to really do that, so don't forget it.

Love,

TENNESSEE

.46.[3]

[1647 Ocean Ave., Santa Monica, Calif.]
[*July 18, 1943*] *Sunday P. M.*

Dear Donnie –

I am sitting at my kitchen table waiting for my lover to arrive with lettuce and tomatoes and rum and sherry wine and a big floury loaf of bread in the fading sunlight. Coffee is percolating gently, and my mood is mellow. I have been very happy lately, just wallowing in it selfishly, knowing it will not last very long, which is all the more reason to enjoy it now. I suppose life always ends badly for almost everybody. We must have long fingers and catch at whatever we can while it is passing near us.

I have your lovely picture (by Lynes)[4] on my dressing table across the room from where I am sitting. You look very sweet in it, not in Horton's way but a nice way. I hope you have not grown to dislike me.[5]

Margo has just about decided to stay over till November which is the time when we could use the main stage. She will

1. An early title of *The Coming of Something to the Widow Holly.*

2. An early title of *Flesh Farewell.*

3. Written on the backs of three handbill "programme"'s for a production of "Rain" at the Beaux Arts Theatre.

4. This photograph by George Platt Lynes is reproduced in the "Memoirs".

5. Why? Had he already learned of the "realistic" omission mentioned in letter 51?

88

give up her $300 a month job at Texas to do this. Then we would have a fine star cast and probably a set by Lem Ayers. Don't you think that is better than putting it on a little sooner in the little Playbox? However if you want to come out here before then, just for a change, why don't you?

Met Ruth Ford and her husband Peter Van Eyck at a cocktail party. Peter is *excruciatingly* beautiful. Do you know what I mean? Ruth is a darling, prettier than Charles.[1]

Later – My landlady knocked at the door and said she'd just now remembered that Mr. ... called about noon to say he was returning to N. Y. tomorrow, unexpectedly, and would have to stay home and pack.

Being a sensible character, I go out and cruise the Palisades and fetch in a pretty little belle with T. B., a brace over one chest where 5 ribs were removed but a pretty ass and a sweet nature. She has just left. Says I am "so restful." Beautiful tribute. For one thing in life, there is always something else not quite so good, but acceptable.

Send me the *Carnival*.

Love –

10.

·47·

Metro-Goldwyn-Mayer Pictures, Culver, City, Calif.
Sometime in July, 1943

Dear Sandy:

Thanks so much for the clipping and your letters. I like all of them, it always gives a pleasant beginning to the day to find a letter from Don or you stuck under my door. I always arrive on the lot too late (sometimes nearly noon) to let the mail-boy in. I like to take my letters over to the commissary with me and read them and read them over while I'm enjoying

1. Charles Henri Ford, her brother.

89

the morning coffee – which, with the morning mail makes up the warmest and brightest part of the day, the time when the nicest part of the personality comes out of all the traumas and mutations we get sealed up in as a result of our mixing with the world we never made.

The interview is like Hopkins and not like her. It's funny. It gives one side of her personality, but certainly doesn't suggest the brilliance and the bubbling warmth that make her unforgettable to me. There were times when she was like morning mail and morning coffee, and again she was like a hat-pin jabbed in your stomach. The quintessence of the female, a really magnificent bitch.

I have come to the roughest part of a new play, assembling the scattered papers and getting ready to prepare a last draft of it. This is always a nightmare to me, for while I am working I toss papers right and left, at the end of each day I gather them helter-skelter and pile them together. So that the ultimate arrangement is a colossal job, which I do with actual groans and muttered curses, sitting on the floor with papers all about me, gradually going into little separate stacks, some order finally emerging, but not till I have died a thousand deaths. I am sure it is worse than child-birth. Reading through it after the assembly is worse still. In fact I usually don't do it, that is why such odd incongruities and contradictions occur in my scripts. – Writing is not a happy profession.

It has just about been decided to post-pone the Pasadena production of "You Touched Me" till late October or November when the main stage would be available for it and better actors. I am wondering how that will affect Donnie's plans to come out here this summer. Perhaps he will prefer to wait till the production, or maybe he will just come out for a change of air and environment, which he may be needing. And how about you? Are you still thinking of coming to the Coast, and when?

I'm supposed to see the producer Arthur Freed today about a new picture assignment. Probably making a folk-opera out of the "Billy the Kid" material, using my lyrics and dialogue with Lem Ayers and Eugene Loring working on it, too.

If I have to write on a picture, I guess that would be as nice an assignment as I could get.

Life here is sort of dream-like, it slips by so easily and effortlessly. That is a peculiarity of California, it makes you a healthy animal, anesthetizing the troublesome little soul, or whatever it is you're conscious of other places.

By all means see "The Ox-Bow Incident". I think it is the finest American film ever made.

Get Donnie to write me soon how the production date will affect his intentions, and do go on writing me yourself.

Salud!

TENNESSEE

.48.

Metro-Goldwyn-Mayer Pictures, Culver City, Calif.
7/28/43

Dear Donnie:

I am glad another letter from you has come as I feel like writing you, it is so much better than talking to anyone else.

My nerves are tied in knots today. I have plunged into one of my periodic neuroses, I call them "blue-devils", and it is like having wild-cats under my skin. They are a Williams family trait, I suppose. Destroyed my sister's mind and made my father a raging drunkard. In me they take the form of interior storms that show remarkably little from the outside but which create a deep chasm between myself and all other people, even deeper than the relatively ordinary ones of homosexuality and being an artist. It is curious the various

91

forms they take – someday, when I have the courage, I will sit down and face them and write them all out. Now I can only speak of the symptoms, for if I look at them too closely, I feel they would spring at me more violently. Now for instance all contact with people is like a salty finger stroking a raw wound. My office is merciful, but whenever the phone rings and someone raps at the door, I shudder and fairly cringe. Back of this craziness is a perfect sanity, untouched and wholly separate, a wise counsellor that looks for causes and tries to side-step effects and says patiently and comfortingly, Hang on, it will pass away! But knows that it will always return another day.[1] Ever since I was about ten years old I have lived with these blue-devils of various kinds and degrees, they come and go, all of them at their crises achieving about the same intensity, none of them ever quite reaching the innermost me. All of us must sadly face the fact that we are make-shift arrangements. That our parents and their parents before them have wantonly bedded together and created anything and everything in the way of descendants that accident might arrange. No regard for good or bad mixtures, no regard for warring elements. Pies, sandwiches, cough syrups are put together with attention to what are congruous or suitable components – but not human beings! We are slapped together by any two bodies that happen to lust for each other. And told to live – and be good and decent and render a good account of ourselves in the world! Naturally we don't. Naturally we have very little integrity, if any at all. Naturally the innermost "I" or "You" is lost in a sea of other disintegrated elements, things that can't fit together and that make an eternal war in our natures.

No, the world hasn't started yet, and it won't start until these incredible fools who run things come to see that all reform begins in procreation.

1. Revealingly close to the remark attributed to the nun on page 305.

92

It has done me good to write this out, I hope you don't mind.

You say that you are pompous, selfish, and stupid. Of course you are sometimes, but at least you have the good sense to see it and the honesty to say it. The innermost "you" is building his world on honesty which is the only good foundation we can find. It is the common level on which occasion[ally] "you" and "I" or somebody else's innermost being can momentarily meet, during the flux and torrent of our disparate parts. Without it – what a grinning desolation! Nobody can honestly blame you for anything that you are. Blame or guilt is all mistaken and false. Even William Randolph Hearst is not guilty, but he is evil. There are a few of us who know this and feel it. I think it is what Isherwood says in *Sally Bowles* and it is what you hinted at in your phrase "the momentariness of truth". We all bob only momently above the bubbling, boiling surface of the torrent of lies and distortions we are borne along. We are submarine creatures, for beneath that surface is the world we live in, with all its names and labels and its accepted ideas. And over it only is the oxygen unadulterated which we can only breathe in spasms now and again, and the only vision which is pure at all.

[—] – a salesman of my father's just called. He and his family will descend upon me this week-end for "a little visit" and a swim. When Parrott and I were at Laguna, [—] and his screaming little family once drove all the way out there to see us, but fortunately we saw them crossing the ranch, and we skipped out the back door and hid in the arroyo till they had given up the search. We saw them poking around the place for hours like ants while we sun-bathed on a big rock. Tonight I will have dinner with Ruth Ford and Peter Van Eyck, another ordeal. They are both charming people, which makes it all the worse. By the way, Isherwood

93

says that Peter was Sally's young lover in the short story –
he knew him in Berlin ten years ago. Seems extraordinary,
for he looks so boyish. I believe I have told you he is the
most exciting man I have ever looked at, and in a way that
you also would feel.

"The Gentleman Caller" remains my chief work, but it
goes slowly, I feel no overwhelming interest in it. It lacks
the violence that excites me, so I piddle around with it. My
picture work is to make a scenario out of "Billy the Kid"
material – as good an assignment I could hope for, but I am
lazy about it and barely am started.

Love –

10.

P.S. Wrote this in depression which is now past and I
am bright and sunny again. But I like the part about procreation so I will send it anyhow.

Too bad about Sandy – or is it? I am maintaining a benevolent neutrality till I know more. But you have "looked on
Beauty bare!"

·49·

Metro-Goldwyn-Mayer Pictures, Culver City, Calif.

8/2?/43

Dear Donnie:

I have just gotten your letter and read it at breakfast in
the commissary, trying to shield from such eyes as Lem Ayers
and Mr. Arthur Freed, and at the same time absorb it fully.
I think it the nicest letter you have written me, and I am
certainly glad you mailed it.

I am sure that at this point the most dreadful thing for you
is indecision, being unable to say, "This I will do!" So it
is just as well to regard coming out here as an eventual

94

certainty, now that you have thoroughly weighed all the pros and cons.

I know you to be a realistic boy but at the same time one capable, to put it mildly, of very intense feelings. So I am a little disturbed about the emotional set-up. Who knows better than I the impossibility of looking objectively at the possessor of a beautiful body that one has been to bed with? But you must try to remember Sandy as you saw and knew him before he became your lover. I think we both judged him correctly to be a charming little fellow with no particular scruples. Dip into his honey-cup but don't let the petals close on you, Brother Bee!

Hollywood is a maelstrom in which you will almost inevitably lose each other. Be *very* sure of that. Constancy is unknown out here, there is too much flagrant beauty and flagrant bitchery all round. Even the normal men are flirtatious with each other. Yesterday afternoon Margo and I had cocktails at Ruth Ford's. She wanted to read "You Touched Me", so we brought her the script, and it may very well be that she would be excellent for Matilda. She is really very beautiful and much like Charles in imagination and background. But Peter Van Eyck, whom I have mentioned before, came in wearing very sheer silky trousers and a pale green shirt unbuttoned to reveal his pale gold chest. Another girl, a house-guest, was there. Margo and I both felt the atmosphere was charged with an almost hysterical sexuality and torment of jealousy and suspicion although there was much exchange of kisses and darlings all around. That is how things are in Hollywood all the time, no peace where sex is concerned, only continual frenzy and intrigue. One must be sensible about it.

Well, everything is settled about the play production. The date is definitely set for October 24 and it will be done in the intimate Playbox theatre and Lem will *not* do the set. He demanded a contract stipulating he would do any set in any production of it, which Audrey thought preposterous and rejected. Margo said without him to design it, she would prefer putting it on in the Playbox, so that is settled. Also I am thinking of changing it back to *after* the war, now that the war appears to be approaching an end so nearly.

I spent all yesterday with Margo, riding in taxis all about Los Angeles county, delivering Ruth and her friends various places and finally taking four of them to the most expensive restaurant on the Strip, then Margo and I to the ballet in the Bowl. The cost of the evening was thirty-five dollars! And I splashed chicken gravy all over my good suit and was so upset by Peter's beauty that I all but wept. And at the ballet we ran into Horton, and after the ballet I sat between two beautiful dancers in another restaurant, and finally ended up having to share a very narrow single bed with Horton, as the buses had stopped running to Santa Monica. After such evenings I say to myself, Yes, verily, I shall live in the Lobos mountains!

Well, I must stop now while I still have some energy and get some work done.

We will not think too seriously of what may happen when you and Sandy and I are sleeping in the same room. A sense of humor and that mutual lack of illusions will doubtless see us through whatever contingencies arrive. In her letter to me K. A. P. says, "It goes, it goes!" And that's how I feel about it.

[...]

With love,

10.

.50.

[1647 Ocean Ave., Santa Monica, Calif.]
Aug. 14, 1943

Dear Donnie –

I am writing in my "Big 5 Pencil tablet" as I am taking several weeks (not exceeding 6) leave (without pay) from MGM. Tomorrow I may start a 2 wk. job at Goldwyn's. Otherwise I'll take a little trip up or down the coast on my thumb, which I would rather do. Audrey writes that I have over $600 in my savings acct. I hope I can run it up to $1000 before I leave for Mexico in November. I'm glad you are coming out before then. We might go together, if the play is sold so we'd both have money.

Right now I am spending a few days with a fellow I lived with in New Orleans 8 years ago. Ran into him in the Brown Derby. He is now a designer at Goldwyn's.

No news on play – Oct. 24 is production date. Ruth Ford will probably play Matilda. I am crazy about her, and she is really lovely. Adores Charles and poetry and insisted I send him some, so I mailed him pt. of a new long poem. I am writing a good deal of verse. Reaction to studio. But seldom is verse any good. I love E. E. Cummings in August *Poetry*.

I have been reading Katherine Mansfield's letters. If you haven't, you should. They are a little gushy but often lovely.

Last night I knocked out my false front tooth by walking into a plate glass window which I thought was an open door. Was replaced this A. M. – $5.00. That's all the news.

Love,

10.

Quotation from Mansfield.

"How strange talking is – what mists rise and fall – how one loses the other and then thinks to have found the other –

97

then down comes another soft final curtain. But it is incredible – don't you feel – how mysterious and isolated we each of us are – at the last. I suppose one ought to make this discovery once and for all, but I seem to be always making it again."

"I am so tired – I have the feeling of dragging a great endless rope out of a dark sea."

"It is so hard to live from one's center of being in London."

I wish I could remember my reaction on receiving this letter. No doubt I was upset. Suddenly "You Touched Me", which I had started and which both Tennessee and I had worked so hard on, in the hope of earning enough money to concentrate on other undertakings closer to our hearts, was his very heart itself and so deeply a part of his life that I could not imagine his discomfort at having my name connected to it! I knew that he was more responsible for its current version than I was; but I don't think it occurred to me at the time, even as a remote possibility, that his emotion came from guilt at having let this fact make him wish I could be dropped altogether, now that the play was about to be produced. There was no question that he was upset, however, even to the point of attacking me on my sexual morality. I must have decided that his intention was to defend himself and not to hurt me, that the "resentments and jealousies" he spoke of were his, and tried to assuage them. Still, I tend to hold my own and say what I think in such matters, and I wish I could read my reply.[1]

.51.
[1647 Ocean Ave., Santa Monica, Calif.]
8/27/43

Dear Donnie:

The studio has exercised the 6-weeks lay-off clause in my contract in retaliation for my unwillingness to undertake another stupid assignment. Which means I am having to live six weeks on one week's pay – till Sept. 24th. Aside from that inconvenience, I find it very agreeable, certainly better

1. The University of Texas has none of my letters to Tennessee among his papers deposited there and I have been unable to discover any elsewhere. (Note: see the Preface to the Brown Thrasher Edition.)

than doing the job they wanted. This will explain why you haven't heard from me lately. Having nobody to put stamps on my letters and mail them, they just don't get off.

I'm glad to see the play is getting some publicity in N. Y. Of course I don't subscribe to the omission of your name in the notice, and I will inform Audrey and Margo again that it should appear in all the press-releases. Of course the omission was motivated, in a realistic way, by the publicity value of my name.

Now that the play is actually going into production two places, and may very well leap into prominence nationally, I think we had better anticipate and prepare ourselves against the little resentments and jealousies, however unnecessary, that may result from the play being legally our common property. As you know, when there is a very decided preponderance of contribution, as well as reputation, on one side of a collaboration, the credit and percentage are usually fixed accordingly. In our case, however – at your suggestion[1] and with my willing agreement – the preponderance is only in the contribution and reputation. Profits will be equally divided between you and me,[2] and you will be given full program credit as co-author. Because of our friendship I am reconciled to that unusual situation. Just the same it may very well happen that more attention, of a less tangible nature, may come my way than yours. I won't pretend to think that would be unsuitable. Unless you keep in mind the equity of the situation, this might make you resentful. So I hope you will bear in mind that my *heart* (as well as so much labor, time, desperation) is threaded into this play. There are things in it, speeches, feelings, ideas, that are as deeply and intensely personal to me as all my past life – or any organ of my body, or life itself! I am saying this with

1. Not true. See page 41.
2. See page 166, footnote 1.

such poetic emphasis so you will be able to imagine the degree of discomfort I have to adjust myself to in having another person's – even a close friend's – name affixed to the work. I'm saying all this now not by way of complaint, or belated squawking, but so you will sense my feelings as well as your own in case a resentment springs up about the division of laurels – *not* money – in case of the play receiving the praise it deserves. This being understood, I don't think anything is going to come up which we can't talk out with our usual frankness and still be loving companions – so much for that!

Margo left yesterday for Texas. On Sept. 13th she goes to Cleveland to direct the production there. She has wangled funds from the National Theatre Conference to pay her transportation, round-trip between Cleveland and Pasadena, to put on the play both places, and she will receive also a very good salary. The girl is rather monumental in force of character. Frankly, I am over-awed by the way she accomplishes things and exerts her will over people. She is never tired or bored herself and can't imagine weariness or boredom in other people. She wore me out this summer! But she will always be, as a personality, the most vital accident of my life. – Incidentally, I saw her student productions at Pasadena and I feel that her direction is better than any in New York, except possibly Mary Hunter's.

The Pasadena cast, so far and subject to changes of heart and mind during Margo's absence, is as follows:

Matilda – definitely Ruth Ford
Emmie – possibly Agnes Moorehead
Captain – probably Carl Benton Reid
Hadrian – probably Henry Morgan
(Morgan played Fonda's partner in "Ox-Bow Incident" and is awfully strong.)

Brother Dakin surprised the family by becoming a 2nd Lieutenant in the air-force and is about to be placed in charge of a control-tower, primary object of assault, in one of the South Pacific bases. Mother is full of sorrow and religion – poor old girl!

I can only advise you to rake up all the money possible before you come out here, as the expenses here are terrific. Could you farm Sandy out at ten percent on his ass? – Christopher says he's gotten very sad letters from [—]. Wrote back to him suggesting masturbation as a relief. Did you realize that [—] was so deeply in love with the boy when you took him over? Sandy being Sandy, and [—] grown up – it seems to me fantastic. Anyway [...]. There is nothing more deadly than a smiling hatred! And I have seen it in [—]'s face for offenses as small as mine.

Love,

TENN.

This explosion sank from sight as suddenly as it had surfaced.
Occasional ripples appear where the unique combination of money
and importance is concerned. (Should I get my travel fare to Cleve-
land – where I had gone and Tennessee hadn't – even if it had to be
deducted from his?)

But for the most part, his feelings about me take the form of an
increasingly abstract insistence on the "purity" of my artistic situation
compared to his – as though it will not matter so much what com-
promises he makes in order to succeed so long as I make none.

.52.
[1647 Ocean Ave., Santa Monica, Calif.]
[*September 8, 1943*]

Dear Don:

Complications and complications! The bearded "Holy
Man" who used to bless our food when I lived at Fritzi's
– Tony! – has shown up here and been here a week with his
mistress, the star of "Oklahoma!" – erstwhile.[1] All sorts of
weird goings-on that I couldn't even begin to write you
about, so I won't try to!

It has been a very thick, juicy slab of a summer, with
too much of everything, sun, sea, sex, neuroses, entertainment, ennui, an overdose of them all, all very thick and
jammy! Everything seems to be good for me in a way. In
spite of basic damnation, I am incorrigibly lucky. I feel
that God should walk into this mellow kitchen of mine with
drawn sword and just wordlessly chop my head off because I

1. Tony Smith and Jane Lawrence, who were married soon after with Tennessee as witness.

have been too fortunate compared with the female members of my doomed house.

But then when I'm in a pretty good humor like this I forget how wretched occasions have seen me. Consistency, thy name is not Tennessee!

My astonishment at life increases daily. – No material for a new paragraph!

Would like to talk to you but don't feel like striking poses on paper just now – bear with me!

Love,

10.

·53·
[1647 Ocean Ave., Santa Monica, Calif.]
[*September 20, 1943*]

Dear Donnie:

The ants are literally taking over my place. I have left the dishes unwashed for about ten days. When I need a clean dish I just turn on the faucet and let one of them rinse off. The ants love it! They are thinking of supporting me for a 4th term! Fortunately I don't dislike them as I do roaches. I respect their social organization very highly and they seem to have an indulgent feeling for my anarchy. So we get on. I have only three sacred articles of food, my cereal, my brown sugar, and my coffee. The ants seem to realize this and respect the sanctity of those articles, never go near them. And I regard their concerted attacks on left-overs as a manifestation of the cooperative commonwealth on a small scale. Tony doesn't approve of all this. In spite of the red beard he dislikes disorder and says that I have grown very much like a Kafka character of the early Kafka period when he was still capable of creating more or less characters. My 6 weeks away from the studio which terminate Monday have been a busmaker's holiday. I've written far more than I did at the studio. My contemptuous attitude toward the world and its creatures has reached an all time high, so that I rarely even bother to button my fly when I go out on the streets and as you know, I have abandoned civilities even in letters. All of this derives not from megalomania but from association with the ants. Of that I am pretty sure.

I have just had an orgy with a Ganymede of 15 years exactly, met on the Palisades. Moaned like a wounded bird pierced twice by the arrow of love, and I have just sent him home to get there ahead of Mama who works on the swing-shift. If Saint Oscar wasn't working with me this summer I would wind up not in Mexico but San Quentin. There are only two times in this world when I am happy and selfless and pure. One is when I jack off on paper and the other when I empty all the fretfulness of desire on a young male body. There must be a third occasion for happiness in the world. What is it and where? I shall have to find it, it is the Holy Grail. Have you any idea where it is?

Zola the Landlady has given me a bowl of ripe tomatoes from the garden back of the house. They are big as your fist, bloody red, and spurt between your teeth when you bite into them. Bits of brown earth are still clinging about the spiky leaves and stems and they taste like the sweetness and pride of all unconscious life which we put so shamelessly to our own uses. Zola is a wonderful character, a lecherous communist woman of about forty-five with a great blown-up body. She sleeps with any man in the house who will have her, and has a frail, sour little husband named Ernie who does all the house-work, bed-making, Etc., while she soaks up the sun on the porch steps or a big raggedy mattress she has flung out in the back-yard near the tomato patch, with a cocker spaniel resting its head on her belly. Right now the wrestling champion of the Pacific coast is stopping here, a big monolith of a body. He stalks down the hall in an electric blue satin robe clinging like a kiss to all the lines of his body and lounges in the hall telephoning his women. While he phones he shifts his body in the glittering robe lasciviously from right to left, the big buttocks jutting out and rolling as he croons into the mouth-piece. He fairly fucks the wall. I always pretend to be waiting to make a call so I can watch, and tonight Zola finally and reluctantly introduced us. Either she has gotten all of it she can take or can't get it. There are two things we agree on, and one of them is communism. The other is our most ardent point of agreement but we only discuss it in knowing smiles at each other and the shyly understanding exchange of drinks and tomatoes, Etc. The little husband is polite and furious and is always trembling a little. There is a tremendous short story in the place for you or Christopher,[1] especially the woman on the raggedy mattress by the tomato patch with the great rocking days of California weaving in and out while she ages and laps up life with the tongue of a female bull.

Probably the greatest difference in the world is the difference between being fucked and well-fucked. This is my best epigram and I give it to you without charge!

Love,

TENNESSEE

Isn't this a *gay* letter? I am back on pay roll at Studio. Play is in rehearsal in Cleveland.

---

1. Also for Tennessee: *The Mattress by the Tomato Patch.*

[1647 Ocean Ave., Santa Monica, Calif.]
[*September 24, 1943*]

Dear Donnie:

Send Margo Jones at once a biographical sketch of yourself and a photo, preferably not too gay, for press-releases in Cleveland.

Think it might be a nice touch to mention your year in the T. B. sanitorium. I am talking about my bad heart in mine. Reasons apparent – stern attitude toward young men out of army.

McConnell has not been too generous about money. In lieu of royalties he has deposited $200 with Audrey, the primary purpose of which is to get me to and from Cleveland for the greater good of the play. It may be more than sufficient for that purpose and you can use it for transportation, too. I think it is pretty essential, though, that I get to Cleveland and approve cuts and changes before the opening, since N. Y. people will probably get over to see it. McConnell has to pay for it as I have already gone into my savings during my lay-off and don't want the middle of November to find me out cold.

McConnell actually wanted to be cut in on the play, but Audrey talked him out of that.

If you are coming to California, why not leave about time of Cleveland production and try to be routed through there on the train so you can stop over? Then I could meet you there, and the three of us, you and me and Margo, could come back West together.

Margo called me long-distance at two A. M. wanting another long speech for Hadrian as he goes out the door, finally. Christ! As if there weren't enough speeches! She said Audrey had failed to get in touch with you about the autobiographical matter & photo. Had called you several times. Aren't you at the office?

Let me hear from you. Pronto.

Ruth Ford just had operation for acute appendicitis. Read me a long letter from Charles Henri about possible removal to Mexico and terror of dysentery being the only deterrent. I think Mexico City is going to be the Paris of World War II! (Post-war).

Love,

10.

·55·

[1647 Ocean Ave., Santa Monica, Calif.]

[*October 22, 1943*]

Dear Don:

You and Audrey have both written me long accounts of Cleveland and Margo has poured out her wounded soul so I feel as if I had really been there, in spite of my cowardly effort to remain away. Audrey seems highly satisfied with how things went and has mailed notices to everybody in N. Y. who read the script. I am more inclined to accept your account as I think our notions of the play are somewhat more – shall we say – crystallized! – than these other opinions. I am quite sure that the girl-scout who played Matilda – I have seen her picture – would not have gone beyond dress-rehearsal if I had gotten to Cleveland. She would have suffered a fractured pelvis or worse by some mysterious accident in the wings, and you would have gone on in her place! I need not tell you the slight revisions in the last act took me entirely by surprise when Margo showed me the Cleveland script.[1] They kept telling me, when I asked about revisions,

1. McConnell and the actors had cut out the entire next-to-last scene and scattered a few speeches from it here and there.

that "the script was still in a fluid condition." How true that was!

Well, I was all ready to catch the train when the morning of departure a final burst of vague but terrifying comments from Margo stopped me in my tracks. I figured I would be more comfortable in Chateau Williams on the Palisades. Under the circumstances I think the reviews are miraculous.

About the transportation money, I have gotten none of it so far. Each of us is entitled to what it would have cost him to make the trip by coach to Cleveland, per understanding between McConnell and Audrey. I have just written Audrey that I hope you have received your allotment. Ask for it. I understand that she and Liebling went by plane and there were hints to the effect that the two hundred was also supposed to cover their expenses in connection with attending the play. I will see to it that you get your round-trip coach fare one way or another, even if it's deducted from mine.

Metro has informed me they aren't taking up my option and I have saved remarkably little. The 8-ball and I shall resume our usual flirtations in a very short while, or I would be more useful in getting you out to the Coast. I am almost as anxious to get off the Coast, maybe more. Winter has come, rain, and bleak foggy weather, and I feel no interest – or very little – in Pasadena and Charles Henri's sister and all the attendant fuss and fume of Matilda Rides Again! I am, however, working out a new last act which puts it all in one scene without the dog and door business, but with a little more dramatic substance than the Cleveland cuts had. I think somebody will finally buy the play! – I am mostly working on "The Spinning Song", which is now all in verse, and a group of short stories Laughlin wants to see – I call them "Alice's Summer Hotel" for this place I stay in.[1]

1. Whatever they were attached to, neither of these titles survived.

What a delightful bit of news I received from home lately! My father is making a trip to the Coast and will call me up as soon as he gets here and perhaps stop at my apartment a while. You can imagine the change that this has affected in my life. I have tried to give the place the outward appearance of vacancy, window-shades drawn, doors bolted, all entrances and exits by the back door and a Spartan refusal to answer all calls to the phone. I have nightly dreams of being surprised at least appropriate moments by his unannounced entrance.

I was amused and highly pleased to see your picture with my name under it in the Cleveland papers. You look sort of Chinese and a little touch of the idiot sister act, but even so the mistake was flattering.

Bigelow's jaw! It is assuming a legendary character like the jaw-bone of an ass that is mentioned in scriptures! It will have to go to the Smithsonian when it finally comes off. No, I haven't heard from him since I arranged for a friend of Margo's to stay at his apt. in N. Y. – brief and gloomy letters from each subsequent to the meeting, – then silence! The young man's naked body will probably wash up on some desolate beach in New Jersey.

Send me a copy of *View* with your story in it. Did you see the blurb Charles Henri got in the *New Yorker*?[1] I am sure that he rose above it, all is gist to the surrealist mill! I mean grist. I do hope you will not become identified in any way with The Movement, I would almost rather see you taking a hand in one of those literary feuds that rage in *Partisan Review*. The clarity and the lovely honesty of your stories is so far superior to anything that Charles has ever printed to my knowledge in *View* that – although I am glad

1. An item in The Talk of the Town, contrasting the prose styles of *View*, edited by Charles Henri Ford, when it discussed art and when it gave the facts of ownership, address, etc.

you are having something exhibited – I feel that you have done the lady too much honor. There is only one standard in art that has never been impugned or grown a day older and that is honesty, and anybody who has a heart really living as you have in your stories wants to speak it beautifully but clearly. For some a kind of surrealism is the natural tongue. That's good. Ten percent of Charles' verse which I've read is heavenly. But the rest – and nearly all his imitators – are recognizable by their odor not as roses. I made this observation in a letter to Charles, a bit less bluntly, and never got any answer! I am afraid that sister Ruth, aside from her looks and her acting ability, both good, has a marked similarity to ninety percent of her brother's verse. Now she wants the Pasadena Playhouse to run limousines between there and Hollywood to get her to and from rehearsals. She's the Bernhardt of Grade B pictures! However – I should not be so catty. I think I resent her possession of Peter Van Eyck, insecure as that is.

Love,

10.

[*At top*] You should have told Margo only thing I really enjoy is a "golden shower" from a black cloud.

.56.

[1647 Ocean Ave., Santa Monica, Calif.]
[*November 3, 1943*]

Dear Donnie:

I am always childishly pleased and excited to get your letters. They always arrive at eleven o'clock in the morning when I am gradually being resurrected from the dead, groaning at the sight of my tooth-brush and the demoniac chaos

111

of the apartment. I put them on the table unopened to encourage me to get my teeth brushed and empty out the old coffee grounds, the two most odious things I have to do – before I read them with the first cigarette. I went to Pasadena this week-end. A crisis had come up. All our movie actors had balked at the prospect of riding buses an hour or more each way to rehearsals and they had to be replaced by Pasadena people. Included in this descent from the band-wagon was the slightly more female member of the Ford family. Margo and I were very evil about it. She approached the subject of her withdrawal with the most elaborate delicacy, expecting wild protestations, but Margo and I received the news as calmly as a weather-report and told her the contingency had been foreseen and another actress already in mind. Margo phoned me this morning that the cast is now complete. It only contains one movie personality, Onslow Stevens for the Captain, but they all live in Pasadena and I think that will make up for their lack of prestige. We barely have three weeks rehearsal. It will not be a brilliant production but it ought to be a fairer representation of the play than Cleveland was. Hollywood people are all bitches and liars and degenerates in the true sense of the word so I am glad we are shut of them. Success in terms of screen credits and contracts is all they live for. Also this week-end I had to see my father twice at a Los Angeles hotel. The first time I brought Margo along. We were entertained by some of the old man's salesmen and Margo was so bored she got drunk on their liquor and performed a wild dance alone around the room. The old man was dreadfully shocked and sent me a wire to see him again before he left, the purpose being to urge me against marrying her. He had the idea I planned to. We had a conversation for the first time that I can remember, and it was rather pathetic. He told me that he had been a slave to drink all his life, that all the Williamses had been terrible drinkers and he hoped I wouldn't marry a drunken woman as the Williams women so far had been a redeeming grace of sobriety, all except poor old Bessie who drank in bed and never got out of it. All during the talk he was drinking continually himself and getting more and more like a maudlin old buzzard. It was shocking and pitiful. He feels probably correctly that his days are numbered, told me dolefully that "the Parson" was 85 but would probably out-live him. It would have been much more endurable, somehow, if he had been his usual self. If a person is hard he had better stay that way! But it was a sad, sad picture. What tragic messes these bourgeois families are! Even we who don't fit anywhere are happier and better off. Now and then it occurs to me that the time has about come to shut the windows and turn on the gas. But that old man in the hotel room, fawned upon and feared by his salesmen and regarded with horror by his family, has probably experienced more bitterness than I could dream of. The loneliness and hunger for affection! There is so much of it out here, more than I ever noticed in N. Y. So many rootless people have come out here. You meet them on the beaches and in the Palisades at night and they are positively gasping, some of them, for a little human kindness and understanding. My social life here is devoted almost entirely to a few odd and anonymous little characters like this that I have casually adopted, and I feel ever so much closer to them than I ever could to the intellectual sort of people we are usually thrown with. I am reading Jung now, the man with the cosmic-unconscious theory – you should try him – and I think he explains logically what Lawrence felt intuitively, that the dreadfully conscious and willful people with the over-developed minds are peculiarly dead and away from the only really warm and comforting things in human life. Competitive groups such as Hollywood and Manhattan sets make a high degree of conscious will necessary. The unconscious that wants other things is more and more lost and thwarted and so the hearts wither up. It must be kept away from, these Lemuel Ayers and Ruth Fords with their fearful conscious egos saying, I will, I *will* all the time. I have instinctively done the right thing out here, kept away from them all and petered out of the studio. I usually feel more or less damned but sort of purely damned, not nastily the way I would be if I got caught in this shit. It is so important, now, that we do sell the play and make some money out of it to build a free life on. But nothing can be counted on. Endurance is all. Anything we squeeze out of bourgeois society in the way of support is a little miracle to be sure! My distrust of the world, however, has plumbed the depths and from time to time I make little discoveries that are surprisingly pleasant. – Enough confessions and self-analysis!

Margo will not be crushed over being left out of a possible Broadway production. I told her right along that she would have to take her chances on that and she knows it. There is a core of real unselfish interest in the woman. Naturally she wants her bone to chew on, but far more than most of us she is capable of an impersonal devotion to something and evidently this play is really in her heart more than her ambition. She has gone through hell with it, certainly, and is still going through it. I will let you know how rehearsals look soon as I get out there again. I take it you are not planning on Calif. now. I never thought it a very sound plan for you to come out here, that is, as a strategic move. If you did fit into Hollywood I would regret it, and while the sort of life I lead here is pleasant – where would it get you? Also the atmosphere makes you lazy. I only work in spasms, not continually like I do other places, and have mostly been soaking up things. I know the difficulty you must have in thinking what is the best thing to do, but when uncertainties are so thick it is usually better to stand on whatever ground you do have.

Love,

10.

[*Upside-down*] *All of my suppers are from the white cafe!*

"The tendency of education has been to create in the young mind the illusion that nature is kind and man is benevolent, which is as it may be, but there comes a time when so much evidence has been accumulated to the contrary that the inexperienced youth bounds to the opposite conclusion." Life of Rimbaud.

[*At top*] Got your letter & cuts. Very pleased. They correspond pretty closely to those we have made, that is, as far as eliminating unnecessary repeats. Don't worry about Wharton. She has been very sweet & generous right along but we know her confusions.

·57·

[1647 Ocean Ave., Santa Monica, Calif.]
Nov. 8, 1943

Dear Donnie:

I cannot tell you how lovely I think your story[1] is! I hope you will realize that this is no shit, that I really and truly mean it. It has the cool and limpid quality that all of your best work has, plus a dream-like quality that is very haunting. Everything in it is so perfectly right, like a Picasso, or one of those delicate pieces by Rimbaud. You have really caught in this little story the infinite sadness that there is in night. There is an abstraction in it of that and numberless other things that a less delicate artist would have tried to put in a flood of lyricism that would have destroyed it.

1. *Night* in *View*: Vol. iii No. 3.

The story has the cool power of sculpture. The details are so stringently and correctly chosen that they evoke a great deal more than is actually said. The inert bodies, only partly revealed, the heat and silence, the desolate calm. "They came by Greenland and did not know that it would be hot here." The sea battle. And then the last sentence, the loveliest of all! I am sure that more has never been said in eight words. The fineness and restraint of this writing, and the inexpressible effect created, is the work of no ordinary artist and I salute you for it with a feeling that I reserve for poets like Crane.

I have read it several times to myself and then aloud to David Gregory and just now to a story editor at Monogram who is a night companion of mine. They were all deeply impressed. I say all because some others were present when I read it tonight. I feel this story will attract attention in spite of the rather unfortunate position in the magazine[1] and it would not surprise me to see it reprinted somewhere. It should be. In fact your stories must all get into print now. Not that that affects in any way their excellence but that it is your due to get some recognition at this point of a sort that will encourage you and make things easier for you. I need not tell you that this reminder of what you are able to do – I had not really forgotten but you and your work have been so removed from me lately – greatly increases my desire for *your* sake as well as my own that we can do something financially with our play, to give us both the freedom we must have. I have committed a thousand crimes against art of which you are guiltless in my long and desperate effort to make a career of writing. I would like now to give that up, and I hope to God that you will never try it. So many abuses are forced upon us by necessity – we must try to avoid inflicting them on ourselves. In a way it seems to me that

1. It was on the "Children's Page".

116

your present situation is not a bad one. Lincoln has been pretty wonderful, whether consciously or not. But tell me, What do you really want to do now? Do you feel that New York is not right for you? I ask as though I could rub a magic lantern. Alas, there is too little magic about me! But our problems are similar and discussion may help. I think the present job – that attachment to something and the privacy of it – are miraculously good and hope the prospects there are not as uncertain as they were. However I know you are not always happy in New York – I suspect less so with Sandy in the army – and think you should have some choice of things and places clearly in mind. I am a fine one to be giving this advice, for I have no idea what I shall do next, where I shall go. It is a blank wall. But I shall try to act intelligently about it.

One good thing has happened about the play – the production date is postponed till Nov. 29th which gives us considerably more rehearsal. The cast is very good, I think, except for one person who plays Aunt Emmie. I am hoping Margo can replace her this week. Unfortunately she is the most devoted of all and her eyes fill with tears whenever she does something wrong, which is nearly always. It is hard to let her go, even if we can find someone better. That isn't easy due to the several other productions at Pasadena. I think you would be satisfied with the cuts I have made. I have been pretty cavalier in disposing of repetitions and dead matter. Margo doesn't want much change in the script and is pretty stubborn against any new ideas I bring in. Which may be good as I am so tired of the play that it is difficult, now, to continue work on it.

If you haven't sent Isherwood a copy of *View*, I will show him mine. And if you have extra copies of other things, I certainly wish you would send me a little portfolio of them. I feel that Laughlin should have one, too.

Are you going to Atlanta for your mother's operation?[1] Dakin is now at Fort Dix which is quite near N. Y. This frightens me a little, it brings home too close to my away-from-home character. Maybe he is wiser than I think. In his little letter recently he spoke of "The young Lieutenant I go around with." They were fabulously entertained for a week-end in the city by our wealthy cousin Mrs. W. Arthur Pearse who invested half a million in Flemish laces that were mostly eaten up by the moths. Give your mother my solicitude in her operation. If I can afford it I shall have another, at least to correct the divergence.

Write me all that is going on in your pretty head!

Love,

TENN.

.58.

[1647 Ocean Ave., Santa Monica, Calif.]
11/23/43

Dear Donnie:

I must write you very hastily, having just gotten your letter, as I am going to leave for Pasadena to spend the week there with Margo. The play opens there Sunday night, and it seems imperative that I attend all these last rehearsals.

A terrifying thing has happened. Jay (James) Laughlin has arrived in town. He visited my apartment last night while I was out and entered and left a note for me. The state of the apt. was indescribable, the kitchen a garden of fungi and a paradise of microscopic organisms, dishes having remained unwashed for weeks, my worst manuscripts thrown about like a cyclone had struck them, joy-rags scattered all about the unmade bed together with all the little accoutrements and conveniences of pleasure and his unframed photo carelessly tossed on a table with Crane's and Chekhov's and Porter's

1. For cataracts; hence his interest.

118

nicely framed on the wall! The very odor of the place was appalling. He left a curt note for me to call him. I have never felt so unlike seeing anybody, not even my father when he was here! However I shall go through with it, and I will discuss your stories with him while I am about it.

I am *not* re-writing the play. I would be quite incapable of it. The final acting version, however, will show considerable change and improvement mostly through cuts and reworking of awkward speeches. I will get this version off as soon as everything is set in it. All the movie crowd will come on Sunday evening. The rest of the performances are sold out to a subscription audience in Pasadena.

I did not praise your story at all too much, believe me. The only thing quite sound about me is my standard of judgement where creative writing is concerned – I do think I am sound about that. Of course this story is communicable to only a few people but so is every really pure thing and its slightness of size does not make it slight in content. Don't worry about the sparsity of your writing. It is a good sign. That is, in your particular case. If you began to write furiously and indiscriminately you would lose by it. I see that you deprecate[1] your work. I understand that, since at the present time I have a positive loathing for all of mine. I wish I could crawl out of it like a snake from an old skin and begin all over again, more with life than with words. I feel that I have reached the end of something, but beginnings are still obscure.

I will let you know immediately how things turn out at Pasadena. My regards to Sandy, and I will write him as soon as my plans are settled. I shall leave here very shortly for somewhere.

Love,

10.

P. S.

Left this unmailed when I departed last week for Pasadena.

---

1. I thought *deprecate* was a slip for *depreciate*. I don't deprecate my work. But that is what he is doing to his own in the next sentences.

The play was very warmly received, in fact both audiences were obviously delighted with it, the Hollywood crowd on Saturday night, and the elegant old ladies even more so on the following Founder's Night. I felt it to be a complete vindication of the script, since the part McConnell had cut out was the part most liked by the audiences here and it played perfectly. There was a great warmth and charm in the play as it came through here and I know you would have been pleased with it, after the mess you saw in Cleveland. A number of studios have phoned Bertha Case (Audrey's Hollywood connection) to get copies of the revised script. I shall have it typed up as soon as possible. Also Mary had me call her long distance – collect, thank God. And it appears that she is securing backing there. If she gets the money, I think Mary would be the best possible producer. It isn't sold yet, but the prospects are certainly much improved by the showing here. No reviewers are admitted, ordinarily, to the Playbox – it is very proud and seclusive – so no reviews have appeared as yet. I am hoping that we can prevail upon Mlle. to admit some during the run. Mlle. is the dragon who operates the Playbox. She passes around between acts offering pillows and blankets to the old dowagers. Applause is not permitted between acts and laughter is discouraged.[1] However even the old dowagers were in stitches during some of the comedy scenes last night. It is definitely a woman's play.

I have written Mary in detail about the production and I am sure she will show you the letter. I am too exhausted, having just returned home, to write anymore. And I have to pack and get out of here very quickly as I am being pursued by the Sheriff. He is trying to serve papers on me in connection with a suit being brought against me by the motor

1. Someone had probably shushed him. No one laughs louder at his plays than Tennessee.

scooter company. So far I have eluded him. If he doesn't touch me with the papers I am safe. So I am packing behind barred doors and planning a midnight escape to Hollywood or L. A. I will only remain on the coast about a week longer: then to Saint Louis – then New York maybe. That is, if something is done about the play. Otherwise, South. Laughlin spent the night with us in Pasadena, saw the play and liked it, though of course he regarded it as a bit too earthy or theatrical. We stayed up all night to see Margo off on the train to Texas: then drove to Laughlin's hotel for a swim and had lunch with Isherwood. I do indeed think Laughlin might like your stories. He promised to read the one in *View*. I will let you know his reaction. He is a terribly sweet person underneath his austere skin – but I think he is rather appalled by things you and I regard as commonplace. He and Isherwood exchanged accounts of my apartment, which Isherwood said he had seen nothing like since he visited a cheap abortionist in the slums of Berlin.

I got no sleep last night so I am barely able to punch these keys. You will hear from me again very soon. Since when has the New School had a job for me? ! ! That belongs in Bulfinch's anthology. But give Berghof[1] my love. – Margo was a life in herself, so when she left this morning, grinning and crying a little and waving out the window like a child, I felt like a ghost. What a person!

·59·
El Fidel Hotel, Albuquerque, N. M.
[*December 17, 1943*]

Dear Don –

I'm pretty sure I never mailed the long letter I wrote you in Pasadena about the play. I went into great and enthusiastic

1. Herbert Berghof, who had worked with Piscator at The New School.

detail which I cannot repeat now; I trust you've gotten the report I sent Mary Hunter. My last two weeks on the Coast were a climax of confusion. For one thing I was being pursued by a Sheriff who wanted to serve some papers on me in connection with a suit brought against me by a motor scooter company. I successfully evaded him. Then James Laughlin arrived on the Coast and I was involved in a lot of entertainments by and for him – also farewell parties for Margo and me. And a lot of moving and packing. I am still trying to catch my breath. Right now I am spending a wretched night in Albuquerque trying to track down some luggage gone astray. As always, the suitcase containing my Mss. has disappeared. I have to meet every bus tonight to search for it. I am planning to visit Santa Fe and Taos to see old friends before I go on to Saint Louis. Soon as I settle down for a moment I will write you a decent letter. When I left, Warners and several others studios were more or less eagerly waiting for revised scripts of the play. They were being typed up. The first batch went to Mary as she paid for them.[1] They were frightfully high, $38.50 for 4 copies. I sent Mary 2 (for her $15) gave Bertha Case one and kept one. More are being prepared for the studios. The audiences loved the play. Unfortunately we got to ask Hollywood people only *one* night. The rest were Pasadena subscription audiences. *No* reviews. Reporters were not invited, a rule of the Playbox. I did not know all the little rules and conceits of the Playbox till it was too late to resist them. Consequently in spite of its very successful presentation there was little could be done to publicize it. I will explain this to you later. The chief advantage derived was the vindication of the script as written which I think was complete – as far as playing well. It played beautifully. The last scene lets

1. I went over this script with her, enlisting her aid in the removal of the additions I objected to.

down a bit – think that could be fixed. Our Matilda was a stick but the others swell.

In letter to you *lost* I asked you to air mail your stories so I could show them to Laughlin. He is definitely interested. I met Man Ray and Henry Miller at Laughlin's before I left. – Spent the last week with Tony Smith and Jane Lawrence while I was hiding out from the Sheriff.

Send your stories to Laughlin at Alta Lodge, Sandy, Utah. He is there now.

Afraid all this is a bit incoherent. I am so exhausted & anxious about luggage.

Love –

TENNESSEE

.60.

Travelers Hotel, Taos, New Mexico
Dec. 21, 1943

Dear Donnie –

You know how hard it is for me to get letters off when I am stationary – when I am moving around it is impossible practically. I wrote you in Santa Fe and dropped the stamped envelope somewhere. It may reach you. And I wrote you twice from Pasadena & Hollywood, neither of which got off. The play went *well*. Some studios were interested when I left. For details see Mary Hunter. I got a long letter off to her about it and talked to her long distance. I imagine you and she have been in touch so I won't go into details.

I am on my way to St. Louis for Xmas. Dakin is leaving for China, a very dangerous assignment, and it is necessary for me to be there on his departure. I am stopping briefly in Taos. It is lovely here, desert all covered with snow. Had lunch with the Hon. Dorothy Brett, and tea with Frieda

123

Lawrence. Tomorrow I have lunch at Frieda's. She still has her Italian lover and they are running a pottery shop. She adores the play and has given me the script of an unfinished play by D. H. which she would like to have written over. Laughlin was in Calif. and anxious to see yr. stories. I wrote you to air mail them to me at Pasadena but that letter I lost. Suggest you send them to Laughlin at Alta Lodge, Sandy, Utah.

I am *not* well – too much strain lately. Will probably have an eye operation in St. Louis and rest – rest –

Write me there, discreetly, you know – 53 Arundel Place, Clayton –

Tenderly,

10.

P. S. Tell Mary that Helen Guggenheim is in N. M. and Frieda will try to get some money out of her for play.

From Taos, Tennessee returned to St. Louis. The future, after his Hollywood parenthesis, was no clearer; but our closeness was intact.

.61.

[53 Arundel Place, Clayton, Mo.]
[*January 3, 1944*]

Dear Donnie:

The clear atmosphere of winter in Taos woke me up a bit and I have considerable new writing on "You Touched Me" which I will either send piece-meal or in new typed scripts. Probably the latter, if I can get hold of a typist here. It seems that some kind of social disturbance is going on in the world and people who used to type scripts are going around making noises and odd gestures in foreign places. I shall have to get in touch with Bigelow and enquire what all this is about. He is usually *au courant* with such things.

I am deeply impressed, if not over-awed, by your new address.[1] You are practically a neighbor of that eccentric cousin of ours, Lucy Pearse, who invested a fortune in Flemish laces that were eaten by moths. I am supposed to get in touch with her my next time in N. Y. Dakin says she is always good for a dinner at Michel's and orchestra seats at the best shows. We will descend on her together when I reappear, just as a neighborly gesture. Apparently not quite everything went to the moths or maybe they got indigestion.

I feel like going to N. Y. but don't know how strategic it would be at the moment. I got off the coast with $800 in my possession and some uncertain amount with Audrey, but I

1. 747 Madison Avenue, a brownstone, the top-floor-through of which we rented for the next fifteen years, at $50 a month.

have two eye operations coming up with hospital bills and am not sure how much that will leave me. I will have the first this week, another needling operation, and another in a few months on the muscle of the eye to correct the divergence. Then I am having my teeth patched up – they were like the Festung Europa – an' that ain't hay neither. I may wind up ushering again at the Strand or battling old ladies to a draw at the San Jacinto. It would not be anticipating too much to make my application now with the Bigelow-Maxwell Genteel Employment Agency, Inc. – Audrey has been dreaming up something about a job with a film company in Mexico starting in April but that is still kind of vague. – Anyhow when I come to N. Y. it would be fun staying with you and Sandy. Right across the park from the Y and with spring coming on and Joe Hazan in Hollywood it sounds like a good deal. Two beds and Fritzi's furniture – heavens to Betsy! – that's not an apartment but an old Etruscan bath-house!

[*The letter switches here from type- to handwriting.*]

I have just been ordered to bed. It is midnight and Mother says late hours will wreck my health – finishing this in Dakin's room which I have inherited since he left. I got to see him. He has gone overseas now. He thinks China or Turkey, but the only real clue is a mosquito net in his equipment and the fact it will take 3 weeks to get there. He is sweet but so reactionary we disagree about everything. He says this country is Christian, Democratic & capitalistic and always will be – I say shit!

Grand is well – and radiantly beautiful, all silvery and warm. Home is pleasant after the mad period past. But the "body electric" couldn't stand it long! Everything starts to itch and quiver and – goodbye!

Hold your stories till I come to N. Y. I *will* – fairly soon – I would like to go over them with you and write Laughlin my *ideas*. He seems to respect them more than I do, although

126

he calls me "a mad poet". He is a strange and beautiful character.

More bleating from Mother – lights out!

Love –

Tom – excuse me! – 10.

.62.

[53 Arundel Place, Clayton, Mo.]
Saturday – Jan. 1944

Dear Donnie –

The news of *Sur* is very impressive and *good*.[1] I remember the story quite vividly, two images particularly, the "sweet and sour cow odor of the mother" and the black pearl sky over the swimming lake. Then of course I loved the little crazy woman who did the jig in the streetcar, though I felt you had a chance there for something a bit more electric. However your *reticence* has always a *power* of its own and is never destructive as out-bursts frequently are. The title is especially lovely with a peculiar significance because of all the bourgeois meanings of Sunday. You have drawn so beautifully from your life in Atlanta. One cannot help wondering if N. Y. offers you as much emotional experience. It never gave me *any* whatsoever. Really *none*. Just a frenzy. On the other hand, *New Orleans*, especially as I first knew it eight years ago, is an inexhaustible reservoir of experience. The leprosy of art is professionalism – and in N. Y. you are too close to the leprosarium for comfort. It is amazing how impervious you are to it. And lucky. Your work, published or not, is important to me and I hope you'll always keep me well-informed of it. I believe you now have about

1. This Argentine magazine had published a Spanish translation of my story *The Seventh Day* in the September, 1943 issue.

6 complete stories, including *Carnival*. I have about the same number which I am not ashamed of. If it is not enough for separate vols. maybe Laughlin would be, or could be, interested in doing them together as "2 Southerners".

My Grandmother died suddenly last week of a lung hemorrhage while playing the piano. I will say no more about it except it was frightfully shocking. I went ahead with my operation – mainly to avoid the bourgeois rituals surrounding death. It was very successful this time. With a thick lens the vision is about as clear as the right eye. Magnifies the eye and gives me a somewhat grotesque appearance, however. I may use a monocle for it. "Y. T. M." rewrite finished – good, I think. Will mail this week-end or Monday.

Love –

10.

(Plans pending Mary's accomplishments.)

P. S. Tell "Bubber" I am not the least bit mad at "Sister". Her defection at the last moment forced us to use a very inadequate student, but I understood Ruth too well to expect any sacrificial allegiance. She has about as much honesty as I ever look for in a woman, and lots more charm.

I have wonderful new sleeping pills which make me feel like I am a water lily in a Louisiana bayou on a summer afternoon! The days here are nice, but the nights make me so restless I need sedatives. The old man gave me $100 tonight to pay for my operation. – Yes, he *is* sick! I sat up with him all one night which made him remorseful. I don't think he will last very long. Dissipation has finally come home. His lungs and kidneys are going. He is pathetically fearful of death.

My Grandmother accepted it all too graciously. She never spoke nor opened her eyes when the fatal bleeding started, though I am fairly sure she was conscious.

You might phone Audrey, if you wish, about my operation and tell her that is why she hasn't heard from me – that and Grand's death. And that new scripts are coming. I haven't felt like writing a letter until tonight.

10.[1]

.63.
[53 Arundel Place, Clayton, Mo.]
2/2/44

Dear Donnie:

You are being very nice about writing me when I need letters most. Yes, I have about reached the end of my endurance here, not that they aren't being nice as they are able, but I am getting unbearably restless. Afraid I will have to remain till a week from this Tuesday for my final eye-test but then immediately make tracks. Margo wired this morning would I consider offer from Curtain Club. Altogether mystifying but letter explaining follows. Presume it involves going and staying at Texas. Only appeal is proximity to Mexico. So I am writing Mary to please be a little more explicit about what is going on in N. Y. If chances of production this season are at least 50/50 I would come ahead. I want to see you and "The Cherry Orchard" and a few other items anyhow. Ask Mary if she can spare you a script to read and then see about getting it to London. There is a man there named Shephard who puts on almost nothing but American plays. I would like to go to London myself: I suspect there is a far more intelligent audience for our sort of thing over there. At any rate I know there is nothing here since the war. I cannot think of anything I really want to write very badly that

1. He enclosed a letter from a poetess written in 1935 (when he was twenty-four) on which he inscribed: "Here's an old letter I found among my juvenile correspondence – thought it might amuse you! 10."

would be acceptable here. Obviously you are in the same boat with your stories. I love the title of the new one.[1] Perhaps you are right about New York. You are so much more self-contained than I am. I always see you being quite separate from N. Y. and yet flowing serenely through it. I seem to flounder in it like a drunk pig: that is, when I am not attached to anything that absorbs me. You keep making little complaints about Sandy, his selfishness, snobbery, Etc. Are you serious about this? Aren't you really very pleased? Will continue tomorrow – Mother is hollering down the laundry chute for me to go to bed.

Later – The book[2] has come and I am endlessly grateful, as it is one of the few things by him I'd never seen, and so far it is the most curiously living thing he has written. What sanity and clear vision that man had, and what a delicate sad humor, what an overwhelming sorrow and disillusionment – of the best sort, the sort that will not admit any comforting lies but at the same time does not turn cruel and fierce as little skeptics do. I have only read a few chapters – will return it when I'm through.

The gloom here is so thick you could cut it with a knife. My brother gone a month and no word, Grand's death and my sister back at the asylum and refusing to eat. My father has returned to work but is feeble and irritable and Mother of course is completely unnerved. This morning all this brought on a crise de nerfs for me – I became so dizzy I couldn't stand up – then a reasonless feeling of panic – palpitations – nausea – chill – finally now a comforting drowsiness and a wolfish appetite. But I cannot live in this situation, I must get out of it quickly or I will go under like I did when Dad put me in the shoe-business. So I leave next week –

1. *New Dominoes.*
2. A paperback of Chekhov's novella "My Life".

Texas or N. Y., New Orleans or Mexico – Nitchevo, Nitchevo!

10.

.64.

[53 Arundel Place, Clayton, Mo.]
[*March 4, 1944*]

Dear Donnie:

The itch is about gone but for the past five days I have written 60 pages of a new play,[1] and while the colored lights are on I don't move. However I am getting packed and at the first good interval I will entrain for New York. There is really only [one] scene left before I have the first draft so I may leave this week-end – but don't expect me till I get there. I will take a room at the Y – at least for a while – but if you want me to, I will put my typewriter and victrola in your apartment and if it is a good place to work, I could work there during the days while you're at the office and we could have supper together. If such a studio life sounds frightening to you, you will surely say so. Neither of us believe in acts of penitence or self-immolation, as it were. When people say, Oh, Tennessee, you must come and stay with me! – I make the sign of the cross on the witless creature's forehead, for well do I know the devil has whispered to him. Ask poor Fritzi. Who holds me directly or indirectly responsible – mostly directly – for the destruction of his electric percolator, loss of electric razor, permanent damage to central nervous system. I hope we can do a little entertaining of an informal nature this season. I don't think one should have an elaborate debut in war-time, I think it is in bad taste when so many are devoting their time and energies to things like the Red Cross and the canteens, as our mothers used to call them. But I

1. Possibly "Summer and Smoke".

131

think it would not be inappropriate to serve a little light wine and biscuits to friends who drop in. In lieu of etchings, I have framed photographs of Chekhov, Crane, and – oh, yes, my Picassos – where are they now? – Speaking of pictures there is one by Cadmus in our local gallery American exhibit – *Gilding the Acrobats*. As for the libidos, mine was considerably repaired in California but New York might cause a relapse. I only had one bad moment in Calif. and that was when I discovered myself to be entertaining an escaped German prisoner, but it turned out – nicely . . . Chop-chop! – However I don't feel at all forward these days. Everything happened so gently on the Palisades that the faster tactics of Glamourburg – what ever became of that actress? – might not find me adequate. In which case we shall simply have to get hold of a new pilot-fish. We might advertise in the classified section of the *Saturday Review of Literature*. "Girls! – Helpless honeysuckle types, two of them! – Want a sturdy oak to cling to! Call, write, *Wire*! – But preferably, *Come*! For Further Information enclose self-addressed stamped envelope!"

PLEASE don't answer this in a similar vein! I'll probably be gone and –

Love –

10.

LETTERS 65-75

In mid-March, Tennessee arrived in New York. The plans for a production of "You Touched Me" dragged on. In May, he took a house for the month at Ocean Beach on Fire Island and invited friends out. One day he came into town to receive a $1000 award at the National Institute of Arts and Letters. I went with him and we found the "immortels" very nineteenth century and comic and got the giggles, but enjoyed meeting Eudora Welty. At the beginning of June, he departed for Provincetown. There, in the calm of his comparative affluence, he finished "The Glass Menagerie". His letters that summer, some sent, some "forgotten", overlap. I have cut them to lessen the repetition; but I have included all of them to show that he produced his correspondence in progressive drafts, as he did his stories and plays, and that those "forgotten" letters were often in fact simmering on his contemplative stove, waiting until they were done.

.65.
[*Note left at 747 Madison Ave., N. Y.*]
[*April, 1944*]

Dear Don –

Searched for you desperately at the Met but presume you had taken refuge in some old Etruscan basket or sarcophagus.

I did the park, a 42nd Street movie – took a ten cent peek at the moon which made me so faint that I required a shot of bar rye at the Pink Elephant to pull myself back together.

Now I shall go out room-hunting again – but in case I don't find one or someone with one, you might leave the key on the post again.

In case I have to creep ignominiously back beneath your red plush window drape.

10.

There is a picture of Margo under this, in envelope.
P. S. I owe 20 ¢ for Sandy's cigarettes consumed here.

.66.

[*Postcard*]
Capt. Jack's Wharf, Provincetown, Mass.
[*June 14, 1944*]

Dear Don –

Fritz has the measles, temperature 104°, so I am staying
by myself. Have a nice one-room studio apartment on
"Capt. Jack's Wharf" where I used to stay with Kip. Seems
a bit haunted but otherwise pleasant. Joe Hazan is here –
Denby[1] out on a dune where I do not intend to disturb him.
I have a bike. *Call Audrey*. Ask for copy of typed plays and
remind her to mail my check *right away*. Address Capt. Jack's
Wharf or Gen. Delivery.

Love –

10.

.67.

[Captain Jack's Wharf, Provincetown, Mass.]
[*June 21, 1944*]

Dear Donnie:

Here I am, back on Capt. Jack's Wharf – shades of 1940.
All a bit nostalgic, or perhaps ghoulish is the right word.
The whole lunatic fringe of Manhattan is already here,
Valesca, Joe Hazan, Robert Duncan, Lee Krasner and Pol-
lock, the Bultmans and myself. Such a collection could not be
found outside of Bellevue or the old English Bedlam. Fritz
has had the measles but is now recovered and they have

1. Edwin Denby had written notes on photographs of Nijinsky for an issue of
Dance Index the year before.

moved into their summer home. I think it is a horrid place, just like a city apartment, neither on the ocean or the dunes, in back of some old queen's antique shop. However they seem to have one or two extra bedrooms and are planning to have you up to visit them. It would be all right as you could be outside mostly. I only have one room with a double bed but you could share it with me if the Bultman ménage was too much for you. I may have to move on the 24th, however, as this place is reserved after that date by another party. They may shuffle me around on the wharf or I may take a room at the Hofmanns.[1] Fritz had diarrhea with the measles. He and Jeanne giggled delightedly over it. – Jeanne dashing back and forth with the bed-pan. I think it was the most satisfactory experience of their married life. Never was there so much occasion for discussion of shit!

Lots of the belles are showing up with wives this season. It is most depressing, the only thing more gruesome than the belles is the wives. I am getting a phobia against them – wives of belles! They run to the horsey blond type, vaguely intellectual or extravagantly Bohemian or both, and Jeanne is really a very superior example.

The sea is splashing right under the floor tonight – the fog squeezing under the door – that's what makes this type-writer ribbon so fucking gooey. The weather has been a mess for three days straight – rain – fog – storms – no swimming, no beach. Just Joe Hazan and Valentine and the Wingfields to keep me busy. I believe [—] is about to offer his beautiful body to me again. [—] has. Outside of that no sex going on right now. Valentine has dictated a story to me which I will offer to *View* as a primitive. It is his story of his love-affair with a whore named Vivian in Providence, R. I., which I have transcribed literally as he told it. I think it makes a pretty good primitive. – I keep telling myself this is better

1. Hans Hofmann and his wife Miz rented rooms to his students.

than Manhattan but I am seldom altogether convinced. If the weather improved I might be. Dakin writes that the monsoon is dreadful. He is now in Burma and a python was killed right outside his tent and he has to walk a mile to take a bath. Why he should worry about a bath during the monsoon I don't understand.

Valesca says she has a 70 yr old female midget employed at the Beggar's Bar. Is called Mme. Pumpernickel, sings and dances grotesquely and screams with jealousy when Valesca is performing. Valesca says they get mad and choke each other.

The sea under my floor sounds like the washerwomen of Joyce slapping wet linen on the stones of Dublin. It is good to go to sleep to. I suppose it is really very nice here except for the weather.

I have been reading Henry Miller. His viciousness, his absolute sadistic violence has some fascination – for a while – then becomes merely tedious and revolting. All in all a poor writer and a fake one. His literary idol is Lawrence – How? Why? – Two more different attitudes are inconceivable! Of course it is nice to see cunt and fuck and prick and shit discussed so freely, but I think you really get the same thing at the Bultmans . . .

Mr. Miller thinks that honesty requires us to behave just as bad as we are, to disown all tenderness because it is partial, to make no pretense of being other than pigs. I agree with him about being pigs but I do think we have to exercise our partial virtues, pretend to be somewhat nicer than we are. That isn't dishonesty but just good taste – or hygiene. – It annoys me that a man like Miller should enjoy such prestige through sheer energy and uninhibited out-pourings. Your short pieces, for instance, are so much better than all his stuff piled together. I think you really should try to work up more steam and get more done, for that seems to be the only way to make a current impression – by a certain amount of

136

volume. Though heaven knows it is unimportant how much paper you cover. I do not know if it is even worthwhile, now, to think of one's self as a writer.

The whole fucking wharf is rocking like a boat now, I suspect it has broken loose and gone out to sea. Will stop and have a look at the distant shore before I go to bed.

Laughlin sent me a picture of himself on skis, up to his ass in snow and the ass turned to the camera and very beautiful.

Love –

10.

I liked the "Three Old Ladies"[1] though it isn't really a very good play – recognize myself in two of them, the ghastly old devil and the timid old ingenue. Can't we do it sometimes? You and Me and Gilbert. You can be the nice one who makes the tea.

MY GOD! WATER IS POURING UNDER THE DOOR!

.68.

[Provincetown, Mass.]
[*July ?, 1944*]

Buddy-buddy-shipmate!

(That is a navy term of endearment which I have just picked up.) I have just returned from a most extraordinary all night party on Captain Jack's Wharf, as a matter the third consecutive one of a series, but this the most extraordinary of all. In fact I doubt that the pair of us have ever gotten into a more complicated rat-race. To begin somewhere, if not at the beginning, a couple of willowy rather pretty Jewish-looking intellectual belles have opened a salon on the wharf, which for sheer chi-chi tops anything of the sort I have yet

1. "The Old Ladies", a dramatization by Rodney Ackland of a novel by Hugh Walpole, which I had given Tennessee.

run into. One of them, to complete the definition, was a fellow student of Fritz's at the Bauhaus and assists Norman Bel Geddes in his miniature panoramas at the Modern Museum, Etc. Well, I have been dropping in there evenings when I knock off work or the beach, as it is literally the only place to go. Usually there is nothing there even to affect your mother's not insensible libido, but tonight they had somehow come into possession of an immense creamy-fleshed blond sailor directly out of Melville. I began having palpitations and other serious organic disturbances the moment I entered the salon but entertained no hope as it was early and the crowd was large, and all the belles present were dripping saliva with the same idea. However I stayed and stayed and the atmosphere became more and more intolerably Firbankian till the field had narrowed down to five or six. In the meantime the less attractive of the two hostesses had made me a declaration of love. Although my impulse was to vomit, crafty thing that I am, I figured that if I did not discourage her too much, I might have an excuse to remain on the premises – the sailor being their over-night guest. (Of course they had both had him in the afternoon but he was obviously not beyond resuscitation.) Well, everyone finally departed but the four of us. One of the belles was unbuttoning the sailor's pants and the other mine – we were all on one enormous inner-spring mattress on the floor. Then all at once things start to happen! The sailor extends his arm, I extend mine. In one dervish whirl both belles are thrown clean out of the charmed circle which from then on consists solely and frenziedly of Tennessee and the navy!

After the sort of dialogue which you can supply as well as a witness, the belles retire to a corner among themselves and the party divides geographically in two camps, one grunting like greedy pigs, the other hissing like angry geese at opposite sides of the room. Well, I shall probably have the bitch's curse on me the rest of the summer but I'm not at all sure I'm sorry! I got through quickly, however, and left the navy still in fighting trim. And returned, now, to my own little bed – but thought I would write you an account of it first, as I felt it was the sort of situation you would appreciate. Only KB[1] could perform a better piece of diabolical strategy!

The town is swarming with belles but trade is scarce as hen's teeth, or rather that which is not too dangerous is. My syntax is yawning! – roosters crowing – birds chattering like outraged belles – so I will finish this when I have had some sleep. Mmmm...

Later – I have waked up at noon and had a breakfast of fried clams and will finish this while I'm waiting for my coffee to boil. I don't know how to advise you about coming here. That is, how well you would like it. If you share my delight in smooth sea-water, dunes, and salt air, you would be satisfied. On the other hand, if you want a mad time of it, – that is, the sort of time we both enjoy – not camping with a bunch of shrill queens – you *wouldn't* perhaps, for society here consists pretty largely of such. I know Fritzi will
[*The rest of this letter is missing.*]

.69.
[Provincetown, Mass.]
[*July ?, 1944*]

Dear Don:

I haven't yet moved into my house by Picasso, it is still being prepared for me. The carpenter is a drunkard. One

1. KB was a friend who had left Tennessee's bed in the middle of the night on Fire Island and come into mine. Refusing to believe that this was in order to sleep, Tennessee had denounced him and ordered him out of the house.

day he saws the door five inches too short, the next he puts the lock in the wrong place. I try to help him and it only creates more confusion. So I have taken another place till it is ready. This is equally nice, however, or nicer. Two rooms with private shower and toilet right across from a clear estuary to swim in. The embarrassment I last mentioned[1] has passed and I feel quite well. I have finished the "Caller" and am slowly re-typing it. I think I will submit the short version first and if people like it, will add the rest. It is not a very exciting business but it keeps me occupied while I wait for the energy to do something more important. I am so glad to hear you are working a little again. I understand how difficult it is, but it is your duty. I don't say duty in the tiresome moral sense but as Lawrence means it, to yourself. So get your stories in shape and let us get them off to Laughlin, for his magazine or something. Charles Henri, his mother, and Tchelitchew were in town today, all looking remarkably well. They took me to lunch. The poor little mother was the first example I have seen of a thoroughly intimidated southern matron. Tchelitchew had her completely in awe of him, she even paid for the lunches. I thought Charles might be interested in Valentine's story, but when I mentioned it, he said, Is it fantastic? How discouraging! I thought they were getting away from that nonsense, at least in their use of primitive material. Incidentally I have read "The Endless Island" by Parker Tyler and was surprised to find he really does have a brilliant style as essayist.

I am *glad* you and the little one are getting along better. [. . .] The circumstances of our lives make all of us bitchier than we really are. I have a little one here, too. But it is so far just a spiritual companionship. Maybe that's why I like it. He is a Harvard boy, looks like a younger, more delicate

1. Probably on the missing page of the previous letter.

Kip. I picked him up wandering along the street one night with intentions of seduction. But we began talking and kept on till daybreak – his emotional crises and I the Father Confessor. He fears women but doesn't want men either. However he *likes* men better. I read him Crane and he has ordered a copy from Boston. It was really better than fucking. He has thick dark lashes and a very soft brown throat, all I really want to do is kiss his Adam's apple or touch it while he's talking! Isn't that queer for you?

[*The rest of this letter is missing.*]

.70.

[*Postcard*]

Provincetown, Mass.

July 20, 1944

Buddy-buddy-shipmate (a navy term of endearment) – Think I am going to Cambridge for about a week as guest of a Harvard student. Hope I will not miss you here. The town is screaming with creatures not all of whom are seagulls but you would like the beach. I am not yet in the cabin – carpenter is drunk.

Love

10.

.71.

[Provincetown, Mass.]

[*July ?, 1944*]

Dear Donnie:

Here is a little note from Mary which I enclose since you may not have been in touch with her. Isn't it dreary?

I am catching a boat this afternoon for Boston, thence to Cambridge for an unspecified interval in a Harvard dorm with a very nice though wildly eccentric student – meant to leave earlier but became involved with a wild group of summer visitors, the last of which drove me out of town and all but out of my mind. He moved into my room. I rode around town all night on my bike to get away from him. Woke him up at six in the morning to catch his bus. Got gratefully into bed, was just falling asleep when this apparition reappears with luggage, announcing that he had missed the bus. Darling, I said, go back to bed – I feel restless and am going for a long walk! Whereupon I got back on my bike and rode all the way out to Joe Hazan's place on the dunes, two miles from the nearest human habitation, where I remained till this morning when I felt reasonably sure last week's storm of belles would be finally blown over. Honestly, they are like a plague of green flies, the sort that torment you on a summer beach, or like Fritz's eternal case of poison-ivy, or woolen under-wear on a fierce sunburn. Pox on all of them – their Lord & Taylor T-shirts, flowered sarongs, baby-blue silk shorts! The Portuguese natives have been beating them up on the streets at night lately and I am not at all sure which side I am on . . . my own or the opposition's.

I wish you would postpone your visit till I get back from Cambridge. I don't think I will remain there more than a week. The latter part of the season will be nicer, particularly September. At that time Fritz and Jeanne plan to move in their new house. They say you could have the present place all to yourself. *That*, my dear, is an *inducement*! With all due respect to our favorite young newly-weds. They keep telling me that their social set here is so much nicer than mine. But the only noticeable difference is that mine is prettier. Their chief follower is an old Auntie, Elmo, who runs the New York Flea Market, a precious old thing who drapes windows with things that look like the Empress Eugénie's underwear. One cannot enter one of his decorated salons without a savage desire to pull, throw, tear, bite, smash everything to chi-chi smithereens! Perhaps I'm being unnecessarily moribund about the social situation here, and at any rate you would benefit – even now – from the travel and change. However I wish you would wait till near the end of summer when we could return to New York together. Fall and winter are becoming a fairly imminent problem. I suppose I will visit home a while and then take the long jump to Mexico. I do not feel in such a Gulliver mood – more like an Alice-Sit-By-The-Fire – only I can't find the right fire, none of the chimneys seems to draw very well. Time is motion . . .

Laughlin has been having trouble with printers again. Two of them undertook "Battle" and then stopped because of the "sinful text". A third is now making progress. Charles, Tchelitchew and Mother Ford took me to lunch one day. Tchel. putting on more airs than ever, Mrs. Ford the first thoroughly intimidated southern matron I have ever seen! They want us to visit them when you come up.

The Picasso cabin is still uninhabitable. The carpenter got drunk and put all the doors on wrong so I have been moving among various rooming-houses. I work in spells – think I will get the final draft of the "Caller" finished at Cambridge.

I'm glad you and the little one are at peace with each other. That should make the hot weather easier on you both. I have never believed it a fundamentally or inevitably bad arrangement, the good points being too obvious to require commentary. You two never really had much of a chance with each other, there being so much interference and irritation from other parties, meaning mostly me. Though I never meant to. My good intentions are so badly handled that they are no excuse.

KB writes he has a good job with the New York *Times*.

Paul Moor is working for Pathe News. Margo is producing "The Purification" in the Pasadena Laboratory theatre. Robt. Edmond Jones has written a rather gushy letter which Audrey forwarded, apparently about "The Little God".[1] Joe Hazan is very wild and sexlessly beautiful in the lamp-light, reading "Moby Dick" and passages from his novel aloud in that voice which is almost like the language of apes. The novel is correspondingly out of the world. Valentine has left town . . . .

Love,

10.

.72.

[*Postcard*]
Cambridge, Mass.
August 3, 1944

Have written and lost letters to you. I am spending a little period at Harvard with a very mad crowd of young professors and students. Heard Joyce recording of *Anna Livia* yesterday – also Cummings, Stein, Millay, Marianne Moore – returning P-town tomorrow. P-town is a little revolting *socially* at present. Think you would prefer it later in season. I may give a $100 reading here if I have courage.

Love –

TENNESSEE

.73.

[Provincetown, Mass.]
[*August 12, 1944*]

Chiquito –

I have had no peace lately and have knocked myself out tearing around between here and Boston and Harvard,

1. The collective title for three one-act plays: "27 Wagons Full of Cotton", "Auto-Da-Fé", and "The Strangest Kind of Romance".

mainly because I had no suitable place to live here. The little cabin I was supposed to have was never made habitable for me. It unsettled and depressed me so, and made work all but impossible, having to move every few days among various ghastly rooming houses and the town full of really *surrealist* belles. I am so glad you didn't get here during *this* period. I was so afraid you would – and you would have HATED it. I knew you would spend a lot of money and be disappointed, so I haven't urged you to come. Truthfully, regardless of what Jeanne and Fritzi may say, the social atmosphere has been utterly vile. They insist that their friends are nicer than my associates have been, but the only noticeable difference is that mine are better looking.

Well, now – tomorrow I am moving back into a divine little cabin secluded from the town – owned by a Bennington art teacher – where I expect to remain through Sept. So I feel greatly relieved. I suppose now I will relax and get something done.

[. . .]

There are two boys here who have "stayed and comforted me" through the phantasmagoria. Fritzi hates them, having known one at the Bauhaus, where they formed a mutual detachment. You might not like them at first but I am sure you would later. They are operating a sort of surrealist salon (both paint) which is my evening headquarters. Then, sometimes I visit Joe Hazan and his mistress on the dunes. Joe has a car, drove us to Wellfleet recently where we visited Charles Henri Etc.

Blanchard[1] wired me that he is arriving here for a few days. Coming this afternoon. I expect my two friends will put him up till I have a place located for him. Town is dreadfully crowded still.

1. Blanchard Kennedy, poet, sculptor, jack-of-all-trades at *View*, and apparently, according to the next letter, a malleable listener.

I saw your new issue[1] at Charles H.'s – lovely pictures and altogether very impressive.

Laughlin has sent me $100 for "Battle" – balance on publication. Several printers have refused to do it because of "sinful text" but a third with less scruples has been set in motion.

As for the Fall, I don't think I will spend more than a week in New York – then home for a rest before I leave for New Orleans or Mexico on my thousand which is still intact. Time is motion! (even when you are a little tired of moving.)

A note from Mary merely reports "nothing new" – dreary? – Hope to see you soon, Chiquito.

Love –

10.

·74·

Provincetown, Mass.
Friday, Aug. [18 or 25] 1944

Dear Stinky:

Fritz and Jeanne lost patience with me and repossessed their typewriter which I had been using, so I now have to do my writing in their apartment. At the moment I am waiting for coffee to boil on their maddeningly deliberate oilstove while they are up farting around the new house. I'm afraid the new arrangement will be mutually disadvantageous, as I always make such a mess of other people's places. However they claim it is the only way they could get me to call.

I was entertaining Blanchard all last week. Do you remember the speech I made to KB one night on Fire Island? Well, that was nothing compared to one I delivered to Blanchard, holding him down on an upper bunk with one arm.

1. Of *Dance Index*: "Taglioni, Grisi, Cerrito and Elssler" by Joseph Cornell.

I told him things about himself and his associates that it would take him a year to get out of a Freudian analyst! The whole *View* staff and set were included in the dissection, and as he departed to their summer colony when he left here, I dare say the benefit will be general. However Blanchard took it quite well. The following morning he began to behave quite humanly for the first time, and I think we parted with at least an understanding. The gist of my sermon, or text, was "The Charming Fallacy" or that beauty and charm is justified in exploiting their homelier but more sincere fellow-sufferers. When I finished I said, "I suppose you think it is very crude of me to discuss you so intimately." – "No," said Blanchard, "I just thought it was a little surprising." In many respects he is the prettiest and most intriguing thing I've met since Kip, and the worst mixed up. I like him a great deal. Do you know he has written a bunch of really excellent poems? He recited them all to me, and several I typed out and will show them to you. I like them considerably better than Charles Henri's. – Please keep all this under your hat, it would not be kind to either of us to have it bruited about. If I am ever again in New York for a considerable period, I think we should see more of Blanchard. In any case, you would find him agreeable when you broke down the reserve.

Did you know that Lamantia has been fired from *View*? Before he left Wellfleet he asked Charles Henri where he stood with the publication and Charles said, "My dear, you stand outside the door!" They claim to have found him to be a little pretentious, so apparently what they wanted was an opposite attraction. Also Charles says that his figure was disappointing. "He is shaped like a little old woman," says Charles. So they are urging him to return to San Francisco. An experience like that could ruin any young poet, and while I don't think Lamantia was anything more than a rather alarming combination of precocity and preciosity, the business still seems shockingly irresponsible.

Joe Hazan and his current mistress, a delightful German refugee, very pretty and intelligent, named [—], are planning to drive to Mexico in January. We have tentatively agreed to all go together, and the two boys I mentioned in the last letter are also intending to go. If it works out we would all take a big house in Mexico City and spend at least six months, by which time the war should be over and things straightening out somewhat.

I suppose you have read about the David Kammerer murder? He was from my home-town, Clayton, and used to go out with my sister. I never knew he was queer, it will create a terrible stir in Saint Louis and probably start my family to thinking along unfortunate lines – may also start another Lonergan atmosphere in New York.

Well, I must get to work before Fritz and Jeanne return.

Glad you may take the trip – it is ever so much nicer here now that the bitches have had their two weeks and gone back to Macy's Etc.

Love,

10.

P. S. Have finished "The Caller". No doubt it goes in my reservoir of noble efforts.

It is the *last* play I will try to write for the *now* existing theatre.

Leaving for Harvard again Thurs. – perhaps won't come back here.

I have some *paintings* for you – one of Billy Budd.

[Provincetown, Mass.]
Sept. [*5, 1944*]

Dear Donnie:

I have taken your suggestion to heart and dug up this unmailed letter[1] which has been lying about for weeks.

I am not surprised you are unhappy: who can be otherwise at this time of year? *La fin d'été* is the saddest thing in the world, and as you grow older it seems to be even sadder. Is it possible that you mean Sandy as "your pillow of solid comradeship"? His status has vastly improved since I last saw you! Even though you have shaved off that beard – according to Fritz and to Mary Hunter – (she says Paul Moor saw you on a bus without it) – I suspect you are becoming a little Whitmanesque in your attitude toward the flesh. Or has the exasperating little boy grown up? If I go home by way of Boston I will see him in "Life With Father"[2] and decide for myself. In any case, I am glad, for it is bad to enjoy someone's body whom you don't care for.

Mary Hunter was in Wellfleet – a few miles from here – early this week and sent me a card requesting a meeting. I rode over on my bike and spent the night there. It was just about like our visits to her apartment except I didn't have your protection and I felt unusually frightened. There she was, in a simple little gingham house-dress, a blue ribbon in her hair, and no stockings – slicing cucumbers – just like the heroine of a wholesome western – our Mary! After lunch we went out to the beach – to my everlasting horror she

1. Probably letter 68 or 69.
2. Sandy was out of the Army, playing Clarence in a cross-country tour of this play.

opened an enormous red bag and produced – guess what! – a copy of "You Touched Me"! – just as if she had noticed it for the first time, with a sort of naive, childish delight! Well – – – I haven't felt such a sensation since I was required to dissect a frog, stinking with formaldehyde, in a zoology course at college. It put me into a state of absolute coma, all I could do was grunt and stare miserably over her shoulder at the ocean, while she rattled brightly along about little adjustments here and there which she felt were necessary to clarify Matilda's character or make Emmie more understandable, Etc.! I tried to get away after supper but was almost forcibly detained. All kinds of bright wholesome people came over and stayed till after midnight. I sat like a backward child, smiling inanely at everybody and saying nothing. Finally – bed! At breakfast the script came out again – no one has suffered this much since the Spanish Inquisition! As for a production, she was just as vague as ever about money. But she did say that she was now going to give the backers a list of actors on the basis of which they would have to decide one way or another. But she has no idea who she would use in place of Reid, and Estelle Winwood, whom she wants for Emmie, has not even read the script. So there you are – she expressed no discouragement, if that is a sign! We marked places where changes could be made if the war ended – and of course it could be made *after* the war with very slight alterations.

I had no sooner returned from this little trip to Paradise than Blanchard arrived from Wellfleet for another stay here. The same old business, except I felt really sorry for him this time. It seems Charles Henri and Pavlik had subjected him to positive torture – persecution! He sat up all night telling me of their cruelties to him – made him wash all the dishes and gave him no liquor and wouldn't drive him to town! All very childish and silly, on both sides – reminded me of that play "Three Old Ladies". Blanchard left this morning and I told him to call you up in New York.

As for my departure, it is imminent. The money I've set aside for the summer is about gone and I must spend a little time in New York.

Don't let this affect your plans if you still want to come here. Fritz has a lovely place for you, and September is said to be nice here. Of course I would want to see you the short while I will be in New York. The last couple of weeks have been very exhausting, emotionally, nervously, Etc. I feel quite weak. Blanchard, Mary, finishing a play, and other complications. I hope New York will be restful.

Love,

10.

LETTER 76

*In October, Eddie Dowling optioned "The Glass Menagerie".
The production, happily, was to have a gestation period about one-
sixteenth as long as that of "You Touched Me". Before rehearsals
started, Tennessee went home.*

.76.
[53 Arundel Place, Clayton, Mo.]
Nov. 3, 1944

Dear Don:

It is raining gloomily here and I find it difficult to adjust
myself to the quiet tempo after Manhattan. I loiter moodily
about the house till mid-afternoon, then give up and go
downtown for a swim at the Y. I suppose I shall have to
start writing if I remain here long, though I wished not to
for another month or so.

Miss Bull-dog is cowering between my feet because the
carpet-sweeper is going downstairs and eight years have not
accustomed her to it. She always expects it to fly upstairs
and attack her. A neurotic little beast! Loves to go walking
but is terrified of the leash – whines and cringes when you
remove it from the closet. About like our behavior on Times
Square. Yesterday a sturdy marine came up to me while I
was waiting for a bus and asked how to get to the station.
I told him briskly but he remained, looking sort of desperate. He finally said, Where is a mailbox? I showed him right
on the corner. He walked away from it, murmuring, That
one isn't the right kind! I guess Oliver[1] is right about this

1. Oliver Evans: Tennessee wrote an introduction to a volume of his poetry
in 1950.

152

town. Found two letters from Oliver waiting for me here. He was going overseas, must have gone by now, for Mother says he called one night from the station, passing through to port. He seemed sort of miserable about it.

The family is terribly upset because they got a 15-page letter from Dakin announcing his conversion to the Roman Catholic church. As my grandfather had baptized him in the Episcopal church he took it as a personal affront that Dakin had had it done over by a Roman. So he packed up and left for the South immediately afterwards. Mother is praying over it and Dad says that the jungle has affected his mind. The letter was all about Transubstantiation and "The Infallibility of the Pope" which he says has not been disproven. It just made me sort of disgusted. I had hoped the soldiers were getting some new ideas and perspectives to bring back with them.

Margo met me at the train and got me to wire Dowling that she was coming and would make him a great assistant. She looked wonderful, and seems to have twice as much energy as ever before. Wanted to know if you liked her. I assured her you did, so be nice to her. It's no telling what somebody like her might get away with in this world! Supreme confidence and verbal witchcraft are useful items.

I have written Dowling a letter about spiritual values in the theatre. That's about all I've done. But I'm going out now to see if I can't do something more! – I am bored.

Love,

TENN.

153

Rehearsals for "Menagerie" began in December in Dowling's New York office and Laurette Taylor's hotel room. Margo Jones worked with Anthony Ross and Julie Haydon in my Madison Avenue apartment. Some of the difficulties, which have been reported as taking place in Chicago, started immediately.

From my letter to Sandy, December 13, 1944: "*We had been to see Margo who was upset because she had been given an outline of a drunk scene which Dowling wants written and put into the play. Tenn hadn't been at rehearsal because he was supposed to be writing it. He thought, the material being so unbelievably out of place, halfway between vaudeville and Saroyan whimsy, that they would drop the idea. He even thought of speaking to George Jean Nathan who he felt sure would not advise anything so corny going into the play. At the theatre, where we had gone to the opening of 'Little Women', Haydon rushed up to us and introduced us to Nathan and said he would like to see us after the performance. Afterward, Haydon rushed up to me and said she was taking Tenn away because 'my escort' doesn't feel like seeing a lot of people and we want to talk to him. I went on to Margo's room where she was giving a party. It was a couple of hours before Tenn got there. Together with Dowling, Haydon, and Singer (the backer), Nathan had given him the works. It seems that the drunk scene is Nathan's idea. He said that he didn't love the play but that if Tenn would put it into their hands they might could make it into something good. He said Tenn didn't know how to write drama, that he was really just a short story writer, who didn't understand the theatre. I guess I hurt you about 'Battle of Angels', he said; but Tenn told him that, no, he hadn't thought it a good play, but just one that had good material in it. It boiled down to that if they could have their way Nathan would give his support, otherwise no . . . Anyway, they missed on their intentions, as Tenn now intends to refuse to give in on the small corny*

154

misinterpreted points that he had let them have and will withdraw the play if they insist on having this put in."

On December 16th, the company left for Chicago.

·77·

Hotel Sherman, Chicago, Ill.
[*December 18, 1944*]

Dear Donnie –

We're having a bloody time of it here – as expected. Yesterday, Sunday evening, I thought the situation was hopeless – as Taylor was ad libbing practically every speech and the show sounded like the Aunt Jemima Pancake hour. We all got drunk, and this A. M. Taylor was even *worse*. I finally lost my temper and when she made one of her little insertions I screamed over the footlights, "My God, what corn!" She screamed back that I was a fool and all playwrights made her sick – that she had not only been a star for forty years but had made a living as a writer which was better than I had done – then she came back after lunch and suddenly began giving a real acting performance – so good that Julie and I, the sentimental element in the company, wept. So I don't know what to think or expect.

She has been tormenting poor Julie unmercifully but I think Julie is getting back at her in her own sweet way. For instance Laurette declared furiously that Julie had called her up at two o'clock last night to enquire sweetly if "she could go out and buy me an apple". I think that is the funniest Julie story that I've heard yet, but they are unlimited. What *characters*! This company is more amusing than the show!

Taylor has been drinking but so far no signs of drunkenness. In fact everyone in the company except Julie and Eddie have been devoting all free hours to drink. Margo is like the

155

scoutmaster of some very jolly but wayward troop. Everybody makes drunken declarations of love to everybody. Such intense and indiscriminate congeniality always gets on my nerves. Tonight I disappeared for a swim and stayed away all evening – a great relief! Our house is in the same bldg. with "Winged Victory". I have met some interesting members of the cast, some of whom stay at the Sherman, so the social outlook is not too disheartening.

I have a lovely room – double bed so you could share it with me – and am living luxuriously on my $10 a day. "Condemned man ate a hearty breakfast" perhaps. Last night, when I was feeling so gloomy, I read your Crane and found it as comforting as ever. Hope you've forwarded my cheque by this time? *Wire* me when you are coming. And *do* come![1]

Love –

10.

.78.
[Hotel Sherman, Chicago, Ill.]
1/11/45

Dear Donnie:

It is four A. M. but I feel like talking to you a little. The show is doing swell now. Week-ends almost capacity and other nights about fifteen hundred and still building. So it looks like we'll remain here – they're selling tickets up till Feb. 10th. Everybody except Dowling is eager to get into New York – especially Laurette. She gets better all the time. However I guess it's wise to milk Chicago a little before we face another set of critics. No important changes in the script – except I've gotten my own drunk scene in place of Dowling's ad-lib – and the second narration, which you didn't

1. I did go to Chicago, for two days, for the opening.

like, has been taken out. Five lines added at the end and the final tableau blacked out – which made Laurette furious. Nobody told her she was going to be blacked out – they were scared to. So they just blacked her – Julie came up to the candles – Laurette comes up right behind her! Last night Laurette got in a fight with Eddie backstage and missed her cue after the love scene – Julie gives Tony the broken glass and says "a souvenir" which is Laurette's entrance cue. No Laurette. So Julie raises her voice and repeats it. Still no Laurette. Tony says – "Thanks for the – *souvenir*". Still no Laurette. Julie drifts over to the glass cabinet and ad-libs – "Here is another just like it." "Aw, gee, thanks!" says Tony. Still no Laurette. Julie is just about to start back for a third souvenir when they get the old bag on – still frothing! But she is the whole show.

Being feted and lionized on a small scale has convinced me or rather confirmed my suspicion that success is a bore. People are never so unattractive as when they think you are worth impressing. So I am avoiding society here, all but the college kids. Bob [—] has been coming up several nights a week for the night. I have never known such a useful child! And I don't get a bit tired of it. Except for that I wouldn't stay here.

Mary Hunter called long distance about some prospect. I don't know if he's the one who says, Little girl, you've got a great play, or not – but she says he is now on the coast and she is holding out for co-producer. That is, he is an angel who wants to produce. And a character named Harry Bloomfield who put on a show named "Many Happy Returns" has phoned Margo and conferred with Audrey about "YTM" also. But he is on the black-list with the Dramatists' Guild because he had his last show re-written without the author's consent. Audrey says not to fool with him, at least till we get in New York with this one. Anyway it looks like the money will come easier now. My recent experiences have taught me how cagey you've got to be with these Bloomfields, Singers, and so forth. Be sure you've got the upper hand with them! Don't mention Bloomfield to Mary. If Mary really has a backer she is still the best bet.

My royalties have started coming but so far haven't gotten past Audrey. She was here and happy as a lark – gave me ten dollars cash and took my 5 % of the gross home with her.

Loved the Lynes issue![1] Let me hear from you.

Love,

10.

·79·

Hotel Sherman, Chicago, Ill.
[January 26, 1945] Friday

Dear Donnie:

Our Mary just called me from N. Y. to say she is now in a position to buy "YTM" and that I should wire Audrey to sign with her. I asked her if she had all the money, and she said, "Well, it's all in sight!" Then one of those wild shrieks of laughter. So I don't know, but let us hope she wasn't training a telescope on Tiffany's window. However I see no harm in signing with Mary. If she doesn't have the money, she'll have to drop the option and in the meantime I am sure getting some option money won't hurt us. We didn't discuss terms but I am sure Audrey will make them as favorable as possible. Of course Audrey is not going to like this any too well, as I don't think she likes Mary – and probably has hopes of disposing of the play elsewhere if "Menagerie" continues to go over big. But if Mary is on the level with us I think we should stick with her. Peculiar as she is, I think she is the one to work with on this show. It is going to take

1. Of *Dance Index*: George Platt Lynes' photographs of ballet dancers.

brilliant direction and the best cast available – and I should say about fifty grand – to put it over.

If you are in touch with Mary – I presume you must be – worm as much information out of her as you can without making her hysterical. It has been rumored around here that International Pictures have promised her 50% backing if she gets the rest of it. They are the new picture concern that Gary Cooper has started. Dowling is scared to death that "YTM" would open in N. Y. before "Menagerie" and I think that is one of the reasons they have signed for a N. Y. theatre. I believe we are now going in the first of March, in spite of doing a land-office business here.

I feel rather sad about leaving Chicago, not on account of the town, but the university kids have been so sweet to me, particularly two of them, [—] and a little blond one I don't think you met. I feel like the Crimson Flash in Emmie's chicken yard! Perhaps it is good I'm leaving before I get twenty years for contributing to the delinquency!

Jack [—] – do you remember him? – an old friend of Criswell's whom we ran into last Fall at the Downtown Cafe Society – was through here last week and we did the bars together. More successfully than usual. He is traveling for some big advertising agency and his next stop is Atlanta. Today he wired me to ask you to send him some addresses down there. Says he is dying of loneliness. Wants you to wire him collect at his hotel – says he told you which one – why don't you get him in touch with that old belle who stays at the Atlanta Y? She could at least tell him where to cruise. [—] is quite a nice person when you get used to him – he is pulling himself together after a long period of deterioration and needs helping.

Dad came up to Chicago to see the show. He was only here one night. I had a date on the Chicago U Campus so I left him with Laurette and she was furious. Called me up early next morning and shouted, "How DARE YOU LEAVE ME ALONE WITH THAT DULL OLD MAN?!"[1]

We are going to open at the Playhouse in New York. I believe that's one of the nicer theatres. I would like to get a room at the Shelton. Wish you would call them and ask if I could make a reservation there – preferably room without private bath or one not more than $3 a day. I may leave here before the company – possibly the middle of February – and will probably visit home for a few days first. Margo is back in New York and working on a plan to get us to England (she and me).

Laurette has got Julie to put her hair up and wear a hat, but I think it makes her look a country school-teacher. It is a plain blue felt hat with a wide brim – effaces her almost completely. We all went to a tea given by a woman's club this afternoon. One of the members was out of her mind – temporarily, the ladies said – and she rushed up to Laurette and started to dance around her singing "Here we go round the mulberry bush". Another one asked Julie if she was really shy and Julie said, "No, it's just my profession"! Julie gave Laurette a nigger baby doll. I think it was a dig at Laurette's nigger accent. Anyway Laurette was furious and threw it out of her dressing-room, yelling "Who put that horrible thing in here?" It was several days before Julie confessed.

That's about all the gossip.

Love –

TENN.

1. Tennessee enclosed a letter from his father in which he had circled this paragraph: "Your Mother said you were a little too free in paying the food and other things for other people. When we tried to get you over the telephone one night last week, and were unable to do so, your Mother was told that you were down at the bar with Margo Jones. She later called Margo and talked with her, but I have stopped at the Sherman Hotel, and I know what they charge for drinks there, and with her capacity it wouldn't take long to break you. She is making a good salary, so let her buy her own drinks and pay for her own food."

.80.

[Hotel Sherman, Chicago, Ill.]
[*February 2, 1945*]

Dear Donnie:

Had another long-distance talk with Mary, mostly about "Menagerie's" opening which I am fairly sure is March 6th. Singer has given that date to Laurette and it has been mentioned in one of the columns. Our box-office continues to grow but I doubt that they would relinquish a N. Y. theatre on that account. I think an April opening for "YTM" would be ideal, though I wonder if Mary can really get a cast and theatre that quickly, not to mention the right amount of money. She said the backers were mainly disturbed about "the porpoise story" and wanted to know if it could be cut. I assured her that I would not put up a life and death struggle for it. But I do think that "bestiality" shit is the silliest thing yet. With a good captain I think the porpoise would play better than anything else from an audience point of view and is badly needed at that point in the play to relieve the stuffiness. I think we should have closed rehearsals and keep it in, if possible. And I hope to God she hangs on to Phil Brown. I shudder when I think of some of the Hadrians we might be stuck with – a swish would throw the play! or anybody who wasn't a damned good actor. – So Freedley[1] is messed up with us! – However you know I still think working with Mary and given a competent bunch of actors the play could be moulded into a success. Margo's remark is silly. Not very much has been done to the play since Pasadena. Willoughby was removed and the tea-scene given more action and humor – the porpoise put in – Matilda run out of the house – and the Capt.-Emmie scene inter-

1. George Freedley was a member of a group that invested in plays.

161

woven with the elopement. I can't see how any of those things has damaged the mood of the play and although some of it may not read as prettily as it used to I'm sure it will play lots better – and that's an important factor. Margo really doesn't know how to read a play script and sometimes she makes me mad when she gets so meddlesome and officious. Her motives are always good and loving – (though not without personal angles) – but anybody who could make such a remark about Naya does not [have] impeccable taste. I think she is just feeling hurt about something – maybe because I haven't written her yet. I did tonight. Did you see the Naya?[1] I wish you would and tell me if they have changed it. I ought to go back to N.Y. but I hate to leave my children. As a matter of fact, I lost one of them when they got wise to each other – but still have [—]. The little blond one is lost. And was such a love! The Sherman offers ideal conditions as nobody pays any attention and room service is wonderful. I have coffee sent up. Then martinis. Then coffee. Then more martinis – when I am working I don't even have to go downstairs. If I ever get poor again I'll be lost. Do you remember my speaking of Andrew Gunn, the Pullman scion whom I met in Acapulco? Well, he is now in Chicago working for his father – they have entertained me and given me a guest membership at the Chicago Athletic Club which is just like the Roman baths! – that is, in luxury – so it is hard to leave here. And I ought to visit home for a week first – though how I could ever endure it after my hours and habits here I don't know!

I loved your expression "ice-hags". Is it from "The Tempest"? Chicago streets are full of them, too. But also lots of fire-devils! You know what I mean.

But a sort of nearly middle-aged but attractive sailor

1. "Quintin Quintana" by Ramon Naya, which the Hedgerow Theatre was doing. Margo, who had returned to New York, had not liked it.

with sweet lonely eyes looked at me across a restaurant counter and smiled and we both went out together but I didn't have nerve to speak – so you see I'm really no better.

Tony just called and said he can't sleep and wants me to walk around with him. It is five A. M. – poor Tony! He has a growth on his nose which may be malignant and is practically an alcoholic – but so damned nice it's heartbreaking. Like Laurette. This letter is a fine example of 20th century chaos!

Blessings and love,

TENN.

Jay Laughlin will be here tomorrow to see show. I met *Nims*[1] (5 Poets) and *groped* him just to get *rid* of him – and *did*! A funny story I'll save till I see you.

.81.

[Hotel Sherman, Chicago, Ill.]
[March 2, 1945]

Dear Donnie:

I am writing you from the dog-house where I have been committed by almost everybody on various charges.

Singer and Dowling are enraged over an article I wrote for Ashton Stevens' column about "business men and gamblers" in the theatre. They have written our N. Y. press-agent instructing him to omit my name from all publicity about the show.

Then Tony and Laurette have decided to get mad at me on the most childish pretext. Tony has become a regular alcoholic here, and inventing all kinds of excuses. He is never drunk on the stage but practically never sober off it.

---

1. John Frederick Nims, who appeared in the same volume as Tennessee of "Five Young American Poets".

He and I have been constant companions till the last three days when he began to get sullen. I think it was mainly because I was getting more chickens than he was. I have three 17 year old ones, including [—], on the string and he seemed to resent it, as he has only two which aren't very reliable. And is so drunk every night he doesn't even remember next morning what he did with them. Anyway he told Laurette that I was preventing him from going on the wagon, that I embarrassed him in public by my outrageous behavior – this after him getting us both thrown bodily out of a gay bar last week because he couldn't keep his hands – publicly – off some horrid little screaming bitch!

So you see –

Laurette doesn't know all the ramifications, including the sex-angle, but Tony has convinced her that I am a dreadful influence and right at the moment our erstwhile wedge formation is broken up.

But I have been buried in a long surrealist poem the last few days, mostly about gay jockeys in a Miami rooming-house.[1] So I don't much care.

There's too much to begin with about "YTM". Briefly, Alex Yokel[2] wants it away from Mary and has offered all kinds of dazzling enticements of an all-out all-star Mielziner-designed production with all the money in the world.

Audrey has sent the play back to Guthrie McClintic. That's all I know and all I can tell you and I think the only thing to do is nothing until I get to New York and we can talk seriously and completely to all concerned.

1. "The Jockeys at Hialeah".

2. Alex Yokel was business manager of the "Menagerie" company. A month later I wrote Sandy: "Audrey and Tenn have received anonymous notes telling them that Mr Singer is a member of Murder Inc. Mr Yokel is suing Singer because, though he was billed as supervisor in Chicago, he gets no billing here. Mr Yokel says he has heard Mr Singer will 'be taken care of', but Audrey thinks they will all be included."

I have had for some time increasing reservations about Mary as a producer-director. Aside from lacking promotion power she is so God damn picayunish about little things – you know what I mean – analyzing and analyzing the juice out of everything! I wonder if that is what it takes to put a show on like "YTM". Still think she may be the best one for it but that we should wait till we're sure and always give the show the first consideration.

SAY NOTHING TO MARY OF THIS! – that would screw things up fine.

I'm having a good time here, spite of all the intrigues and counter-intrigues that make the world go round counter clockwise!

All I can say is – Don't be a lush! Ever!

Thought for the day: It is hard to tell a beau geste from a belle gesture!

Love,

TENN.

.82.

[Hotel Sherman, Chicago, Ill.]
[March 15, 1945] Thursday

Dear Donnie:

I am back in the Loop in a race-track suit! – loud black & white check job I bought in Saint Louis. Dowling gave me a sour look and said, Are you gonna wear *that* to the Opening?

Things are in a state of chassis here – Tony Ross is in the hospital and Randy Echols is playing his part. Tony has been going to pieces for quite a while – getting drunk every night – unreasonable and persecuted in his relations with everybody due to his nervous state – heart-trouble and now dysentery which final item has put him in the sick bay. He hopes to be back with us tomorrow but I am naturally very

165

concerned over the situation – Randy is doing a noble job but just isn't right for it. I may have to go in the trenches again – if they want to keep him, Tony not recovering.

"The menagerie" is no lie about this company – and neither is glass! I sometimes wonder if we'll really get to New York in one piece. The play back-stage is far more exciting than the one *on*!

Well, I got the McClintic signed contracts yesterday[1] – isn't that one for the books? – and sent them on to Frieda! Also a hurt little letter from Mary. She called me twice long distance and I've never known *less* what to say in a delicate situation. Naturally I'm sorry for her and Helen[2] but no

---

1. On March 12, I received a card from Audrey Wood asking me to come to her office at noon and sign the McClintic contracts. When I arrived, she also asked me to sign three copies of the following letter, which her office had prepared.

March 12, 1945

Mr. Tennessee Williams
c/o Liebling-Wood
551 Fifth Avenue
New York City

Dear Tennessee: –

As you know, on September 17th, 1942 we entered into a Dramatists' Guild collaboration contract concerning the play "You Touched Me" based on the story of the same title by D. H. Lawrence. This contract provided that any and all receipts from the play should be divided as follows: –

Thirty (30%) to Donald Windham
Thirty (30%) to Tennessee Williams

In consideration for the great amount of work you have done on this play since the above mentioned date I now wish to change the distribution of royalties to read as follows: –

Forty (40%) to Tennessee Williams
Twenty (20%) to Donald Windham

All the terms and conditions of this contract in every other respect shall remain intact.

My signature at the bottom hereof shall make this a binding agreement between us.

Very truly yours,
Donald Windham

I told her I would prefer to talk to Tennessee before I signed them, and took the copies with me.

2. Helen Thompson was the American Actors Company business manager.

166

reasonable person would act otherwise – after all that hedging and procrastination and really no visible results – just vague promises or hopes! And after all – McClintic! Where they really fell down was putting on "Only the Heart" first when everyone knew it wasn't a horse for a slow track. I hope something can be done to make the girls feel better about it but don't see why we should have hurt consciences. C'est la Jerry – as they say.

The university kids gave a home-coming party for me last night. [—] was acting strangely – got very drunk and gave a demonstration of drooling which horrified his play-mates but which I thought very cute. He blew spit-bubbles and slobbered all over his clothes! This new generation is very, very different from mine – probably even yours. But I find them adorable. Do you know Four F's – almost regardless of physical condition – can get in the field-service and go to Europe or Asia? I am definitely interested as I want a good, definite and long change.

I went out every night during my week at home – mostly with Inge and an amazing widow named [—] who is like a one-woman Court of Charles II. Goes hog-wild in the presence of gay boys, flitting from one to another, offering herself and whispering demurely, Do you suppose he'd fuck me, do you think he could do it?

She is also a willing and talented procurer. Fixed me up with a charming Captain in the air-force and having no other place of refuge we ducked into an empty building on the campus of the Lutheran seminary. In exchange I fixed her up with Jimmie [—] – do you remember him? – was in "Wallflower" and is now playing Saint Louis with "The Searching Wind". When I briefed her on his manly attributes, the poor girl practically went out of her mind. She drove me down to the station and the last I saw of her was driving her car right over a curb-stone in her haste to get back to

167

the American Theatre where we'd left him. Really simple!

It is grey and rainy here but Saint Louis was all blue and soft like your Mother's first kimono.

Love,

TENNESSEE

After Tennessee arrived in New York many people, including Audrey Wood, telephoned me looking for him. I hadn't seen him. For some reason, he was hiding out at the Brevoort. He surfaced after a few days, in his race-track suit, and established himself at the Shelton. When I saw him, I asked about Audrey's suggested change in our collaboration contract. He said he would have to question her about it, and never mentioned the subject to me again.

The afternoon of the opening, Saturday, March 31, he and I searched the Second and Third Avenue junk shops for a lamp shade for the second act of the play. Tennessee had only two tickets for that evening and took me with him. Horton Foote was outside the theatre, watching people enter, and Tennessee slipped him in to stand. Mary Hunter was in the lobby. Tennessee and she embraced, which was emotional. By Monday morning, when the reviews were out, Tennessee was a celebrity and began to be the target of strangers; but the people I saw him with that spring were old acquaintances, Fidelma Kirstein, Margo Jones, Jo Healy (who had been the switch-board operator at the Theatre Guild at the time of "Battle of Angels"), an old sailor friend, etc.

The middle of April, Tennessee gave an interview to the New York Times and caused his first off-stage sensation. "The real fact," he said, "is that no one means a great deal to me, anyway. I'm gregarious and like to be around people, but almost anybody will do. I'm rather selfish in picking my friends, anyway; that is I prefer people who can help me in some way or another, and most of my friendships are accidental." I had a hard time convincing outraged acquaintances that he was saying no one meant a great deal to him compared to his work, that he preferred people whose private responses helped him with this private vocation, not who helped him worldlily, and that it was by the accidental patterns of such responses that his friendships were made.

At the beginning of May, he entered the hospital for another eye operation. For several days, while his eyes were bandaged, I went in the afternoon and read Plato to him. Then, as soon as the bandages were removed, he was off to Mexico City, in search for "The Paris of World War II (Post-war)".

.83.

[*Postcard*]
[Mexico, D. F.]
[*June 1945*]

Made a brief appearance at Opera last night with 2 generals & 6 duennas but in spite of most discreet behavior there has been a wave of suicides & duels & every time I go out my carriage is drawn by students. What shall I do?

10.

.84.

Hotel Regis, Mexico, D. F.
June 6, 1945

Dear Donnie:

I wrote you a long letter in Dallas but it was still in my trunk when I crossed the border and the immigration authorities held it for further inspection along with some other papers which struck them as being suspicious. However it was not in an addressed envelope so don't worry. The censor, who was a Mexican girl, read every Ms. I had with me and I had to catch a later flight out of Laredo. The poor girl, especially when she got to my journal, kept looking at me over the papers as if I were an uncaged monster which perhaps I was. Unfortunately no one had warned me of this procedure, but I have become such an alligator that I was not embarrassed but just annoyed at waiting.

I flew down here from Dallas,[1] though I still hate flying. But my stay with the Project had exhausted me so that I couldn't face a long train-trip. Margo has just about decided on "Battle of Angels" for an opening production and I have prepared another version, without the prologue and epilogue and eliminating Val's book and the fire phobia. There is a new ending with a totally paganistic import which ought to blow up the Project, if it's not already blown up by that time. Margo got drunk at a swanky party given by the richest and most influential old Auntie in Dallas. This Auntie had a young soldier staying with her, and Margo began to make subtle comments across the tea-table, such as, Honey – I hope you'll get out of this mess you're in! The Auntie's composure was admirable, but I hardly believe these delicate hints escaped her or that her attitude toward the Project will be improved. The old girl happened to be the art, book, and drama editor of one of the two leading papers!

Reforestation is not such a bad idea.

I haven't done very much here and have seen only one person, who is a friend of Margo's with not very much to offer, though sweet and diligent about showing me the town. I ran into Nicky [Magallanes] (of the Ballet) at a symphony concert here, but he was complaining of a tooth-ache and not inclined to be of social assistance, though he made a half-hearted attempt to find Balanchine who was there also. Anyway I heard Shostakovich's Fifth Symphony, conducted by Chávez – and was really thrilled by it. And yesterday went to the bull-fights, which were sickening and fascinating as ever. One matador wore white silk with silver sequins and bougainvillea pink stockings. He had to stab his bull nine times before he killed him, and the crowd was disgusted with him, but my attitude was indulgent. After each fight

1. It is on this visit that Tennessee says in his "Memoirs" that he saw a production of "Summer and Smoke".

171

the matador marches around the ring, bowing at each section to receive his plaudits. This poor youth was hissed and booed until he came to my section. I stood up and yelled "Bravo!" so fervently that he made a bow directly to me. I am sorry you weren't along for the two of us could have staged a real demonstration.

Write me c/o Wells Fargo, for I'm not sure just when and where I'll go. May try Chapala which is on a big lake near Guadalajara. Wells Fargo will hold or forward letters from here.

Have just received an invitation from the University of Tennessee to unveil a portrait of my great-great-grandmother Polly McClung in a hall that is named for her at the University. Seems that she was the first American co-ed. This is supposed to take place in the Early Fall, so the future is very bright for me.

Love,

10.

If you ever leave N. Y. I think you would love Mexico. The people are gentle, humorous, and beautiful – *sympatico y hermoso!*

McClintic wired me that Catherine Willard has signed for Emmie.

.85.
[Hotel Lincoln, Mexico, D. F.]
Junio 19 (Martes) [*1945*]

Dear Donnie:

Just got your letter from Wells Fargo after it had apparently been over a week in transit. Your situation sounds quite heavenly. Wish I had tried Nantucket instead of the Cape so many summers.

So much has been going on since I last wrote you. It all began with Leonard Bernstein's arrival in the city, of which I heard through Nicky. I wrote him a note (having never met him) and he responded immediately by inviting me to lunch with some friends in the International Set. From then on I have been going out socially all the time and with very interesting people. For instance this week-end I went to Rosa Covarrubias (wife of the painter) where I met Dolores Del Rio and Norman Foster. I don't suppose you remember Foster, but he used to be what I thought was about the most attractive man on the screen. He is now 41 but still looks like trade in a way that you would particularly like, I believe. (I wonder if the censor gets this?) Since quitting American pictures he has gone into directing and is doing art films in Mexico quite successfully. As for Dolores, she is even slightly older but her appearance is miraculous, the way Maxwell probably thinks he looks after the Boncilla treatment! And an afternoon in the sun. Also she is intelligent and charming, comes of the highest Mexican society. Balanchine was also at this luncheon, complaining terribly of Mexico, hates it, says he likes only N. Y. Pauvrecita! Says all the girls (in the ballet) are sick with sumzings! After lunch we all lay on grass-mats in the patio and nobody bothered to talk to anybody, which was wonderful. I have also been to several gay parties, the only nice ones of the sort I have been to outside New Orleans. Really attractive people, and tequila and dancing. No camping or anything of that sort, which ordinarily takes the fun out of such gatherings. As for Bernstein (he has now departed for Cuernavaca) he is nice, but, oh, what an egotist! When not getting all the attention, he sits in a chair with closed eyes, pretending to be asleep. At least so he did, on one occasion, when we were being entertained by Bobby Lester who is a famous play-boy formerly of Paris. But he knows and quotes Hart Crane fluently and is a passionate revolutionary so – although too self-sufficient to be really lovable – I am mostly in favor of him. For private occasions, I have found a little Indian who speaks no English at all, not the least of good qualities. So with all this society, of a refreshing sort, and the Sunday bull-fights,[1] I am finding Mexico more than tolerable and I'll probably stay on here till it is time for "YTM".

I have gotten a series of cables from Guthrie. In the first he was considering Gilmore and had signed Willard. In the second he was undecided between Clift and Brown and wanted my opinion. I wired him to decide himself. In the third or fourth, the English actor Flemyng had come into the foreground and was Guthrie's choice provided his release could be obtained from the British army. I didn't answer this wire as Guthrie is the only one who knows anything about Flemyng, though I suspect he would be the best. It looks to me like Guthrie is doing a brilliant job of casting,[2] and if he directs equally well, there is nothing to worry about. I also got a charming wire from Katharine Cornell (signed Kit) saying that she had just seen "Menagerie" and would I write her one. When people are as nice as all that, I become embarrassed and it frightens me! I have spent so many years making myself over in such a way as to get along with bastards, cultivating a tough skin, rejecting my tender responses before they are rejected by others, assuming indifference so well that I have actually come to feel it most of the time – that now when I discover I have done more than was necessary – it is quite a shock! But life is not half long enough to even make the beginning of understanding yourself in relation to others, and the more

1. Enclosed were photographs torn from news magazines of bullfighters, Pepe Luis Vázques ("This one is my favorite") and Alfonso Reyes Lira.
2. Virginia Gilmore read for Matilda, who was played by Marianne Stewart. Catherine Willard was Emmie. Of Montgomery Clift, Phil Brown, and Robert Flemyng, McClintic chose Clift for Hadrian. And Edmund Gwenn played the Captain.

complex you are – *Basta*! (Spanish for enough of that shit.)

I suspect you will have money enough to travel in the Fall, and it would be nice if you could visit Dallas a while, for "Battle" and then come on down to Mexico. The more I see of the places and people here the more certain I am that it would please you enormously. Perhaps Sandy, too. *Come non?*

Margo called long-distance and while the Project had not exactly blown up, it was definitely passing through a little crisis. Mielziner had come down there and declared the intended theatre to be impractical and Margo had just flown to New Orleans and back on some desperate errand affecting the rental of another building. (Don't be misled – Project is still in Dallas.) She was very gay over the phone, but having known Mary I don't regard that as necessarily nor even probably a good sign.

Incidentally, Covarrubias (his wife says) has been engaged to design for Mary's [Katherine] Dunham show which is supposed to start rehearsals about the same time as "YTM".

Get plenty of sun and Sand, a nice combination.

Love,

TENN.

.86.

The Hamilton, Laredo, Texas
July 28, 1945

Dear Donnie –

I have just come from throwing the most violent scene since the time I dragged KB out of bed on Fire Island! When I got to the border last night a customs officer confiscated all my Mss. for inspection and I had to stay over in Laredo till they were cleared. When I called for them just now I discovered one was missing, the story *One Arm* which I had just gotten into final shape when I left Mexico. Of course I suspected it was being held because of its subject matter. A perfect fiend took possession of me and I began to shout and rage. It must have been a terrific polemic for in a few seconds I had the whole U. S. Customs gathered about me, some shouting back, others just looking like you and KB. One was in favor of throwing me in jail for peace disturbance but the Chief was conciliatory and begged me to rest in his office while the search was continued. He gave me a shot of whiskey and sent a wire to the train and my hotel in Mexico to enquire if the script was left there. I had assured him that it was my life's work and that existence without it was unthinkable. At last he suggested the inspector might have overlooked it and it might be still in the trunk at the depot so I was sent off in a jeep with a most attractive young officer to take a look. Fortunately the officer waited outside while I opened my trunk for, sure enough, there was *One Arm, virgo intacta*, beneath a pile of dirty shirts in the top tray.

I came out, exhausted and wildly exhilarated, and said faintly that I had an idea I might have already mailed it to my agent.

It was such a heady experience, blowing off all that steam, that it will probably cast a pink glow over everything for the next few weeks. Of course, on the other hand, I may be taken off the train somewhere between here and Dallas and put under observation in a state hospital!

Mexico is not as physically healthy as a summer on the northern coast but it has a richness that soaks into you and makes you feel as if your spirit had been feeding on something after a long starvation. Things that happened there were not repetitions of repetitions like happenings had begun to seem in the States. I have left there physically tired (from the activity and the altitude) but rested in my heart, as it were! The best good is knowing that there is a place I can go to and be in tune with when I've got to rest somewhere. I hope this feeling will last when I return to New York. If it

2/27/42

Dear Donnie: I meant to be in N.Y. by now - suddenly broke
out with a dreadful itching rash. I thought sure I finally
had the old Joe so I rushed to the family doctor. He sent me
to a skin specialist and it was pronounced to be The Seven
Year Itch! - There is an epidemic of it here among school-kids.
And other undeveloped types. So I got it. I had to spend three
days in long underwear and a coat of grease without bathing. Now
I have graduated to lotions and ointments and bathing is permitted
and the itch has subsided to where I can think of other things.
If it has become non-infectious by this week-end I can leave town.
But Gracious, what a mess! Me and the lower organisms have always
had trouble. Fortunately they say you can rid of it entirely in
three weeks instead of the original long term with options. Have
you heard of it in N.Y.? It is terribly prevalent here, even among
us suburban bath-takers. But of course the family is outraged and
appalled and I am told that gentlemen just don't have such things!

We've finally heard from Dakin after six scarey weeks of silence.
He has arrived in India after "a long voyage with lots of nice
officers".

I am reading "Moby Dick". Have you ever? It is lovely writing,
and the tattooed cannibal in it would please you, as he apparently
did the hero if I understand him correctly.

How is N.Y. now? But I will find out - won't I? Here it is really
nice at last, smokey gold afternoons with plum-colored sunsets
through the oaks on the campus - dogs and children chasing around
the yards and nobody, nobody I know anymore but that crazy old woman
who writes me the letters - Alice! - she calls me twice a day. I
will be ready for some society when I get to N.Y. - that is, if I've
stopped itching.

Jenn -

What a lot of itching
there is in life!

T.W.

"The Life of a
Sitting Target"
(my auto-biog.)

lower organisms
(one is on skates)

Dear Donnie —

We're having a bloody time of
it here — as expected. Yesterday
Sunday evening, I thought the
situation was hopeless — as
Taylor was ad libbing practically
every speech and the show
sounded like the Aunt Jemima
Pancake hour. We all got drunk —
and this A.M. Taylor was
even worse. I finally lost
my temper and when she made
one of her little "insertions" I
screamed over the footlights —
"My God, what corn!" —— She
screamed back that I was a
fool and all playwrights made
her sick — that she had not
only been a star for forty years

but had made a living as a
writer which was better than
I had done — then she came
back after lunch and suddenly
began giving a real acting
performance — so good that Julie
and I — the sentimental element in
the company — wept. So I don't
know what to think or expect.

She has been tormenting poor
Julie unmercifully but I think
Julie is getting back at her in
her own sweet way. For instance Laurette declared furiously that Julie had called
her up at two o'clock last
night to enquire sweetly if
"she could go out and buy me
an apple". — I think that
is the funniest Julie story
that I've heard yet — but they
are unlimited — what characters!
This company is more amusing
than the show!

Taylor has been drinking

but so far no signal of drunkenness
In fact everyone in the company
except Julie and Eddie have been
devoting all free hours to drink
— Margo is like the scout master
of some very jolly but
wayward troop. Everybody
makes drunken declarations of love
to everybody. Such intense and
undiscriminate congeniality always gets on my nerves — tonight
I disappeared for a swim and
stayed away all evening — a
great relief! Our house is
in the same bldg. with "Winged
Victory" — I have met some
interesting members of the cast,
some of whom stay at the
Sherman) So the social

outlook is not too disheartening.

I have a lovely room — double bed so you could share it with me — and am living luxuriously on my $10. a day — "condemned man ate a hearty breakfast" perhaps. Last night, when I was feeling so gloomy, I read your Crane and found it as comforting as ever. I hope you've forwarded my cheque by this time? Wire me when you are coming. And do come! —

Love —

10.

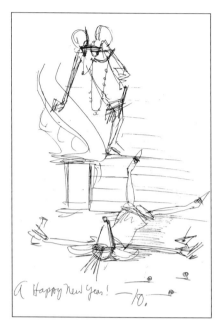

Greeting drawn by Tennessee
Williams, December 1958

Tennessee Williams, Marlon Brando,
Jo Healy, 1947

Frank Merlo, Donald Windham, Maria Britneva, Tennessee Williams,
and Sandy Campbell, New York, December 1948

Gore Vidal, Truman Capote, and Tennessee Williams, New York,
October 1948. Photograph by Jo Healy.

Donald Windham and Tennessee Williams, Rome, 1948.
Photograph by Sandy Campbell.

Tennessee Williams and Donald Windham in a Times Square
photo booth, New York, 1942

Fred Melton and Tennessee Williams, Band Shell, Central Park,
New York, 1940. Photograph by Donald Windham.

Sandy Campbell, Rome, 1948. Photograph by Donald Windham.

Donald Windham, Rome, 1948. Photograph by Sandy Campbell.

Margaret Phillips and Tony Smith at party for
Summer and Smoke, October 1948

Frank Merlo, Tennessee Williams, Mary Grand, and Bill Caskey,
Key West, Christmas 1949

Paul Cadmus and Donald Windham on Fire Island ferry,
1941. Photograph by Margaret French.

Tennessee Williams, friend from St. Louis, Fred Melton, and Donald
Windham celebrating option of *Battle of Angels,* Village Barn,
Greenwich Village, New York, May 8, 1940

Guthrie McClintic, Tennessee Williams, Thornton Wilder, and
Donald Windham at dress rehearsal before out-of-town opening of
You Touched Me, Boston, 1945

Donald Windham and Tennessee Williams with Edmund Gwenn as
Captain Rockley in *You Touched Me,* 1945.
Photograph by George Platt Lynes.

Donald Windham and Tennessee Williams, Houston, 1953

does I will know that this very broad-minded God of mine is still with me!

Aside from the panic over the script, the night here was nice. I have a room on the 12th floor, and the bed is right against a big window so that lying down looking out I seem to be floating between the stars and the desert which are the scene beyond. Such HEAT! But it moves, there is a desert breeze all the time, so it's almost agreeable to be burning. And in a way it is the sexiest Texas town I have ever been in. It is like something hot and soft and wet that has just been removed from something with the same dear properties and nothing has yet been covered or put away!

Perhaps I will stay over another night for such an atmosphere shouldn't be too casually discarded, not even for all the glories of "The Project".

If only Margo could get something of this quality into "The Project" but "The Project" for all its high fervor is more like a sonnet by Rupert Brooke than a painting by Gauguin. It is a dry fuck, really!

But maybe something can be done with a 10-cent tube of something.

We will see!

Love to you and *hasta vista*!

10.

The sun is right outside my bed which has a light pink counterpane on it which does something wonderful and extraordinary to the light in the room, makes it have a cloudy Renaissance glow, and there is a faint hum and vibration, everywhere. Hidden among the trees of the town are little glitters and noises and cries as if precocious children were doing lovely things to each other!

The desert horizon is just as straight and flat and brown as the edge of a big table, with all this excitement on it.

177

Both Tennessee and I were in Boston for the last rehearsals and out-of-town opening of "You Touched Me". It was a touchy time. Complex feelings rose again. Then the play opened in New York, was compared to "Menagerie", and flopped. There was hope for a run at the beginning, but in December the production laid off for ten days before Christmas.[1] It closed in New York on January 5, and a month later on the road. Either I had brought failure on Tennessee or he had brought it on me. Both versions contained emotional difficulties. Undoubtedly, he preferred for a while to know me "at a distance"; and the result is quite funny when he tries to write friendlily and at the same time suggest that I should leave New York and come South – anywhere except where he is. But all this is soon spilt milk to him. By March he is suggesting, although not another collaboration, a joint production.

.87.

Hotel Pontchartrain, New Orleans, La.
[*December 18, 1945*] *Tuesday*

Dear Don –

Sorry I didn't see you before I left N. Y. I felt in some vague way that we knew each other better at a distance, at least for a while, it would be difficult to say why and probably no need to.

I am sure it is good for me to be out of New York. Broadway seems like some revolting sickness, that involves vomiting and eating and shitting all at once. One's ego becomes so sickly bloated with it, little vanities take the place of any real truth in living. This can be anywhere but for

1. For one week, our 30% each royalties had dropped to $36.94.

me it happens more easily there than elsewhere. Many little distractions make it unnecessary to think or feel. Which you accept because thinking and feeling is dangerous and hard, and sometimes frightful. N. Y. holds me only by the balls, but that is sometimes a hard hold to break. There is so much sex there: I was running quite a little establishment at the Shelton, what with Oliver's raids on the steam room and the bar and my own chicken run. That part was hard to relinquish for I – alas – am not yet ready to forswear all fleshly attachments.

However N.O.L.A. is not strictly celibate. My old friends have disappeared but while apt. hunting I ran into a group lying on the floor drinking wine, one of them in a Carmen Miranda head-dress devised from window-drapes. And to-night I am being taken out to a place called "The Goat House" where everything goes on, including "Ether parties", which is something I haven't seen yet. Town is *wide* open!

I get an apt. in the Old Quarter on Jan. 1st with 4 rooms and a balcony right behind the cathedral.

Munsell asked me to make a few changes in "YTM" to make it post-war for London production.[1] I did this on the plane coming down here and mailed it right back to Audrey.

Love –

TENN.

.88.

710 Orleans St., New Orleans, La.

Jan. 3, 1946

Dear Don:

I wrote you an ecstatic letter about the Japanese wind-instrument soon as I unpacked it, but I moved that day and the letter didn't get off somehow. I wish you could have

1. Nothing came of Warren Munsell's proposed production.

seen me with the wind-instrument! I had a belle and a bell-boy helping me move, also a taxi driver. They took the luggage, I walked serenely behind them, holding the wind-instrument over my head, never setting it down for one moment till it was safely hung in the brightest spot in my new apartment. It is a joy forever! I will tell you a funny thing, though. I had it hanging in the second room, the parlor, and it never made a sound, the wind never hit it – never a tinkle out of it! Then the belle who was with me left town. It was my first night alone in the apartment. I was propped up on pillows in my big four-poster bed consoling myself with literature and cigarettes. All at once, in the big dark room beyond the folding doors – I hear a ghostly tinkle! It is the Japanese wind-instrument beginning to talk to itself for the first time since I hung it up four days ago! *Well*! I turned green as a ghost! I was scared to look in the next room! Why should the wind-instrument start tinkling at midnight with me alone and no perceptible wind? I got up and peeped through the folding doors. Sure enough, it was swaying and chattering girlishly to and fro! The mystery is still unsolved, but I have moved the wind-instrument into the bedroom where I can keep a closer watch on it. I have an idea it is the ghost of some lovely dead boy! I like to think so. I love it more than any other of my possessions except possibly my collected poems of Hart Crane. And by the way, it arrived without a thing broken or displaced. Thanks for it. I also loved the card of "The Peaceable Kingdom" although Miss Lion looks as if she was about to *start* something.

I didn't know you were going to leave *Dance Index*. If you are not going to work there I should think you would leave N. Y. for a while. In memory of Bigelow I never suggest that anybody go any particular place,[1] but I do think the

1. !

South is the best place for a writer, and I hope that with new experiences and places more of those matchless short-stories will be forthcoming. You are so young and wise! And your taste is the most impeccable I have known. So put yourself some place where the air is in motion.

With love,

TENN.

Please let me know how the road actors look.

.89.

[710 Orleans St., New Orleans, La.]
[*February 15, 1946*]

Dear Donnie:

I ran into Fritz and Muriel[1] at the Symphony last night and they said you were going up to Provincetown. Is this true? If I were you I would go to Mexico if I wanted to get out of New York. Or Santa Fe. Witter Bynner is back there now and would be nice to you. I'm afraid you'd be bored with it here because of the society. It is perfectly frightful. I was very lucky in meeting a young Mexican whom I have stuck with almost exclusively. That and the weather and my apartment (which was another rare piece of luck) are all that is really pleasant. Fritz will confirm my opinion of the people here. There is the dreariest bunch of belles anywhere to be found, not one – literally – that you could get down with brandy. All the cute or interesting ones have departed. However I am well-adjusted here because of the items mentioned above. I had a little whirl in high society and went to some of the big débutante parties but that blew up when Santo and I entertained a couple of the society beaux after a party

1. Fritz Bultman's sister, Muriel Francis.

in my apartment. They seemed to enjoy themselves but did not hold their tongues and I am told that my name is now mentioned only in whispers in mixed company. It is just as well as the crowd was unbearable.

Have you heard of Barbette? He was a famous trapeze-performer of the 20's in Paris – of international fame. He was in New Orleans last week and stayed at my apartment and is a character like Bigelow only even more astonishing. You may remember him as one of the ladies who occupied a box over the snowball fight in Cocteau's film "Blood of a Poet". He is really the only interesting person I've met here, and the poor thing has contracted some mysterious disease and is supposed to be turning gradually to stone. I could not see it was impeding her movements very much so far. She was on the street constantly and turned into every men's room. "I am like a Good Catholic passing a church," she said. "I always have to look in!" She told me that Proust had the same custom, went out every evening in a cab, from pissoire to pissoire. Each time he got back into the cab he would lean over to the driver and say, "*A l'autre*!" I wish I had taken down some of her remarks, such as, about Hollywood, "Between the ass-licking and the throat-cutting there is never a dull moment!"

I have seen the Bultmans' child. It appears to be normal but there is entirely too much discussion of its bowel-movements, as I expected.

If you come across any notices of "27 Wagons" will you send them to me, no matter how bad? I am working every day: the town is good for that. And the weather and the physical aspects of the city are really dreamy! If you go to Mexico or Santa Fe you ought to pass through here. I really don't see any sense in Provincetown at this time of year! Better even some unpopular little town in Florida, or Biloxi on the Gulf-coast! Reports of the trade there – a big air-base – are hardly even credible! Santo and I are taking a week-end trip to investigate.

How's Jane? Give her my love. Oh! – dear me! – I almost forgot to tell you, Jimmie [—], asst. st. mgr. of "YTM" sent me a wire recently that said: "Financial condition chaotic. Unemployed for five weeks. Girl-friend pregnant. Need three hundred for operation. Please wire me one."

I started to wire him: "Have you ever read 'An American Tragedy'?" – but thought it better just to act as if I had not received the message. It was the last thing in the world that might wring a sentimental tear from my old heart! Another good answer would be: "Fucking good here, too." In fact I have never received a wire that suggested so many barely resistable means of severing an acquaintance!

Audrey has written me a couple of times asking permission to return some royalties to the McClintic office – for very trifling amounts. I ignored the request as I think it is disgustingly squalid of them. Then she wrote that they had said the amounts were "very important" to them and she had taken the liberty of returning them without my OK.[1] I suppose it was the only thing to do, but it certainly turns one's stomach. In fact the whole thing does! So wretchedly abortive! But it is spilt milk now. I hope you have accumulated a little capital on it.[2]

Love,

10.

1. These amounts, the royalties for the last week in November and the first two weeks in December, allowed by the Dramatists' Guild without consent, had also been returned from my share. It is possible that Tennessee is upset because he had been asked for further returns to keep the play running on the road, where it had just closed.

2. My earnings from "You Touched Me" at that point, including the advance on amateur rights from Samuel French, totaled $4,239.73.

[710 Orleans St., New Orleans, La.]
March 25, 1946

Dear Don –

Happy to hear from you after such a long time! And that you have finished a draft of "B. B.".[1] Funny, I was reminded of that work recently while reading over Crane's "Cutty Sark". I hope you have caught the atmosphere in the closing lines of that poem – such as "baronial white on lucky blue" and lots of polished brass.

I have only finished one medium length play about 70 pages.[2] The hero is "Kilroy" whose name you see inscribed so often in public places. It is a freakish thing that only a few may like, maybe you will. Audrey thinks the best scene is "too coarse".[3] If your "B. B." is also fairly short perhaps we could get them tried out together at an off-Broadway house.

I am working slowly on a longer play.[4] As hot weather approaches the Quarter becomes a bit miasmic, and also the prolonged Mexican affair. The stage of intrigue and stratagem has crept up. I may go to Chicago, stopping off home, to create a change.

Oliver Evans is here! I have a mattress stretched on the floor for his amazingly frequent convenience. Brought in two big ones last night. "Wonderful night of fun!"[5] I am terribly uneasy and will be till he leaves.

1. An adaptation of Melville's "Billy Budd".

2. "Ten Blocks on the Camino Real".

3. This statement, combined with Tennessee's suggestion in letter 92 that I ask Audrey for a copy of "Camino Real", contrasts markedly with his version of her reaction to it in "Memoirs".

4. "A Streetcar Named Desire".

5. The first sentence of an obscene inscription Tennessee had read on the wall of a Turkish bath in Boston.

Audrey says I can afford to buy a car – so perhaps I will. Would like a second-hand "station-wagon" – to put a mattress in the back and go Gypsying.

There is a London interest in "Y.T.M.". They want to change the locale to New England. Hope it goes through.

I am still enjoying the wind-chimes – nicest present I ever received! I have one for you – a beautiful picture of Herman Melville removed from one of his biographies, whiskers and eyes like Whitman and a nose like yours!

Had ordered "Berlin Stories" for you. Laughlin mailed it mistakenly to me. As I can never mail a package, will have to deliver it sometime.

Love –

10.

.91.

[*On an oversized postcard of Canal Street, New Orleans, La.*]
[*April 11, 1946*]

Would love to read "Billy". Air mail to 53 Arundel Place, Clayton, Mo. as I am going home (!) for a short stay before other places (?). Will return to you promptly with care in total contradiction to my usual habits. It is *very* sad here now – hot and desolate. Think I will go out West.

Love –

TENN.

.92.

[53 Arundel Place, Clayton, Mo.]
April 1946

Dear Don:

You have the form and content of a good play here. At present only the second act is anywhere near completion.

185

The scene of the drum-head court is the best one and is the only one that has a really theatrical quality. That is the weakness of the play all through, a lack of translation into theatrical values, that and a pronounced tendency to be stilted or didactic in the dialogue. Your great talent is for prose writing and your particular weakness is dialogue so you have three strikes against you when you are working in a dramatic form. There are passages where the lack of naturalism in the speech is effective, where it gives a classical Greek quality; perhaps I like it better than other readers would, however. The work's best qualities are a classic atmosphere, a dignity, coolness, thoughtfulness, and the elemental nature of its problem of good and evil. In the way of understandable characterization I think you have done as much as Melville but not more. Melville's characters were understandable only between the lines, and you have made an omission that increases the mystery rather than suggesting a reason. In Melville there was a mysterious, closeted interview between Vere and Billy. Melville made a point of not disclosing what happened between them. It was this mystery that gave the story much of its powerful suggestiveness. You and I both have the same idea of what probably took place. That alone makes Vere's and Budd's final attitude understandable. My interpretation is that Vere was also in love with Budd and knew that only if Budd died immediately afterwards could anything happen between them. I thought that was why he directed that Billy be put in his own cabin, and I thought that the drum-head court would end with the others' dismissal and Vere's (Curtain) entrance of the cabin, alone with Budd. This, of course, could follow some preliminary talk between them in the outer chamber. Such a proceeding of course blackens Vere's character almost to the shade of Claggart, but at least it creates something tangible and comprehensible. There was never any doubt in my mind as to this being what Melville had in mind and is the thing most necessary to give the story a psychological purpose and validity. Otherwise it is arbitrarily idealistic as "Antigone", which it somewhat suggests.

You have worked out a good formal pattern of scenes in the last two acts. I would put it aside for a month or so as it is nowhere near a stage of completion. Let it rest in that condition until you can take it up again with a really fresh attack. In the meanwhile work on your stories for which you have so much more facility and which can receive so much more of what you have peculiarly to offer than Broadway can. It's really the same problem as mine except that I have been at it so much longer. You may think that I am advising you not to write for the stage. But I am only saying I think your stories are better handled. I wish you did not have to try to think about making money as a writer. "YTM" should have solved that problem for you, but I don't suppose it did more than temporarily until it goes on in England and has a much bigger success.[1] For it is hard to see how a talent like yours can ever be converted into cash at this time in this country. Which is really a tribute. But I am not forgetting that you want to devote yourself to writing and as yet no way is clear except by making money out of it. That is a problem few people look at sensibly. I wish you would read an article in *The Sewanee Review* current Spring issue. An article about Broadway by a professor named Eric Bentley. It shows how fundamentally stupid they are about this problem. There is a lot on "Menagerie" and something worse about "YTM". When I have the time I am going to compose an answer. These professors who write verse and criticism of verse and everything else do not realize that there are a number of artists who cannot teach school and yet have to eat, drink, wear clothes and live in houses or at least rooms of houses,

1. To date, there has been no English production.

and who need a bit of comfort and dignity in their lives in order to bear them. From the haven of the academy the rough edges of the problem are not apparent. I know them all too well, I have all but killed myself contending with them for a good many years. The only answer is toughness and then more toughness. That is how alligators were made through many ages, not one healthy poet in the duration of his lifetime.

I drove home in a super-jalopy, a 1937 model Packard convertible roadster which I purchased in New Orleans. I am intending to leave the middle of next week for another trip, to Taos, New Mexico. The Mexican companion has already preceded me out there. When I got home I found a telegram – opened and read by the family – which stated that he had quit his job and was leaving for Taos and would I please wire him some money to live on till I arrived there. I need not tell you the reception this wire had in the bosom of the family. They have cross-examined me about Santo and the wire ever since I got here. He has called me long-distance collect a couple of times, with Mother scuttling downstairs to grab up the downstairs phone so she could listen in on the conversation. Naturally I would have to practically hang up on the poor kid, especially when he burst into tears and begged me to leave here at once as he was lonely and hungry in the middle of the desert! I guess the cat is all but out of the bag, although I have covered up as well as I can – you know how well that is!

Fortunately nobody here is very bright, but somebody gets anything after so long a time! I mean anybody gets something! I have never felt more anxious to move along, but the car requires over-hauling and a week here is about the minimum I can stay. Dakin is home from India and planning a trip to New York. He grins sort of foxily every time he looks at me and I prefer not to guess what is going on in his mind. He showered gifts on Mother, a bracelet of opals, a sapphire, and a ruby ring set with two diamonds. Also a fur cape in which she looks like a duck! Spent practically all his savings buying presents for her. Dad has retired from business and spends all his time listening to the radio or drinking in nearby bars where I have to deliver him and call for him and poor Grandfather still has to stay in his room all the time to avoid running into him. Lovely family!

I would be happy for you to read "Camino Real". Ask Audrey for a copy of it. It is not good, about as unfinished as yours, though its defects and virtues are practically opposite, which is curiously the case with our writing in spite of the fact we have similar ideas.

It is funny about the passage you used from my letters.[1] I recall an incident of that sort. I have an idea it happened in Jacksonville Florida but I have forgotten who was downstairs and why I wanted to make trouble, if I did.

Love,

Tenn.

---

1. In "Billy Budd", the passage about the sailor in letter 27.

The incidents related in this letter become, with the passage of time and dramatization, a central point in Tennessee's private "Bulfinch's anthology", turning up in his 1955 letter to Kenneth Tynan (p. 306) as "where the desperate time started, and how it started", and in various interviews, until finally, in the "Memoirs", he cites it as the beginning of a three-year period during which he was so sure he was dying that he was reluctant to buy a new suit of clothes as he didn't think he would live long enough to justify its purchase.

·93·

Holy Cross Hospital, Sisters of Nazareth, Taos, New Mexico
May, 1946

Dear Donnie –

The last two weeks are like a fearful nightmare, and I came about as close to death as anyone ever does more than once in his lifetime. I took sick night before I left St. Louis but left anyway as I was so anxious to escape. Got steadily worse on road, knife-like pains in abdomen that doubled me up. Country doctor said I had kidney stone and doped me up so I could go on. Got as far as Alva, Oklahoma when car burnt out its bearings. I was stalled there three days, in agony. Finally went up to Wichita by train, leaving car in garage, and entered hospital. They gave me a cystoscopic examination, running a catheter up in my kidneys, but found nothing. In hospital there three days. As there was no swelling they did not think it was acute, but low grade appendicitis. So I went on to Taos. Here the pain suddenly stopped but I had high fever and blood count of 18,000 so local doctors said appendix had probably burst. Had to operate immediately. Doctor was just a kid and admitted he did not know where appendix was located and that whole case was very mysterious. I thought I was done for. Made my will. When they cut me open discovered I had not only leaking appendix but something called "diverticulum" which was also infected and about to burst. Both removed. On table two hours and just barely pulled through. Santo was with me all the time and Frieda has called every day. Now just third day after operation I am sitting up smoking and writing, but feel profoundly changed in some way. I did not know life was so precious to me or death so unalluring. It is good to be back!

I am going to stay on Lawrence's old ranch, in the very cabin he and Frieda lived in. Santo will be with me but my car is still in Oklahoma. We have rented one here.

Taos seems lovelier than ever but I don't know how long Santo will stand the quiet. I think I could stand it forever.

Please let me know that you received your script. I mailed it from Springfield, Mo. About 10 days ago. Loved your card. The "sisters" have taken it to pass around the ward. One of them is very worldly – winked at me and said, "I know you are a little pansy!"

Oliver has gone to Woodstock and loves it. Why don't you try it? Should be a good place to work.

Well, my head is spinning so goodnight, with love –

TENN.

Late in 1946 I went to visit Tennessee at St. Luke's Hospital in New York (where he was recovering from his summer on Nantucket with Carson McCullers) and found him rather regally withdrawn. Our lives had gone different directions that year, and on several occasions Audrey Wood had seemed to me to be giving official stamp to his attitude when she slighted me in business matters.[1] I, alas, wanted Tennessee to behave rationally toward me, even if he didn't toward himself. And he, alas, insisted upon using me as a projection of his conscience. (His "beach at high tide" remark in letter 94 shows him in the process of transferring one of his self-judgements into an opinion of mine.) The division was slight – even if symptomatic of others to come. My tension was eased by my beginning to have a little success with my stories. The finishing of "Streetcar", which Tennessee takes so calmly that he hardly mentions it, made him more, not less, outgoing; and as its production approached we drew closer together again.[2]

·94·

Hotel La Concha, Key West, Fla.

28 January 1947

Dear Donnie:

Fritz showed me your letter with the various complaints against the "powerful queen". It is gratifying to learn that

1. From my journal, November 22, 1946: "I hear Audrey refuses to let Equity Library do a production of 'Y.T.M.' – says she has to protect Tenn's reputation. When told I would watch rehearsals, she said I was a sweet boy but didn't know anything."

2. From my journal, October 15, 1947: "Went to Tenn's and after supper to see a rehearsal of 'Streetcar' last night in the theatre on the New Amsterdam roof. Enjoyed talking to him very much. Our senses of humor coincide so much that we sit in a room with a French woman producer, Jane, Tony, Sandy, Theatre Arts editor, Irene Selznick, etc. and giggle at the ceiling like children in grammar school."

she could still give an impression of power when laid out at St. Luke's after twelve days on liquids. Maybe it was that Dextrose Infusion they gave her! I have always thought she was more of a "Mad Duchess" than a "Powerful Queen". But that is a trifling point, like most differences of opinion among old friends. Every once in a while a heavy chalk line is drawn through our lives separating one part from another. Our real trouble is that chalk line which circumstances created: time, separation, Sandy, Santo, the misunderstandings that come from lack of communion. Sometime ago I was reading back through my old journals and I came across this rather conceited entry: "Donnie is the only one of my friends who would understand what I was saying about certain things if I should ever be able to say them." That was a lot more important than any present estrangement. The past doesn't seem dead to me, but on the contrary, has more reality than the present with all its momentary distractions. I didn't mean this to sound so like an essay! Proximity to the sea makes me kind of cornily philosophic. If you wish to be catty, you may remark that I must have done most of my writing on the beach at high-tide.

I have just driven down here with Grandfather and the place is even better than I remembered it. The military atmosphere has relaxed and all the sailors appear to be walking to the tune of "Managua, Nicaragua". If you ever come here insist on getting room $\#$ 602 in this hotel. It has windows on both sides that look over a clean sweep of the sea that covers the bones of Crane, and a lighthouse and, right now, a carnival. I went there last night and it made me think of your story. I went in the side-show and was the only one in there. The first exhibit was a child called the "Lobster Boy" for some reason. He had immense hips and belly and tiny atrophied limbs that were like flippers and he flopped around in a sand-pit in a bored fashion while, to my horror, the lecturer began to deliver a long speech about him directly and solely to me. I was so embarrassed that I walked right out and the barker went back to his platform and started shouting furiously that "they didn't want no smart-alecks who think they're too good for the show!"

I can understand your irritation with Audrey. She will sometimes volunteer information but is likely to be evasive when asked a direct question. It is a professional habit, but I don't think anything really insidious is going on behind the Iron Curtain. I know less than you do. The first I heard of the Swiss production was through your letter to Fritz and I never was asked to sign any foreign contracts.[1] I guess Audrey signed them for me as she has my power of attorney. I might as well trust her implicitly and I do, for I think she is thoroughly honest and about as good-hearted as anybody working in the theatre can manage to be. If these foreign productions go on, you should be able to go over there and live on the royalties, as Carson McCullers is now doing on the foreign royalties for her novels. Her books sell over there, just as well or better than here. And she is living in style in Paris in a hotel suite with gilt chairs, rose wall-paper and a big fire-place.[2] And she says that writers are regarded as Princes in Europe. Here they are only sometimes mistaken for Queens!

Ever lovingly,

TENNESSEE

P.S. Please give Jane a message for me. Sometime ago she sent me a bunch of poems by some youth. The message

1. I must have signed a contract and not received money. I find nothing in my contemporary journal, but four years later, December 17, 1951: "Unexpected checks from Audrey for 'Y.T.M.' amounting to $109.73. One check ($20.11) says 'for Switzerland advance, 1947'. No use looking this horse in the mouth, however."

2. I stayed there in 1948, on Carson's recommendation. It was all Tennessee describes; the rent for two people was $1 a day.

is that I still have them in New Orleans but I could not conscientiously submit them to Laughlin as they reminded me unpleasantly of my own long poems. As Isherwood said after reading my verse, "I have an idea you would write good prose."

The mad Miss Hopkins (Miriam) is down here with her new husband and is honoring Grandfather tomorrow afternoon with a cocktail party for 60 people, mostly naval officers. I don't think she is at all satisfied with the husband. She is looking astonishingly well, but seems nervous.

·95·
The Royalton, New York, N. Y.
[*Late February or early March, 1947*]

Dear Donnie –

Don't forget to send me the stories. I am crazy to write something about them – always did want to.

Sorry I hadn't more time here.

If you go South, let me know. Perhaps you could get to N.O.L.A.

Love –

10.

.96.
[632½ St. Peter St., New Orleans, La.]
March 26, 1947

Dear Donnie:

I have just finished reading *The Starless Air* and I don't know when I have ever been so moved by a short story! It is much the best you have written, I think, for it has not only your usual qualities of startlingly fresh and keen perception but also a formal pattern of great strength and clarity and there is a lyric power in some passages that I don't think you have touched before. The dialogue is flawless, and the little scene of Audrey and Cy (over finances) is a perfect bit of theatre as well as commentary on southern family life of a kind that I think is totally original. It is the sort of writing that I thirst and hunger for! I am afraid that I shall not be able to write about it at all adequately, but it will be a joy to attempt it. I think my favorite part of that story is where Lois retires to her bedroom with the bottle just wrested from Bobby and recalls "her melodrama of marriage in the barren landscape of Florida". There were phrases, suggestions, in that little passage that gave me shivers. And they are all so beautifully drawn! At first they all run together in a group that is not very clear – which is good at that point – but as the story advances it is amazing how the individual ones separate themselves and become separately quite vivid and distinct. – You must be very happy over having done such a fine piece of work. I think this story should be published separately – in advance of the others. For one thing, you can get an excellent price for it from some place like *Harper's Bazaar*. I shall write an editor there about it whom I know of through Carson. I think also you should have a good literary agent. Not Audrey necessarily, although I think this work would interest her. But I don't think she is the ideal person to handle it and I don't know just who is. I agree with you about Laughlin. It is better to get a commercial publisher who will really spend money on promoting a volume, for one cannot live on prestige. Laughlin simply does not advertise enough to make much money for his writers. Also this volume is far from being "special". I mean it can have, in my opinion, a fine critical reception and a wide sale. *The Starless Air* will certainly interest publishers in you as a prospective novelist. I would go about the whole thing very carefully and leisurely. First have *Air* typed professionally – and edited for spelling. And see that a few of the right people read it. I am sure it will provoke enough excitement to spearhead the volume. In the meantime I will *try* to write a foreword, but if you find someone who does this sort of thing more professionally and with an influential name – don't hesitate to change.[1]

While in the East I talked to Sandy a little about your economic position which he says is most insecure. I do think you should continue to devote yourself entirely to writing for a while longer and I hope the enclosed check will help you to.[2] Regard it as the sort of loan that can be paid back when and if I should ever need it and you don't. It is a really small return for the satisfaction I had in reading the first story. (I haven't yet gone into the others.)

My plans for the summer are still unsettled. Grandfather is leaving me tomorrow. Santo has threatened to leave several times lately and I have twice bought him railroad tickets which he has subsequently cashed in and remained. I am not sure how I would feel if he left. Probably I would want him back. When we are alone he is usually very sweet and amenable: lately I have been philandering a bit, here and there. I think it is an excellent thing for a relationship to have little side-dishes now and then, but not everybody can see it that way. However I intend to suit myself in the matter.

I will write you again when I have finished the stories and started on the foreword.

With love,

TENN.

How is the novel coming? I would go on with that now.

1. Tennessee did not write an introduction to my stories, but in 1959 E. M. Forster offered to and did.

2. From my journal, May 19, 1947: "Tennessee likes *The Starless Air* very much. After reading it he sent me $300 so I could get along longer."

Piedmont Limited, En Route
April 10, 1947

Dear Donnie –

I have just passed through Atlanta on my way to Charleston, S. C. I am going to meet Mrs. (David) Selznick who wants to produce my New Orleans play. She is supposed to have 16 million dollars *and* good taste. I am dubious. Audrey and Liebling will also be there. The "Princess" was very upset that I left her at home this trip. In fact she left me at the station with the baleful threat that she might not be there when I got back but it was impossible to take her as Audrey repeated twice on the phone that I should come *"alone!"* The Princess was inconsolable. She has been reading movie magazines, every one that comes out, since she was a child and knows the complete history of everyone in Hollywood. I did not know that Mrs. Selznick existed but the Princess even knew that her first name was Irene! (The same as Buffie's cat.)[1]

I have read all the stories now and have been working on a foreword. It is hard to define the best qualities in the stories in the usual language of criticism. Of course I *loved* the one about Gilbert. I don't think it needs much if any improvement and I think you should submit it also to *H. Bazaar*. The editor is named Elizabeth Aswell – I am fairly sure but check on it.[2] I will write her a note mentioning Carson. I showed *Starless Air* to the editor of Appleton-Century who was in New Orleans. He thought it extraordinary and said he would get in touch with you in N. Y. about writing a novel.[3]

1. Buffie Johnson, a friend from Provincetown, whose New York house, remodeled by Tony Smith, Tennessee later rented.

2. Mary Louise Aswell. She wasn't interested in the story, *Single Harvest*, but Cyril Connolly published it that October in the American issue of *Horizon*.

3. Nothing came of this. He wanted to talk about Tennessee's social life.

I think if you work hard this summer you should have one ready. Let me know if you run out of funds. I can give you another "advance" sometime this summer, when you need it.

Am undecided about my summer plans but will leave N. O. this month.

Love –

10.

P.S. I may ask Fritzie to find me a house at P-town for the summer. If so hope you'll visit me, you and Sandy.

.98.

[*Note left at Royalton Hotel, New York, N.Y.*]

[*May 29, 1947*]

Dear Donnie –

Had to go out for a reading and then a screening so will not get back this P. M.

The novel gets more and more exciting as I read along.

I think we ought to wire Laughlin asking if *he* would give advance on it. It is really too good for textbook publishers.[1]

If I leave tomorrow will put script at desk for you, with any suggestions I can think of. Get Isherwood to read it. (And stories.)

Love –

TENN.

Hope to see you in P-town if we don't meet again here.

---

1. I submitted Laughlin only my stories, one of which, *Flesh Farewell*, he accepted for "New Directions 10".

99

Provincetown, Massachusetts
[*June 6, 1947*]

Dear Donnie:

I am enclosing a note of apology from Santo. It is the first time I have ever known him to apologize for any of his frequent and fantastic misdoings. I hardly expect you to forgive him as his behavior was unforgivable being without any reason whatsoever.[1] You should have seen my hotel room! It might have made *your* injury seem less bitter. Real demolition! A portable typewriter borrowed from Audrey had been smashed, a new suit and hat torn to shreds, all my books torn up including one borrowed from Fritzie, vase and glasses smashed. For some reason he neglected to attack my manuscripts. Of course if he had I would have thrown him in jail and perhaps he knew it. Altogether about a hundred and fifty dollars worth of damages! I am taking it out of his allowance, gradually. – Of course this is an impossible situation to which there isn't any happy solution. It is just a matter of deciding which is the least painful and taking it. Perhaps for the time being no action at all is better. My life is already so involved that I want as little melodrama as possible even if it means seeming to be very weak for a while. When you analyze his behavior it becomes so pitiful it makes you more tearful than angry. He has never had any security or comfort or affection and he thinks that the way to hold it is by standing over it with tooth and claw like a wild-cat!

You write very well about violence so I think you understand it better even than I do!

Ever,

TENN.

1. He had denounced me in the lobby of the Algonquin Hotel, where I was having a drink with Tennessee.

[c/o Irene Selznick, 1050 Summit Drive,
Beverly Hills, Calif.]
July 15, 1947

Dear Donnie:

I discovered a letter I wrote you over a month ago, stuck among your short stories. I was wondering why you hadn't answered!

Santo and I are now in California and the house at Province-town lying vacant. Perhaps you and Sandy would like to use it till we start back around the first of August. If so, wire me c/o Irene Selznick, 1050 Summit Drive. I can arrange with the Provincetown realtor to let you in. It is a good house, right on the beach, about a mile out of town.

We have two places here. One is my own little hide-away. Santo does not know where it is located. The other a small beach house in Malibu, next door to Fanny Brice. That one was provided by Mme. Selznick who also gave us a little car, as our own was left somewhere on the Cape. I came out for the casting of "Streetcar". Yesterday met Garbo. She goes under the name of Harriet Brown and sneaks around like the assassin of Bugsy Siegel. The meeting was arranged very carefully and privately like an audience with someone superior to the Pope. She is still very beautiful. She drank straight vodka and said she would like to make another pic-ture if the part was not male or female. Regrets that she was not able to play Dorian Gray. She was very cold to me, I thought I had made a very offensive impression but when I left, she asked if she could visit me at the beach-house. Another meeting is being arranged there for this Saturday. In appearance she is really hermaphroditic, almost as flat as a boy, very thin, the eyes and the voice extraordinarily pure and beautiful, but she has the cold quality of a mermaid or something. I am sure you would like her. She scares me to death.

I saw your story in *Horizon*.[1] How is the novel going? If you need this check or can use it, please do: but make no allusion to it. Would like to hear from you, especially about your work.

Love,

TENN.

.101.

[Santa Monica, Calif.]

[*July 29, 1947*]

Dear Donnie:

I hope you all have found the cottage comfortable and will stay there till we get back. We plan to leave here July 31st in order to be in Dallas August 2nd to see "Summer and Smoke". Chances are we'll remain there a couple of days, also in New York a couple of days. I doubt that we'll get back on the Cape before August 8th or 10th. I will let you know the date by wire when we leave Dallas. There is no reason to rush out of the place because we are returning. Santo is happy that you are there. I am sorry we did not leave the car in P-town so you could have used it. There was a great deal of work to be done on it so we left it in a garage on the way down the Cape and will pick it up on the way back.

It has been a pretty fabulous time here. Have gone to some of the biggest parties and met all the big stars and Santo says, "It is like a dream come true!" It has put him into a wonderful humor and we have both gained about ten pounds so that we look like the big pig and the little pig. Only one misfortune marred the trip. I broke off a front tooth eating corn on the cob. It had to be removed and I am having

1. *The Warm Country*.

another taken out to accommodate a very fancy bridge. Have had to spend many hours in the dental chair and I have become such a bad patient that I actually took a sock at the dentist. He was making a plaster impression of my mouth and I started choking on the plaster. They tell me it costs you one hundred dollars to hit a Hollywood dentist!

We have got Garfield and Tandy and the rest of the casting will be done in New York.[1]

With love,

10.

.102.

[Provincetown, Mass.]
[*September 2, 1947*]

Dear Donnie:

We found the house in perfect order, the letter and the money. I am sorry you didn't stay on a few days though I can't blame you for avoiding the unpredictable.

We now have a house full of guests. Joanna[2] is with us, also two henchmen of Mme. Selznick's and tomorrow a young actor is flying in from the coast for a reading.[3] Margo just got off the phone and said she would arrive here this weekend. She and Joanna have apparently separated, amicably and perhaps only temporarily. When I was in Dallas, Margo had established herself in an air-conditioned suite at the best hotel while Joanna was sweating out the summer in the cottage which they had formerly shared. Joanna says "a mysterious wall" has risen between them. Margo, lucky

1. John Garfield made increasing demands – limited run, the role in the movie, etc. – until Irene Selznick decided against him; Jessica Tandy, of course, played Blanche.

2. Joanna Albus, Margo Jones' assistant in Dallas, who became a stage manager for "Streetcar" and later opened her own theatre in Houston.

3. Marlon Brando – but he only came from New York.

girl, is on the air-conditioned side of it. She says her Daddy recently divided his property among the kids and Margo got the 5 oil-wells. However three went dry right after she got them, the fourth is irregular but the number five well is a gusher that comes in all the time.

Butch sent me a magazine illustration of a lady named Frou-Frou, which was the first indication I had of his return to New York. Is Bill the one that took him from Sally? He deserves credit for that, regardless of how capricious he may be in his choice of careers. Does he have the "Macon ass"? That is a narrow ass that sticks out like a plump Shetland pony's! If he has that he can become a literary figure without Lincoln's influence, valuable as that may be.

Where is Isherwood and what doing?[1] Have to close this as I hear the rumor of returning troops.

Love,

TENNESSEE

.103.

Hotel Taft, New Haven, Conn.
[September ?, 1947] Sunday

Dear Sandy –

I would love to have you in the part[2] if it were at all suited to you but if you remember the scene, the boy's name is *Shapiro*[3] and Blanche says "he looks like a young prince out of the Arabian Nights!" He *has* to be dark.

But thanks –

TENNESSEE

1. He had been in Provincetown while we were there.
2. Of the Young Collector. Sandy, his hair dyed dark, played it, replacing an earlier actor, in the Broadway company from August 1948 to June 1949, and again with Tallulah Bankhead in 1956.
3. The name was deleted during the out-of-town tryout.

Tennessee broke with his Mexican friend during the rehearsals of "Streetcar". !⑥?☆!! But whenever I saw him he was happy and party-giving. Then he was off to Europe. "The Paris of World War II (Post-war)" did not turn out to be Paris any more than it had been Mexico City. But when he reached Rome he found it.

.104.

[Hôtel Lutetia, Paris, France]

[*January 17, 1948*]

Dear Donnie, Sandy, Jane & Tony
(Les deux ménages de mon coeur) –

I am writing this lying up in bed because it is too cold to get up or out except to piss and only when the bladder is about to burst. You may gather from this how comfortable Paris is. I have been moving from hotel to hotel hoping to find one that is heated. The radiators, at best, are about as warm as Mary Hunter's left tit! And the chill, damp air seeps through you. Under the circumstances – cold, bad food, no satisfactory company, no milk for my coffee – it is hard to find any charm in the town. On the credit side, there are about three lovely clubs where the boys dance together. I spend the early evenings there and have brought one home, a couple of times, but he was very unimaginative in bed and also stole from me 10,000 francs. Sounds like an enormous amount but actually only amounts to about $30. But such experiences always make one sad. The poor thing was not getting enough to eat and I tempted him by leaving my roll on the dresser. Ah, well.

I think I will leave this week for Italy, to warm up and

find some softer company. These Parisians are all like fam-
ished wolves or foxes. They *love* Americans – the way a fox
loves a rabbit. And it looks all sort of 1890 and 1920-ish.
The theatre is 20 years behind even *Broadway* – chi-chi
as hell and bad acting. Saw Louis Jouvet last night. He
talked to the audience and the scenery, never once to a
supporting player, and he rolled his eyes and kept his head
back at an almost horizontal angle to keep up his sagging
chin, I suppose. Once he forgot his lines. At least five different prompters started screaming at him from the wings but
he haughtily ignored them, said "Excuse me" and walked
off to study his "sides" for a few minutes; returned much
livelier. I hate to say this, but Dallas, Texas, is better.

A few good things – the bookshops, the night club entertainment, the weird old ladies on the streets all in moth-eaten
black plush coats with black umbrellas and noses that nearly
touch their chins. The Norman type boys with apple cheeks
and silk pin-cushion asses, like the young Rimbaud must have
looked when he was raped in a barracks.

I am getting sleepy at last. Will write you from the next
place.   Love to you all –

TENNESSEE

Audrey will have my next address.

.105.

[Via Aurora, Rome, Italy]
[*February 20, 1948*]

Dear Donnie:

I don't know how many times I have started letters to you,
some of them even finished. Italy and Rome are full of such
infinite and agreeable distractions that practically nothing
is ever finished. I have been traveling around a good deal.

I flew down to Sicily last week and returned through Naples. Since then I have been apartment hunting. I have now found a nice two-room establishment with bath and shower but no kitchen and only one bed. I shall keep on looking till I find another bedroom and cooking facilities as I hope that some of you all will be coming to see me this spring or summer. Honey, you would love Rome! Not Paris, but Rome. The pin-cushions have been justly celebrated by artists for many centuries and there is nothing I can add to the statements of Michelangelo except a corroboration in modern times. I have not been to bed with his David but with any number of his more delicate creations, in fact the abundance and accessibility is downright embarrassing. You can't walk a block without being accosted by someone you would spend a whole evening trying vainly to make in the New York bars. Of course it usually costs you a thousand lire but that is only two bucks (less if you patronize the black market) and there is never any unpleasantness about it even though one does not know a word they are saying! You may wonder how I ever get any work done here. The answer is I don't get much. Perhaps now that I have an apartment I will settle down and be a little more studious. The weather, however, is usually glorious, like the weather in Renaissance paintings, pure and distinct in color and line with great distances and much blue and gold. There is a lovely swimming pool. I have an attractive masseur who comes in three mornings a week to give me massage and exercises. He came yesterday and I am still aching all over! I have lost about 15 pounds due mostly to lack of fat in the diet but my clothes all look as if they had been designed for the fat one in Laurel and Hardy. Clothes are almost impossible to get over here, fabulously dear. That is one problem. Your friends all want to take your clothes not only off you but away from you altogether. Soon as they enter the room they start trying on everything you have and pretend they can't understand English when you say "No!" However Italians are such sweet people that I am afraid I shall become a sentimentalist about the human race if I stay here. They have lost their Empire but they have kept their dispositions and their figures, for which a world is well lost. The *women* are ugly as crows! I just don't understand it. Well, I think I'll stay here till I have to come back to the States. I needn't return till the middle of August when Margo starts rehearsing "Summer". I tried to talk her out of it but it was no use. So I am doing what I can to improve the script. Bowles is in North Africa and if he writes a good score and Mielziner designs a good set the production should help the script a great deal. Honey, my fingers are getting stiff. This is the first cold evening we have had in Rome and my new apt. is not well-heated. I will have to stop now and do something to warm up.

I wish you would see Carson. Her condition is much more serious than anyone of us realized in New York. Her Paris doctor says she may never be able to walk again and that she has a vascular disease of some kind which is dangerous. She liked you and she needs all the attention and sympathetic interest that one can show her now. I try to write her often. Her phone number I believe is Nyack 436 R but you can get it from Audrey more definitely. Call her and say that I sent her my love, will you?[1]

1. From my journal, March 8, 1948: "Saturday I went to see Carson McCullers, with Tenn's blessings and because he insisted she likes me. Of that I am not sure. She was in bed, no better than before, or at least very little. Most of the time – I was there from noon to 8 P. M. – I talked with her sister Rita. Learned innumerable incredible things. They all, like Audrey, think Bigelow 'sweet'. Sweet as arsenic I dare not say. Audrey and Liebling came in the afternoon with Carson's doctor William. Audrey is taking Carson over and helping her out of difficulties with her collaborator and agent. After dinner William had an attack of indigestion (concealed from us all until Mrs Smith asked madly if I could drive) and Liebling drove us home."

My trip to Sicily was very interesting but I have written it up in an article I sent Audrey so you will probably see it somewhere.[1] I miss all of you. Be patient with your book! It is worth it.

Love,

Tenn.

I meant to enclose a cheque with this letter but somewhere on the devious trail I have lost my checkbook. I shall have to ask Audrey to write one and send it to you. Have just heard from Paul Bowles. He is in Fez, Morocco with his wife, Jane, and Edwin Denby, of all people to be with in Fez, Morocco! Doesn't that sound like an extraordinary little entourage? Paul wrote that Jane and Edwin were "not venturesome" and stayed in their rooms! Doing what, I wonder! It all sounds deliciously mysterious, and very Kafka! I wish you could have been here this morning. There are six or a dozen very strange women on these premises which are called a pensione. Their attentions and ministrations are inexhaustible. I go in the bathroom to take a pee and one of them is washing the tub. I go in the bedroom and one of them is changing the bed-linen. I go in the front room and one of them is dusting the carpets. Five or six times before I get up in the morning they call to inquire if I am ready for breakfast! Courtesy is exhausted. I grimace and groan! And their intentions are so wonderful!

.106.

[Via Aurora, Rome, Italy]

[March 9, 1948]

Dear Donnie:

Dear Sandy:

I am surprised and delighted that your plans to come over have matured so quickly. Primavera is here and I am sure it

1. A Movie Called "La Terra Trema" in '48 Magazine, June 1948.

is much better than either Spring or Printemps. I think you are wise in planning to settle down immediately. That is the only way to live economically. It is the moving about that is so expensive in Europe. The items here that are most costly are, first of all, clothes. Be sure to bring with you all the clothes that you will need for your entire stay. Then cigarettes and whiskey. Unfortunately you are only allowed to bring about 4 or 5 cartons through customs. Perhaps you can sneak through with a bit more. Taxis are another costly item. That's why you must get a central location wherever you go. They are about twice as high as N. Y. cabs. I am trying to buy a Jeep and perhaps by the time you get here I shall have one.

There are a great many Americans here and I advise you not to repeat my mistake in getting to know them. None of them has anything in particular to do and they are incessantly calling on you and ringing you up at the least favorable moments. Three different sets of them visited me this morning before I had even gotten out of bed and it is unnecessary to offer them a drink. They walk automatically to the cupboard with a straighter bee-line than Blanche could make for the nearest bottle of liquor and uncork the bottle while they are saying hello and pour down the second shot before you have said, How are you? By the time you have gotten one foot out of bed the bottle is empty and they are looking around for another. If you leave the bedroom to take a pee you return to find them in bed with your boy! Now this applies more to the English than it does to the Americans but as a general rule one does much better knowing mostly Italians and *not* giving parties. I have given several big parties which turned into orgies and have been pestered to death ever since. I remind myself of that lady who Oscar Wilde said had tried to establish a salon but only succeeded in opening a saloon. The main trouble is that it makes it so hard to work. I must have tranquillity over my coffee in the morning or I don't write a line all day! Perhaps if you all like Rome we can find an apartment together with two bedrooms, and a kitchen and do our own cooking. My little Italian friend Raffaello is a good cook and I might take him in. You would love him. I think for about $150 a month we could get a really swell place with perhaps a sun-terrace and a nice location. I could pay a hundred and you all fifty and we could sort of live apart from the rest of the English speaking society which is pretty much as I have described above.

Two notable exceptions are Gore Vidal and Frederic Prokosch whom I see every day. I am crazy about both of them. Gore is a beauty and only 23, the author of three novels. Prokosch is much nicer than I had expected and quite simple and kindly. If one is selective he can have excellent company here. I made my usual error of indiscriminate cordiality à tout le monde!

Double ménages are always a bit of a risk and you may very understandably prefer to stay by yourselves. We can talk that over when you get here and if you will let me know just when you are arriving I will try to locate a good and reasonable hotel for you here.

I suppose the cheapest way to live is in a pensione but I doubt that you would like that as there is not much privacy about it.

I have to return to the States about August 1st for the production of "Summer" but I shall probably come right back to Italy when it has opened and if you all are here I can leave my stuff with you, including the Jeep. I would advise you to stay – to make plans for staying – at least six months or a year for otherwise there is no economy in coming over and no chance to absorb the country.

I am so happy for Jane.[1] I have been wanting to write her

1. Jane Lawrence had just gotten a job in "Inside U.S.A.".

but I have never gotten her address. I can never think where they live in New York! Let me know.

This morning I am cross as two sticks because of all the disturbance before breakfast which prevented me from doing much work. Otherwise I would write you much more about Rome. Suffice it to say, now, that I feel reasonably sure you'd like it better than any place else in Europe. While in Paris – you ought to stay there a night or two – be sure to visit Madame Arthur's where they have a really excellent drag show and the most beautiful male whores and the boys dance together. Also Le Boeuf Sur Le Toit where you may see Jean Marais with his patroness, Jean Cocteau. Marais was the actor in "Carmen" and "Bête". A good hotel there is La France et Choiseul where Carson stayed – she'll tell you about it. Have you seen her?

Hugh Beaumont is interested in getting Monty for "Menagerie" in London. Do you think Monty would be interested? I liked Monty so much better when I saw him this last time in New York. He seemed a lot sweeter than he used to be and more natural somehow.

Thank you both for writing me and I shall be so happy to see both of you again and for the first time *not* in New York!

With much love from

10.

107.
[Via Aurora, Rome, Italy]
3/29/48

Dear Donnie & Sandy:

I guess you will be landing in France today or tomorrow. I don't know what your immediate plans are, of course, but I suggest you stay in Paris until the political situation here in Italy is a little clearer. Practically all my friends here (Americans) are getting out until after the elections which are April 18th. As you know, it looks like the Communists will get in and if they do it will probably be impossible for an American to stay here safely. I haven't made any decision but think I will either fly to Paris or North Africa about the second week in April leaving my things packed here so they can be shipped out easily if the Commies win and I can't return. I don't think there will be any danger at least until after the election but I know you don't want to make unnecessary trips and for that reason you may prefer to wait in Paris (if you like it there) until the 18th. Personally I'd say the chances are about 50/50. Right now there is no apparent antagonism toward Americans. If any develops it will be because of repercussions following the election, such as war-threat, Etc. Those things can blow up with lightning speed, however. Prokosch is driving to France this week and Vidal has booked a flight to Cairo next Monday (week from today). I will stay longer than the others, simply because I am lazy and find it hard to believe that any of these sweet people would really hurt me. Let us hope it all blows over favorably for the warm months here are going to be so delightful, now that the boys are beginning to put on shorts and the days are a succession of gold. Let me know right away what you think, your impressions of Paris. I think you might enjoy meeting a couple of people I know there, Michael James who works for the New York *Times* in Paris and Michelle Lazareff, 37 Rue Lapérouse, whom I visited in the South of France. A precocious girl of 18 who is charming. I have a Jeep. I hope I don't have to leave it here. However I'm not at all sure it is capable of carrying me out of the country. It sounds stronger than it is. I think it is one of the original Jeeps.

I was at St. Peter's Good Friday and saw a very funny

ceremony. A cardinal sat on a throne in a little fenced-off section with a gate on either side and there was a line of people, about half a mile long, moving at a slow trot through one gate and out the other while the old girl hit them over the head with a long stick like a blackboard pointer. She was evidently in a bad humor because she cracked one old lady over the head so hard that she became confused and started to trot back the way she came, against the current. Then the cardinal gave her a second whack to set her straight. A young American priest told me that everybody that got hit by the stick had 300 days knocked off his sentence in purgatory! Italy is a mad country.[1]

Tell me, how is the food in Paris, now? Can you get coffee with cream? How is the France et Choiseul, the hotel Carson recommended? If I return I think I will try it there.

With love,

10.

.108.

[Via Aurora, Rome, Italy]
April [*10*] *1948*

Dear Donnie:

Well, I am glad that you all have made the crossing safely and I hope that the worst of the perils lie behind you, although one cannot be certain that that is the case under the Truman administration of Europe.

Paris does not sound much better than it was during my stay there. The rain I think is a permanent thing. It was raining when I came and when I left and apparently still is and probably still will be. As for the election situation, things

1. Enclosed was a photograph torn from a Roman newspaper of two priests kneeling beside the deathbed of a cardinal with Tennessee's balloon caption: "Sister Belmont is not looking well tonight!"

appear less alarming in Italy than they did when I last wrote you. Now the general opinion (which is totally unreliable, however) is that the Communists will not blow up till a week or so after the election. Frankly one feels more danger any night of the week on Times Square than you do at the most excited moments in the Galleria, which is where the party groups assemble for their discussions. There are about six very fast little Jeeps full of soldiers called the "Nucleo Celere" – I believe that means Rapid Center! – which go dashing about making a display of force and severity but nobody pays any attention to them, just getting out of the way quick enough to avoid getting run over. The biggest and loudest talkers are the "ragazzi", the young male whores and hoodlums, who hang out for sale in the Galleria at night. They are always having hot arguments of some kind but I doubt that they are invariably concerned with politics.

The Americans I knew here – such as Prokosch, Vidal – have disappeared and I don't particularly miss them. Vidal is in Cairo and I got a card today from Prokosch who was in Florence and on his way North to the French border. He says that Florence is full of blue-eyed blonds that are very tender-hearted and "not at all mercenary". We were both getting an appetite for blonds as the Roman gentry are all sort of dusky types. It sounds good to me. I think I will drive up there in the next few days and come back to Rome just a little before the election. If you would like to join me in Florence we could drive back to Rome together in my Jeep, and at the same time it would give you a chance to see the great art of Italy which is mostly in the two big museums of Florence. Michelangelo's David is also there in one of the big squares. I will probably leave Raffaello in Rome. He is the boy that comes in every other night with metronomic regularity which becomes a bit tedious especially as I am becoming fond of him and that is something which

I wished very much to avoid. You can't take them with you, and their future is something you don't dare to think about, although most of them seem just as careless as birds, and as brainless, too. Italy is very tragic now, but at least it is also very beautiful which I don't think France is. The South of France is only good if you like to swim and gamble and consort with chic tourists, which Prokosch does but I don't. I have not yet heard from Vidal about Cairo. He is such a lunatic that anything he says is partly discountable. I liked him but only through the strenuous effort it took to overlook his conceit. He has studied ballet and is constantly doing pirouettes and flexing his legs, and the rest of the time he is comparing himself and Truman Capote (his professional rival and Nemesis) to such figures as Dostoevsky and Balzac. I wonder if the Egyptians will be interested!

God knows what I will do if Americans do have to get out of Italy quick. You should see my place! It will take a couple of Jeep trucks to take care of all the stuff I've accumulated in two months.

Write me c/o American Express in Florence if you want to join me there. I cannot give you any advice because then I would feel responsible if we all get in trouble down here and I had urged you to come.

There is a French circus here. We went last night. A great lot of animals, none of them very bright and performing listlessly as if they had had too much food and not enough sleep. Some chimpanzees came out all dressed up in organdy frocks and corduroy suits, with a lot of equipment such as skates, furniture, baseballs, but they just fingered the stuff in a sort of perplexed and lackadaisical fashion and then dropped it, although the trainer kept grinning and bowing as if they were performing miracles.

Audrey wired me that Helen Hayes is just about set to do "Menagerie" in London opening around July 15th, so I will probably go over there before I return to the States. Well, I am looking forward to seeing you all *somewhere*!

With love,

10.

.109.
[Telegram]
Rome, Italy
April 17, 1948

JEEP BROKE DOWN FORCED RETURN ROME WHAT ARE YOUR PLANS? TENNESSEE

.110.
[Telegram]
Rome, Italy
April 21, 1948

WILL MEET YOU IN FLORENCE – TENNESSEE

Perhaps it was lucky that we arrived in Italy after Tennessee's new friends had fled. We walked into a social vacuum and found happiness. Italy, along with its other blessings, conferred upon us the pleasantest extended time we spent together. For the next six weeks, the three of us and Tennessee's Italian boyfriend passed every afternoon and evening in each other's company.

Early in June, Tennessee drove in the Jeep to Naples to meet Margo Jones, and Sandy and I started by bus toward Venice. Sandy left me there, to return to New York, and I concentrated on finishing my novel, an incomplete carbon of which I had left with Audrey Wood in the spring, hoping she would obtain me an advance on it from a publisher.

.111.

[*Postcard*]
Capri, Naples, Italy
June 3, 1948

On the road to Naples in Jeep.[1] We are now at Capri but leaving tomorrow for Ischia (an island). Beauty of Capri is strictly scenic but the swimming is buonissimo and the atmosphere tranquil. "Ella" seems happy. Margo and I still will leave for London next week. Write you before then.

Love,

TENN.

1. Refers to a photograph of Raffaello and Margo on the reverse, taken on the trip.

[Via Aurora, Rome, Italy]
[*June 7, 1948*]

Dear Donnie:

Margo and I are leaving early tomorrow morning for Paris and London so as to arrive before Miss Hayes who is apparently anticipating some battles with the producer over the question of the 5 Canadians and wants whatever immoral support I can offer. Perhaps I can take care of the 5 Canadians outside the theatre.

Margo's visit has been a strange one. I would not think it possible that anyone could react as little to Italy as she has. If you tell her something is beautiful she agrees with you without even turning her head to look at it. We took a trip in the Jeep to Capri and Sorrento. On the way back we took a wrong turn and got lost in the mountains and a rainstorm. It was quite indescribably beautiful but Margo was still thinking about ANTA and the Project and when we had to stop for the night in a mountain village named Frosinone (which name you should remember) she was afraid to occupy a room by herself because the town had been heavily bombed and she was afraid the vengeful natives might attack her. We all three slept in one room, which bewildered Raffaello no end. He never quite understood the situation and every few minutes he would pop up on his elbows to look across at her and then flop down again with a startled giggle. In the morning he told me, "This donna molto strana. This donna like parlare, like mangiare, like drink, però no like amore, no like poesia!" However this donna is very useful and obliging in such matters as packing for trips and making arrangements. We have our tickets and reservations straight through to London without my lifting a finger.

I certainly hope I can return for a few weeks in July. Write

me care of Hugh Beaumont, H. M. Tennant Ltd., Globe
Theatre, London until I can give you another address, so I
will know where you have settled. I think you should select
some place that will offer a good background for work.
Does Venice? It sounds a bit feverish. Frosinone the mountain village I mentioned might be too lonely socially but not
sexually.

This week I got a wire from Santo saying, "Important call
me immediately Hampshire House New York". Then a letter
from Audrey saying that he and a travelling companion
were in town and planning to sail for England June 11th –
terrifying! If he really shows in London I will join you
sooner than expected if I don't just drop dead at the sight of
him! Audrey's letter also contained word that Buffie has
sailed for Genoa. Does she know where you are? – The Jeep
has arrived for its last work-out. So long.

Love,

TENN.

.113.[1]

Savoy Hotel, London, [England]
[June 22, 1948] Sunday

Dear Donnie –

Are you still in Venice, is Sandy, and are you still happy
there? To really appreciate Italy fully you should come to
London first. Christ, what a dull town and what stuffy
people! I have actually been compelled to start working
again, which is a sign of real ennui. However they have
really been awfully sweet, that is, the theatre and literary folk
I have met and there are several compensations, such as

1. To Venice.

Isherwood, Caskey,[1] and Gore Vidal who are here. I have only had one lay since I got here – in fact since I left Raffaello. There is a good chance I may get away for a week or two, leaving here on Thursday. Will you wire me here if you are still in Venice? Gore and I may fly down to join you there. That is the *present* plan.

Hayes seems okay. Cast 3 Americans 1 Canadian. Opens July 13 at Brighton – will have to return for that. Please send Raffaello a postcard. He is Raffaello [——], Via [——], Roma, Italia. I am worried about him, poor baby.

Isherwood looks fine but is usually drunk. I think Caskey *madly* attractive!

The new Sartre play[2] is divine but there's nothing else worth seeing in London.

Love –
10.

.114.[3]
Savoy Hotel, London, [England]
[*July 9, 1948*]

Dear Donnie:

God knows if I shall actually be able to make the passionately-longed-for trip to Italy. I was not able to get a booking out of Naples early enough to get me back to N. Y. in time for rehearsals of "Summer" so may have to sail from England or France.

Sandy left today for the States. He came to rehearsals a lot and dropped in here now and then to write you a letter on this machine. I got to know him and like him better than ever. There are some very fine qualities in Sandy, and he has developed humor and real independent intelligence which I

1. William Caskey, an American photographer traveling with Isherwood.
2. "Crime Passionnel".
3. To Venice.

think you may have helped him to grow. Gore has also left, returning to Paris, Isherwood and Caskey have departed and my little red-headed boy has shipped back out for Montreal. A month from now he is due in New York. I am quite forlorn here. In spite of almost continual society. It is "Haute Bohème" in which there are only middle-aged fags who still think they are young and pretty. The pretty young ones just don't go out, apparently. I asked them why they don't go out and they replied sadly that they can't afford to. I then asked why the middle-aged fags did not take them out and they said, "Oh, they do, but only very late at night and places where nobody sees us!" I suppose the rest of the time they stay home and bugger each other, and perhaps that is really more sensible. Now I have to go down to BBC and deliver a broadcast talk with Helen Hayes and John Gielgud. The script, supposed to be conversation, was prepared in advance and they have given Gielgud all the bright things to say. Poor Helen and I, being Americans, are given only the most innocuous things to say. I hope I shall think of some funny ad-libs, such as "Oh, John, is it true that you are wanted by the vice-squad in New York?" (As [—] claims.)

You can write me at the Royal Crescent Hotel in Brighton, after tomorrow.

Love,

T.

.115.[1]
[Hôtel de l'Université, Paris, France]
[*July 25, 1948*]

Dear Donnie –

It is after 3 A. M. so I can't type. Have escaped from England for 10 days between the London and Brighton

1. To Venice, forwarded to Sirmione.

openings. I never thought Paris could be so nice. It is really enchanting now. I have found such a nice hotel – the management is ideal. They frankly state that they prefer young bachelors "a little bit pederastical" is how they put it – and that is all they have. I have two huge rooms, windows ceiling to floor and mirrors same size, for only 1000 francs a day. Today gave a cocktail party attended mostly by theatrical folk. Cocteau came by this A. M. to say he could not attend but invited me to his place tomorrow. Sartre did not show up, although reported to be in the neighborhood. The swimming pool *Bains Deligny* contains some rare beauties and one finds at *Boeuf* the handsomest kept boys of Europe like jewels in Tiffany's window to be admired but not touched. I am working hard for the first time since coming to Europe. May return on a small Polish ship the Sobieski, [*Between lines:*] (P. S. Now *booked on Queen Mary.*) sailing out of Genoa on the fourth of August. Takes 12 days on the sea. But surely there must be one nice Polack aboard to divert me. It seems we are fated to occupy Buffie's residences. Margo wires that she can get me Buffie's N. Y. apartment while I am there.[1] It is not exactly my period. I am more of an 18th century girl. But – – – (does Buffie know about this?)

Gore is still here in the same hotel and with the same lover. Truman[2] is reported to be returning – a little too soon, I suspect.

The show seemed headed for a big success when I left. Mother & Dakin are in England. I am told she is "furious". I don't know about what! Have not yet collided with them.

Has the Togliatti business disturbed the serenity of Ven-

1. I had been staying in a room of Buffie Johnson's apartment in Venice.
2. Capote and I had met in Venice and gone to Sirmione, where we stayed two weeks, I working on my novel and he on a story, before we continued separately to Paris and Florence.

ice?[1] How I would love to be going there instead of back to the States. There is much to tell you but I am too sleepy at this moment.

Love –

10.

.116.[2]

[235 East 58th Street, New York, N. Y.]
[*August 19, 1948*]

Dear Donnie –

I cannot remember ever feeling quite so tired so this must be a very brief letter. Here's the important news (relatively, I mean). Audrey says Capote has given Random House an enthusiastic report on your book and today they called her about it, wishing to study it again. Also she showed me a long, pedantic letter from Harcourt Brace, demonstrating great (and genuine) interest but not ready to commit themselves till they see more. Audrey thinks it wiser to hold back script till finished. Don't you agree?

Ordinarily I would doubt wisdom of Audrey handling this book but she is now really excited over you and thinks of you as one of "her boys". Under those circumstances she becomes an excellent and sometimes inspired agent, particularly in handling favorable contracts. That's between you and her, of course. (I mention this because Truman seemed skeptical of her taste.) I do not believe in the taste of *any* agent.

The town is depressing. The beauties have dissolved or gone back to Texas.

1. It had. A general strike closed the town for two days. I wrote an article about it, *Violence In Venice*, in *The Hasty Papers: A One-Shot Review*, 1950, and Truman an unrecognizably romantic one, *To Europe*, in his book "Local Color".
2. To Florence.

Grandfather flies up Thursday. Carson is a continual problem, however lovable. Unfortunately her new stories are not quite stories and she is so hypersensitive that I don't dare talk frankly about this. I believe she really wrote all but one of them at least 10 years ago, the quality is so immature. PLEASE don't speak of this!!! It is terribly upsetting.

Love –

TENN.

.117.[1]

[235 East 58th St., New York, N. Y.]
[*October 19, 1948*]

Dear Donnie:

It is all over now, that is, the play[2] has opened and is a part of history. We got pretty bad notices. Atkinson raved, and so – of all people – did Coleman, but Barnes and Chapman and all of the afternoon papers panned it. Nevertheless we have not had a vacant seat since the opening and one night there were 30 standees. I am afraid Margo did a rather mediocre job. Not inspired, not vital, as Kazan would have been and as the play so dreadfully needed. Nevertheless a certain romantic and pure quality was there and a great many people, I would say about 60% of each audience – practically all women – are more or less – and sometimes to the point of tears – moved by it. All in all I am not depressed or unhappy about it but I regret that it was not converted into the exciting theatre that the best direction could have made it. I always believed it was a play that could live in production (though utterly dead on paper) and what I have seen bears out that conviction. Although what happened did not give it a fair chance.

1. To Rome.
2. "Summer and Smoke".

225

Tonight I gave a "bad notice" party. A caterer came and served hot ham and turkey and champagne and whiskey. And I distributed gifts to all of the cast. I invited the critics who gave us the two worst notices – (Nathan's has not come out yet) – but they had to cover another show – Jane's opening in "Where's Charley?" – a dreadful musical based on "Charley's Aunt" – so they did not come. The party was really swell. Jane came after her opening and sang. So did two other girls in the show. Marlon came on his new motor-cycle and took us all riding in turns. I enjoyed the ride, clamping his buttocks between my knees as we flew across the East River and along the river drive with the cold wind whistling and a moon.

My closest friends remained after the party – Jane, Tony, Sandy, Joanna, and the boy living with me named Frankie Merlo – Merlo means blackbird – and he is a Sicilian from New Jersey. We went to Times Square for Jane's notices which were pretty good. Sandy was very drunk and so cute I had a letch for him. That is I felt like I wanted to kiss him and hold him in my arms but of course I didn't. He is yours. He brought two of your letters, very beautiful ones, and we read them aloud and were all deeply impressed by the description of your night walk through Naples. I am sorry to say that I was not moved by Naples as I was by Rome. Perhaps I didn't give it a fair trial.

I am mystified and amazed by your failure to receive the manuscript.[1] Surely you have got it by now! Audrey told me she sent it air-mail. She told me that quite some time ago – I should think at least two weeks. Don't worry. There are several copies. I have not gotten one yet. You have no idea what the pressure has been! Simply terrific. I even stopped writing Raffaello. I shall get a copy, now, and read it

1. I had mailed the completed manuscript of "The Dog Star" to Audrey Wood to have typed and to mail me a copy to continue work on.

through carefully and write you about it. I told Audrey to continue the monthly checks until the book was disposed of, so don't hesitate to write her for what you need. I don't think you should come home unless you feel like it. Sandy misses you, we all miss you, but it is important that you should stay where you live and work best and Italy seems like that place from your letters. Sandy is in raptures over the completed script and I feel sure I shall be, too. I will read it this week.

Well it is now six o'clock, getting daylight. But it has been so long since I have written you that I would like to go on for several more pages.

I don't think I shall come back to Europe until after Xmas, and then with a car.

Much love,

10.

I returned to New York in mid-November. In early December, Sandy and I saw Tennessee and Frankie off on the Vulcania for Europe. Tennessee suggested in the spring that I return to Italy, but I wanted to stay in New York until I found a publisher for "The Dog Star".

.118.

[Via Aurora, Rome, Italy]
1/26/49

Dear Donnie:

This is actually the first letter I've written besides a few brief necessary advices to Audrey and a postcard to Carson and Grandfather. The report of difficulties in Africa were all too true. We arrived at just the beginning of the rainy season and for reasons of economy (the Bowles') we put up at a perfectly ghastly hotel called The El Far-Har, (rhymes with horror) at the top of a very steep hill over the ocean. Spectacular view: every possible discomfort! The meals were about 25¢ each but were not worth it. I got ill there. A dreadful cold, still coughing from it, and I developed a peculiar affliction – vibrations whenever I lowered my head, running up and down my whole body like an electric vibrator! I really left Africa on that account as the doctors just laughed when I described my sensations, nobody would take it seriously except me, and I thought surely I was about to have a stroke. So after another rainy week in Fez (following two in Tangiers) we drove on down to Casablanca and shipped ourselves (Frank and I) and the Buick to Marseilles: then drove straight on down to Rome. Morocco is wildly beautiful: I want to go back in the Spring when it has stopped raining. One night in the Casbah of Tangiers was really worth all the difficulties, when we were climbing up a steep, narrow street of mysterious white walls and arches and heard someone chanting the Koran. – I believe Paul was quite cross with us for leaving. He has not answered our letters. But can you seriously blame a girl for pulling out, under those circumstances? One can take just so much: then no more! (As Bigelow would phrase it.) You really should have been with us: not bodily but as a disembodied spectator: the night that we first tried to cross the Spanish-Moroccan frontier. Raining skinned cats and alligators and blowing cross-eyed hyenas! We pull up at the frontier. They insist on everything being hauled out of the car, all *fifteen* of *Paul's* suitcases and our four or five pieces. We had to do the hauling as the Arabs had all disappeared for the night. Everything was thoroughly searched, about half the stuff confiscated. Wild arguments, hysteria! In the middle of this, a scream from outside. The Buick had slipped its moorings and had started sliding backwards downhill. Frank rushes out, races it neck and neck down the hill, finally executes a flying leap into it just in time to prevent a serious crash. – We have finally cleared customs and are permitted to go when it is discovered that the car-keys are lost. We're sure the Spaniards have stolen them so we turn around and drive back to Tangiers to complain to our consulate. In the morning we found the keys had fallen into the window socket of the car. Next day we have to go through the whole procedure again. It was that next day that my vibrations started! – We are now back at Via Aurora, the old apartment. Eyre de Lanux, Donald Downes, the preposterous dikes, Sibyl and Esther – all your dear old friends – are still here and "Streetcar" is playing at the Eliseo with Stanley wearing the tightest pair of dungarees I've ever seen on the male ass, including Sandy's,[1] and Blanche making more gestures and grimaces than I thought human hands and face could manage! Successo clamoroso.

There has been nothing but bad news from the States. First, the closing of "Summer and Smoke", which I had half expected, but only half. Then the news that $110,000 had been paid to the government and I was again broke (except for my $65,000 in Gov't. bonds). I had placed all my financial affairs, before I left, in the hands of Dakin, hoping that he would effect some savings for me. The result is that he agreed to pay the lawyer, Colton, exactly double what he had been getting and also put himself on the payroll for a thousand bucks and I certainly paid as much taxes as I could possibly have paid under any circumstances. However I did manage, before I left, to discover that I could make contributions through the Authors' League to other writers: fellowships, which are tax-exempt and therefore cost me nothing. I gave them five thousand for that purpose and it was my understanding that these grants were to be made to a list of people I gave them, Carson, you, Oliver Evans, Paul Bowles. So far neither Oliver nor Paul has received anything and I am wondering if you[2] and Carson have. If not, it is outrageous, for I had a clear understanding with Miss Sillcox on that subject before I left and it is the one thing I accomplished in the States, this time, that seemed to me gratifying in any respect.

Grandfather writes that he is miserable at home, as Mother is continually nagging at him. She claims that he is only pretending to be deaf and will not repeat anything to him so that he lives in a world of mystery and silence which the Audiophone has not penetrated. I sent him today an enormous

1. Another transference: although many people, *including* Tennessee, used to wear tight dungarees, Sandy didn't.
2. I did shortly afterward, a grant of $500.

box of chocolates containing liqueurs as a measure of comfort. Nor have they carried out my instructions (including a trust-fund) to REMOVE my sister from the sanitarium to a private retreat I found for her, but some action on that is in progress.

Love,

10.

You are mistaken about Paul[1] not liking your novel: he was deeply impressed by it and said it was beautifully written. Carson is not well enough (too depressed) to take much interest in someone else's work, I'm afraid. Not many writers do. Especially those who have social roots in New York. Soon as you sell it, will you come back to Europe? I hope you will.

.119.
[Via Aurora, Rome, Italy]
[*February 20, 1949*]

Dearest Donnie:

Frank has been in Sicily for about two weeks and I have come down with either the clap or a non-specific infection as the result of a return engagement with Raffaello. I don't know which it is yet, the discharge not yet being sufficient to provide a smear-test. I go back in the morning. Isn't that sweet and lovely? Raffaello is the only one I've had sex with so it must have been him, poor kid. I can't blame him because I guess he has no alternative in the way of an occupation, and of course he cannot be as monogamous as before. Otherwise I am well. I still have the curious vibrations whenever I lower my head but they don't seem to affect my

---

1. Bigelow, I should think, rather than Bowles, although it could only have distressed me if he saw the manuscript.

general health as I feel pretty good most of the time in Rome. I work more than I did last year in spite of the Buick and have two plays pretty well under way, one being mostly for amusement as it is much too wild, I'm afraid, for presentation. Perhaps both of them are. Poor little Frankie has been sick with the flu ever since he arrived in Sicily and a plaintive postcard says he has only seen it from his Aunt's windows but they are planning a big dance for all his relatives to celebrate his arrival and recovery when he recovers. He has been such a good kid, invariably sweet and patient and although he gets nervous headaches when I am in one of my moods, he stands up remarkably well under the pressure. I wonder if he will come back to Rome? I shall have to leave if he doesn't. I am so happy that you have finished the story about Fidelma on Fire Island.[1] I knew it was going to turn out good for she is such a perfect character for one and I am crazy to see it. I got five sets of notices on the Arthur Miller play.[2] Five different people sent them. It is hard to analyze one's feelings about the triumphs of another artist: even though one may like the artist there is likely to be a touch of the invidious in your feelings which makes you feel cheap and shameful. I liked the play, when I read it, but I must say the great success of it is a surprise as I felt the retrospective scenes were flatly written and that the whole thing lacked the dynamism of his other play. It did, however, have a great genuine warmth of feeling. I think Gadge must deserve more credit than the notices give him. Please see it and let me know. I wish that you were among those coming this spring to Italy. Do you want to? Oliver Evans is coming soon as he finishes his spring term. We could all take a trip in the Buick if it would hold that many. It is still a glamorous article. I've found that you don't have to

1. *An Island of Fire.*
2. "Death of a Salesman".

cruise in it, you just drive slow, like Charles Henri Ford walkin' on Times Square. De Lanux has gone to Paris for a while and promises to buy me the Genet book, "Miracle of the Rose". Peter is here and suffering terribly from his ulcer. Sooner or later I shall have to put him in a hospital I am afraid, though it does not prevent him from descending upon the Galleria like the lion of Judah, as often as night descends on it. There has been nothing but sun, in fact such a water-shortage that the electricity is cut off frequently and I spend many evenings very becomingly by candlelight. Love to both of you,

TENN.

P.S. FALSE ALARM! It was only an irritated urethra due to using too strong a prophylactic. Peter and I celebrated by picking up three golden panthers disguised as Italian sailors. When Peter discovered that I had chosen the nicest he flew into a rage and declared that this sailor had confided to him, privately, that it was really he, Peter, that he had desired. Do you know that wonderful odor your fingers have after you've caressed one? Mine are reeking with it and I hold them to my nose like the rose that Mary Pickford was always sniffing in her "stills", which of course you do not remember. Today a long letter from Frank. He says all his male cousins are beautiful and they danced with him at the party and kissed him – but that was all. The letter indicates that he will be back in a few more days and I am glad for I wouldn't trade him for all the slightly sweaty golden panthers here or in Paradise.

I am glad you got my victrola. Wasn't it impudent of Maria to give it to that maid? Now if you can only extract from her greedy kunt my Hart Crane. He does not want to be there.

Any news or, rather, publicity about Margo and Dallas?

We haven't corresponded since the Happy New Year wire that I got from her which arrived simultaneously with another wire from Audrey saying that "Summer & Smoke" had just closed. Today long letters from Jane and Paul Bowles. Jane is on the Mediterranean, going to Marseilles with a dike named Jody and Paul is still at Fez. They are taking off for the Sahara desert soon, THAT IS, Paul and Janie. But in June Paul is coming to Paris for the presentation of his new concerto and I will probably see him there. Love, love.

[*At top*] A new record has come out called "Addormentarmi così" (Sleep with me like this) – The words are "Mouth to mouth, heart to heart, and to wake never more". Thrilling?! – When you think in terms of Italians.

.120.

Hotel Excelsior, Napoli, [Italy]
3/23/49

Dear Donnie:

I have been in a state of depression lately and have not written for that reason.[1] The life in Rome has gone stale. I tried a few days in Florence. That was worse. Now I am trying the sea-coast. Tomorrow Frank and I are going over to Ischia to try that. Truman and his new lover, whom he imported here from the States, Jack Dunphy, are already there. We drove them to Naples but I fell out with Truman last night in a very silly fashion. I don't know who was to blame, probably mostly myself for taking offense so childishly but he told what I thought was a rather vicious anecdote. Or rather he gave an imitation which I thought was tactless to

1. From my journal, March 29, 1949: "Depressed letter from Tenn in Rome. How unfailing his instinct for the failure which keeps feeling and life going. This time he took with him someone who would be understanding and stick to him, just the thing which would be most suffocating for him in Italy . . ."

234

say the least of it. It was Anne Jackson's imitation of Margo, at least Truman says it was hers, in which she is supposed – Margo – to make a speech to the cast about "Summer & Smoke" – saying that it is "the work of a dying writer". It struck me as an ugly thing to repeat, but I needn't have been so indignant. But I was, and I refused to leave with them this morning on that account.[1] On further consideration – and Frank's importunities – I am reversing that decision and we are going on over tomorrow afternoon. Tell me! What do do you think Truman is, a bitch or not? I can never quite make up my mind about it.

I hope you don't think I am getting morbidly irascible, falling out with everybody, Etc. I'm not really. I've just lost a little patience with the callous sort of bitchery that so many – well, at least a few! – of our acquaintances go in for.

I don't feel called upon to console you about your novel. It is a work that any writer would be more than proud to have produced and you must only keep faith in it and not be discouraged by lack of sensitive response from the first few publishers you show it to. If it is not a hauntingly beautiful book, why, then I am already out of my wits altogether!

My own efforts recently have been middling to poor: I have two plays, perhaps even three, pretty well mapped out and one of them in rough first draft but that sounds considerably better than it actually is, for the writing lacks fire. I have had very few good writing intervals since I came to Italy. Perhaps it is the debilitating climate and perhaps when I go to Paris, soon, I will be stimulated again as I was last year. But I am worried and depressed and I don't feel at all well.

1. From my journal, May 9, 1954: "Last night at Carson's reading at the Y.M.H.A. auditorium, Tenn laughed at the anecdote which once, in Naples, made him turn over the table and stamp out of the restaurant because Truman told it . . ."

I am terribly fond of Frankie but I am afraid "it will end in tears" – to quote Maria.[1] He hates the dependence involved in our relations. I make a sorry companion these days, and when I see him enjoying so much more the company of others, such as Truman, it is naturally a bit hard on me, since I believe that I love him. Forgive me for all this complaining! I feel sure either Guggenheim or the Authors' League will see you get to Europe if the book doesn't.

Love,

10.

.121.

[Via Aurora, Rome, Italy]
4/8/49

Dear Donnie:

I read your letter and story[2] this afternoon in the bar of the Inghilterra which is Frankie's social club and where we leave messages for each other such as "Gone to the movies. Meet you here at seven, Etc." Or "Too beautiful to stay indoors. I took the car." I was literally trembling with excitement over the story and it seemed like the best you had written up till about page 20: in fact till exactly that page, where he cannot get out of bed and starts dying. All the stuff about the drugstore, the motorcycle, the cold wet road and the rides and the girl and the incredibly perfect dialogue between them which is the best negro dialogue I've ever read – all of that is simply breathtaking in its simplicity and its rightness and its enormously real atmosphere. But I feel that somewhere around page twenty (as you probably feel yourself) that a wrong turn was taken, some kind of unnecessary, *evitable* turn, perhaps in an effort to make it more of

---

1. Maria Britneva, young actress and friend of Tennessee's from this time on. "She was an actress until she married the Lord St. Just, then she became the Lady St. Just" (Williams: *Memoirs*, p. 149).
2. *Rosebud*.

what magazine editors think of as a short-story, and quite precipitately *you* went out of the story and it turned to writing instead of being. If you just chopped it off at page 20, you would still have a fine story, but I am sure you will find another way to end it, for it is, up to that point, even better than that other negro study, *The Warm Country*, in my opinion.

I don't remember what all I put in the letter from Naples. I was almost hysterical with hurt feelings and rage at Truman and perhaps also exhaustion from the much travelling we had been doing. The next day I got over it, the rage, and we proceeded as planned to Ischia and Truman was all sweetness and light, we embraced, and there was at least an apparent reconciliation but that mischievous tongue of hers remained fairly active the whole time we were there. I think you judge Truman a bit too charitably when you call him a child: he is more like a sweetly vicious old lady. But Ischia itself is a dream. I'm sure you'll like it best of anything in Italy. The place to go is Forio where they have a lovely pensione with a roof on which you can sun-bathe. The water is still too cold for swimming but there is a long walk you can take among the hills to some radioactive hot springs. They are supposed to give you marvelous and quite indiscriminate sexual energy. I expect Truman's lover will be making frequent excursions if the affair is to be one of extended duration. Truman was wrapped around him like a boa practically every minute except when he was making invisible little pencil scratches in a notebook that was supposed to be his next novel. We left them there, when we left, and we are taking bets on how long both or either will stay on the same island. The English-speaking colony consisted, aside from our party, of Chester Kallman (the perennial Auden lover), and a wee wisp of an American belle whose lover had practically beaten her to death with a bottle of Grappa the week before we arrived and she was still looking happily dazed. The lover had left the island and had written to ask if it was really true that they were through? The lover, incidentally, had only one arm. There was so little to gossip about that we discussed the Grappa-beating almost the entire two weeks. I had a feeling, from the look on Chester's face, that he had somehow managed the whole thing and that it was only the beginning of far more intricate and violent and far-reaching events to come. The island is an extinct volcano, but plenty seems to be popping or going to pop.

Frankie's passion is clothes, and this week we have been on a haberdashery kick.[1] Two suits being made by Carson's tailor, the one that turned her out of his office when she first appeared there, thinking that she was a street-beggar. Also a suit for Peter [—] who is still wearing the same old rags he slept in that night in the bull-pen. And today we bought yards of blue and beige shantung silk to have suits made of that, so we will be known as the Shantung sisters in Paris, when summer comes. This evening Frank said he needed a dozen suits of underwear. Then I blew up and I said, Honey, you should have married Harry Truman before he went into politics. And he is now looking quite sheepish and has washed his old jockey shorts and hung them all over the bathroom to dry.

Cheryl Crawford was in town this week, looking very feminine and bursting into tears over Keats' grave. I got to know and like her tremendously. There is a rumor that Eyre de Lanux had her face lifted while she was in Paris for a long stay. Certainly she looks far more youthful, but that might come from nothing more drastic than her beautiful young Italian lover. She was looking at some of Gabe Kohn's sculptures and she said to him, Gabe, this is a very unartistic

1. The three years referred to on page 190 is up.

comment, but the sexual parts on your (statue of) St. Sebastian have such a weak look about them!

If you are coming abroad this spring or summer you had better see about boat reservations immediately. I shall write Audrey this week to intercede with the Authors' League in getting an extension of your grant if you let her know that you want it. We are planning to leave for Paris late this month, for I have to be in London on the 25th for a conference with the Oliviers, Beaumont and Irene: God knows why! But I am hoping the northern climate will stir me up. I have been working so sluggishly. I have completed an introduction to the reprint of Carson's "Reflections in a Golden Eye" and the first draft of a short story about [—] which won't be good for a long while yet. But the play just creeps along, still. – I must get to bed.

Love and goodnight!

TENN.

.122.

[London, England]¹

5/8/49

Dear Donnie & Sandy:

I have just taken a sleeping pill and am beginning to feel like a water-lily on a Chinese lagoon, so you mustn't expect too much from this letter. I left Frankie and Maria at Piccadilly Circus. I suddenly began to feel very nervous and said, Leave me alone, good night! We had just tried to get in three restaurants that were closed. We finally found one that was open. Then we got into a fight with the waiter, just as the food was being served, and were thrown out after I had taken

---

1. On envelope: "Return add. Am. Ex. Paris for 10 days".

exactly one bite of some fried onions. Consequently I had a crise de nerfs and fled back alone to the apartment.

We spent the entire day, Frankie and I, at the Oliviers' place in the country. They were very charming to us, but nevertheless it was an ordeal; ordeals always make me terribly hungry and terribly nervous. I do hope they bring me home a dry piece of bread. They gave me a very strange look as I galloped off in the opposite direction!

Sandy, I have discussed your case with Irene. Her argument is that this will be a very critical summer for "Streetcar" and that Uta[1] will feel more comfortable with the boy she is used to and that they wanted to send you on the road but you refused it. I take it the road job is still open, but it sounds dreary, doesn't it? Professionally I suspect you'd do better to try something else, as you are young and should keep doing new things and Marlon is leaving the cast and I shouldn't imagine it would be very interesting anymore. Of course there is the salary. What shall I do, shall I urge Irene to offer the road job to you again? I guess it is too late, now, to do anything about the other.

You may be interested to know that Madame got food poisoning here. She blames it on some pâté that she ate at the Oliviers a few nights ago but I think it was mostly annoyance because when we arrived they had already eaten and Sir Laurence had gone to bed. Quelle insulte! The Madame's diamonds were flashing with rage! But she had kept us talking for an hour and a half in her hotel room before we went, so we were quite late. Today she had the doctor three times and is eating charcoal biscuits. I think it is nothing but the annoyance. She seems to like you, Sandy, a great deal and has great admiration for your work. I think if you don't get cross with her something can be worked out some way. I

1. Uta Hagen, who had been playing Blanche in Chicago, was replacing Jessica Tandy in New York.

guess it never does any good to get cross with managers even when they are shits which most of them usually are. But Irene tries to be fair and is usually quite nice.

I feel sorry for Maria. She detests London and has fallen out completely with the Beaumont office so she has no prospect of work here. Only a television job, three weeks rehearsal and entire salary amounts to one hundred dollars. (One performance.) Seems to have no interesting friends here, nobody she likes much and her family is quite poor, except for an aunt who treats her rather coolly. Poor child. I think she may go over to Paris with us for a couple of weeks, but when we return to Rome I don't know what her plans will be. London is just as amazingly dull as ever! And to live here, Oh Jesus!

I have been to the theatre every night and matinee. Nothing new is good but the Old Vic is doing a magnificent "Richard III" in repertory. Vivien Leigh is not really good in "Antigone" but I have a feeling, now, that she might make a good Blanche, more from her off-stage personality than what she does in the repertory, though she is quite good in "School for Scandal". She has great charm. Sir Larry is a bit on the grand side, but today he let his hair down and we became quite chummy. They live in an old abbey that dates from the thirteenth century. Danny Kaye, who is the rage of London, was present but was extremely quiet. Larry acted continually, even imitating the horses in "Henry V" which he did very amusingly and Vivien was extra sweet to Frankie, which pleased me even more than it did him.

I am so glad, Donnie, that my suggestions for *Rosebud* seemed helpful. I felt very foolish making any at all, for it is such a beautiful, beautiful story. I am sure that when you eliminate the unnecessary literary passages after page 20 it will be one of your two or three best.

As far as we know Truman is still on Ischia, and Auden

241

has now joined them and it is reported that Truman is working hard on a new novel. For several months I have not heard a word from or about Carson. Have you? Long letter from Margo. Her season was positively brilliant, everything was a huge success and she is spending the summer in New York. Could I possible close this letter on a brighter note?

Much love from

TENN.

.123.

Rome, Italy
June 10, 1949

Dear Kids:

After my trip to London and Paris and the long session with Irving Rapper, emissary extraordinary from Warners who came here to consult about filming of "Menagerie", I feel quite drained of vitality, and just yesterday morning came a cheery wire announcing the imminent appearance of guess who! Tone was, Oh, so right. She is on the Orient Express right this moment, and Frank is out trying to book her a room in a town already seething and boiling with "stranieri". It is quite hot. The town does a slow burn every day. The out-door pools are open and so is the big closed one at the Foro Italico, and a great crowd of American sailors [are] in the tightest and most transparent whites that I have yet seen except in the very hot weather in the bars on Sixth Avenue when they seem to be wearing wet fish-skins. The Roman whores, my dears, have gone mad! Their price has jumped up to 10,000 lire, but the sailors are not having any. They are mostly just out of boot-camp and are scared to fuck although they get big erections and tell the girls to feel them. The girls call them "bambini". Even the one-legged whore has left her usual stand at the Caffè Notturno and hobbles up the hill to "Il Rifugio" which is the sailors' hang-out. Frank says last night she lost her balance and fell on her ass after groping one of the boys. Personally I see no superiority or even equality with most Roman trade, but it is a change. Peter [—] has really gone out of his mind. He claims that Irving Rapper has offered him a job as dialogue director for the "Menagerie", that Irving was madly infatuated with him, continually squeezing his arm or pressing his knee. I think we shall soon have to send him to Ischia with Auden and Chester and Truman. It is reported that Truman is being released and is going to Paris in a few days, still with his friend, Jack Dunphy. Gore is there now and no doubt there will be a joyful reunion. Though Gore says he is coming South. Oliver Evans is landing in Naples later this month, so I can promise you plenty of American company when you come over, unless you go straight to Sicily. I have not yet heard any news of the boys going there. They all go to Ischia now, but they don't seem to stay very long, and they come back with a dazed look as if they didn't know what hit them, Capote or Auden or one of the natives. And usually afterwards they retire to some unheard-of little village in the hills or a farm in Brittany. Raffaello went straight from Ischia into the army after spending two months on Ischia with Booboo Faulkner. Do you know that one? I think I shall go to Vienna, quite alone, even sans Frankie, as soon as I can politely slip away. I wonder how Maria will like Vienna?

Love,

TENN.

LETTER 124

A subplot surfaces here. Early in the summer, Montgomery Clift had told me he was trying to option the film rights to "You Touched Me", in order to offer producers a package deal of himself and the script. Audrey Wood was putting him off, he said, using as one excuse that Tennessee was already in too high a tax bracket that year. Audrey had not mentioned a film offer to me, and when I mentioned it to her in August she replied that she had been trying to sell me to Warners to write the screenplay of "Menagerie"! Soon after, Clift wrote me from Berlin that his lawyer had finally managed to make an appointment to discuss his offer with Tennessee and Audrey. But I felt insecure. The first of September, I withdrew my novel from Audrey to handle it on my own.

.124.

Hotel Bel-Air
[Los Angeles, Calif.]
[*September 25, 1949*]

Dear Donnie –

Audrey says "Y.T.M." deal seems hot, involves possible 50 G's. We leave here Mon. I go first to Chicago. Then I go St. Louis for location shots. Frank on to N. Y. to scout for apt. Tell Jane have bought her some Chinese things.

Love –

10.

*I sold "The Dog Star" to the first publisher I submitted it to,
Doubleday. In October, Tennessee was back in New York. It was
the season of Alice Astor and Gloria Vanderbilt. When I tried to
see him he was usually busy, and when I did see him my feelings were
hurt.[1] Then he was off to Key West.*

.125.

[1431 Duncan St., Key West, Fla.]
[*November 25, 1949*]

Dear Donnie –

Whenever I find time for a letter I am too tired to write it.
We are living a rich, full life! Asleep by midnight, up about 8,
work mornings, afternoons at the beach. I have taken off 10
pounds and feel very rested. Grandfather is with us and
usually goes along to the beach. This morning was cruising
the park. S[—][2] is here. He is on the shit-list of the local
queens, who do not like to hear so much about "Alice"
(Astor) and "Gloria" (Vanderbilt) and he further endeared
himself to them by going to a party and walking off with the
most attractive (butch) sailor about fifteen minutes after he
got there. The older girls did not like it. Society here is
avoidable. Sailors seem more approachable than I remembered. But we are still on our honeymoon and do not take

1. From my journal, November 4, 1949: "The other night when I joined Tenn
at a Times Square movie, he decided to leave and go to a nightclub where he
thought Gore would be. I said I had no tie on so I could not get in but I'd
ride uptown with him. When the taxi stopped in front of the Blue Angel he
said why didn't I walk home and get a tie and come back and join them."
2. A young writer whom the fashion magazines were grooming to be the new
Truman Capote.

full advantage. I am taking down addresses for reference when Frank goes home for Xmas. I am not sure what my Xmas plans are. In any case, even if I go to St. Louis for Xmas, (which may be necessary) you and Jane and Tony could occupy the house while we're home. If I don't go, there would be room anyway. It is a tiny house but very charming. We have a colored maid-cook, Charlene Marie. She cooks *too* well. My reducing diet is agony.

I'm afraid my accusation of Gore was unjust, for I got proofs of the Bowles review, coming out Dec. 4th, just about as I wrote it.[1] Feel very badly that I attacked him. Laughlin rejected his novel, the one I liked whose classic image was perhaps not conceived altogether independently. You must be careful of your work, before publication, although I don't really think Gore did any culpable (conscious) borrowing from it.[2] Off to beach!

Love –

10.

1. Tennessee had accused Vidal of sabotaging his *New York Times Book Review* article on Paul Bowles' "The Sheltering Sky" and having the editors delete the allusion to "several literary seasons given over, mostly, to the frisky antics of kids, precociously knowing and singularly charming, but not to be counted on for those gifts that arrive by no other way than the experience and contemplation of a truly adult mind."

In 1960, when the write-up in the *Times* of "The Hero Continues", which Howard Thompson wrote me was in galleys, slated to appear soon, and "very good. Repeat VERY GOOD," never appeared, I remembered Tennessee's belief that reviews could be sabotaged there.

2. Earlier in the year, Tennessee told me Vidal had read "The Dog Star" in the office of an English publisher, to whom Cyril Connolly had submitted it, and had written a novel "borrowing from it". This upset me; but when my novel was to appear before this supposed one by Gore, I forgot about it. To edit this volume of Tennessee's letters, I looked through Vidal's novels published shortly after 1949. I found no trace of any borrowings from "The Dog Star". Either Tennessee read an unpublished one, or, more likely, this is another example of his transference. Anyway, if Tennessee ever complains of my editing of this book, I shall say to him: Greater love hath no man than this, that he try to read the novels of Gore Vidal in order to edit his friend's letters.

(over)

Lemme know how you all feel about coming down. The maid would stay on. We would leave here about Dec. 20. Does that coincide with Jane's vacation?

.126.
[1431 Duncan St., Key West, Fla.]
Dec. 8, 1949

Dear Donnie –

Have only time for a note. I am, at long last, winding up a first complete draft of a long play,[1] and I am elated and desperate, by turns. Do you know what I mean? Ha ha! ⑥?☆!!

I *may* come to New York some time between the 20th and Jan. 1st. I want to see Carson's opening in Philly and a rehearsal of Inge's play.[2] The Carson opening should be, in *more* ways than *one*, one of the great dramatic spectacles of our time! Can one afford *not* to be there?! Question, what to do with "Grampa"! Throw him off the 7-mile bridge?

I hope you will come down. I have deposited money in the Authors' League fund. We can arrange transportation through them, if that is a detriment [*sic*]. But I will write you as soon as my own plans are clear as that proverbial crystal.

Love –

10.

1. "The Rose Tattoo".
2. "The Member of the Wedding" and "Come Back, Little Sheba".

247

At Doubleday's request, I had written and asked Tennessee for a quote to put on the jacket of my novel. When the deadline for copy arrived the middle of December, he had not replied. Sandy, knowing how distressed I was, wired Tennessee, urging him to respond. The following telegram revealed what Sandy had done and I wrote to Tennessee, apologizing and assuring him that I would not use it.

.127.

[*Telegram*]
Key West, Fla.
December 16, 1949

QUOTE WINDHAMS FIRST NOVEL INTRODUCES FINEST YOUNG TALENT SINCE CARSON MC CULLERS UNQUOTE

TENNESSEE WILLIAMS

.128.

[1431 Duncan St., Key West, Fla.]
12/20/49

Dear Don:

Since we are old and close friends and both writers with an unusually sympathetic appreciation of each other's work, what could have been more natural than Sandy's wire to me or the similar suggestion that you made in a letter earlier? I don't see how it could possibly be interpreted as what you call "pressure". It was just a friendly gesture, nothing more nor less than that, and the fault is entirely mine for not responding immediately, for not sensing that a delay in responding might be interpreted falsely. The reason is very simple and terribly characteristic. Both letter and wire reached me during a time when I was even more than usually preoccupied with my own affairs. I wrote you recently that I have been finishing up the first complete draft of a play since "Streetcar" and "Summer", but I didn't give you the full background except by implication. For two or three years I have almost despaired of finishing a new play and due to a resurgence of energies here I have managed to push this one through. It is not yet ready to show but at least I have it all there, and the emotional repercussions, or psychic disturbances, blinded me to a great deal else that was going on. Frankie "could a tale unfold"! Ordinarily my ratio of concerns is something like this: 50% work and worry over work, 35% the perpetual struggle against lunacy (neurasthenia, hypochondria, anxiety feelings, Etc.) 15% a very true and very tender love for those who have been and are close to me as friends and as lover. But at a time like the recent time there is a great dislocation and the ratio changes to something like this: Work and worry over work, 89%: struggle against lunacy (partly absorbed in the first category) ten percent, very true and tender love for lover and friends, 1%. A stranger would doubt this but you have known me and observed me for a long time. Surely you see how it is! You must not think that I am trying to butter you or soften you up when I say that nobody, as artist or friend, and as both, has meant as much to me as you have. Neither of us can help it that the same kind of intimacy doesn't exist, now, that existed in the time when neither of us was "married" and when the world demanded less and the heart gave more, and neither of us can help the way things are in New York, which is the only place we meet, and I, always, with my trunks packed for imminent departure, and neither of us can help it that I am a fantastically self-centered but not and never disloyal friend.[1]

With love,

10.

.129.

[1431 Duncan St., Key West, Fla.]

[*January 1950*]

Dear Donnie:

I just wrote Jane and Tony saying I would send them this in their care, as I did not know whether your mood was at all accessible now in this matter. But on second thought it seems like a false delicacy of a sort which neither of us cares for. I like what this says about this book, and I think, unconsciously, it was my desire to say something better than what came immediately to mind that caused the delay and the very inadequate first effort in a wire.

Frankie is back and life is resuming its old pattern which was a good one, although the wild roving of streets was also a good interruption of pattern.

I got a wire from Margo this morning that might amuse you. I had finally written her, saying that I imagined from accounts of her recent activities that she must be beginning to feel like the title of her next Broadway production.[2] She

1. Among some papers that Andreas Brown, who was sorting Tennessee's manuscripts to be deposited at the University of Texas, gave me a few years ago there is a draft of this letter from which one variation seems worth quoting: "You are by nature far more detached, and far more self-sufficient than I. You grow more integrated, I think that I grow less. I haven't made a single new friend except Frank. I am more alone and more lost than I ever was, and know hundreds more people! This letter sounds like an entreaty for understanding or pity. The first is sometimes impossible and the second never desirable, and both are quite necessary."

2. "Southern Exposure"?

wired back: "Yes, honey, I sure do feel beat up and I love
it!"

Love,

10.

.130.

[1431 Duncan St., Key West, Fla.]
1/18/50

My dear, dear Donnie:

    I felt quite emotional when I saw your letter with the
familiar handwriting on my threshold when I opened the door
this afternoon to take a look at the weather, for I had almost
despaired of hearing from you again. I don't think you could
easily imagine how much your friendly feeling means to me
now and always. If I try to tell you I will probably sound
like Margo, but you represent a kind of absolute value, an
integrity, which I feel lacking. This is aside from you and
me: an almost abstract thing which you and your work mean
to me.[1] I hated to think that out of sheer, unmitigated failure
to *think*, on my part, I should have placed myself in such a
detestable and wrong position, for if I have ever been moved
by the work of another artist, ever been thrilled by truth in
it, it is your work and Carson's alone among living writers.
Tony explained to me why the wire was not right, but in my
mind the link was inevitable because it has really been only
you two and I did not stop to think that for a publisher this
was not the right thing. I do hope the later one is better.
I am almost sure that it is. At least because I have made a
better attempt to say (however briefly and inadequately)
something about the quality of the work itself.

    You speak as though you were ashamed of caring about
your work! How silly of you to feel that anybody could

---

1. A clear statement of the degree to which he thought of me as his conscience.

251

successfully pretend to feel as much enthusiasm for it as I have always felt, or, that feeling it, I would in any way hesitate to declare it. But your silliness (which is the expression of a morbid humility) is outweighed by my own (revoltingly self-absorbed) negligence which made me seem to hesitate when I was actually just sitting in a sort of timeless stupor and stew, eyes glassy and saliva dribbling from my chops as I continued my own prolonged masturbation at the Remington portable.

After writing me only three days previously that he was catching a boat for Ceylon, close on the fugitive heels of Paul Bowles, Gore Vidal suddenly startled me out of my wits and my power of speech when he stalked into the living room a few days ago without ringing or knocking and immediately began to browse through my manuscript which I was checking over. He said he had missed the boat. Since then he has divided his time between the sailors and the notices of his latest book:[1] I don't know which excites him the more but I suspect that the sailors taste better! There is a widow of sixty named Erna Shtole or Shmole or something like that who arrived in a great burst of hysteria with an entourage of young queens recruited from the summer colony at Cherry Grove. Frank and I have sunk into utter social eclipse. The Shmole took a dim view of us, particularly of me. She said she had met me twice in "Tony's". I chose to forget her, and she would be God damned if she would remember *me* in *Key West*! She gives great parties almost continually to which we are rigidly not admitted so we sit alone on the beach, or, at best, with Grandfather and a former wife of Newton Arvin's named Mary Grant,[2] the one from Provincetown who asked Santo what reservation he came from and to whom he said, Did you come out of Grant's

1. "A Search for the King".
2. Mary Grand.

252

tomb?! Under the circumstances I find her more agreeable than I used to. She amused me yesterday when she complained that eight women at a party had told her, at various points during the affair, that she was a bitch. I asked her, Was that a quorum? She is the one in the picture I sent you which included also (besides us two) Bill Caskey who was here until his father died [. . .]. I believe that he has inherited some land and horses, which ought to be nice for Christopher if they can get a fox and a couple of red jackets.

I started for New York last week. We drove as far as Miami and I decided that was far enough and we came back the next day, but I believe we are going to hop over to Havana in the next week or so. I must see that exhibition Tony described in which they crawl around sniffing and barking and the whore says, "Dogs!" Tell Tony that I got a letter from Jessica Tandy, thanking me very warmly for the Havana post-card and sending him her greetings. Said the studio had dropped her contract, but she was glad.

Audrey has said nothing to me about the "YTM" deal but I am so happy to hear that it has gone through. Have you received any payment? Surely there must be some coming and I should think it would be a pretty good amount. I shall ask her immediately for some report on it.

With love and many thanks for your letter,

TENN.

Hello to Sandy! I have some good pictures for Jane, taken of her on the beach & will send them.

[1431 Duncan St., Key West, Fla.]
2/2/50
(or fight!)

Dear Donnie:

I am glad to hear that you have made definite plans for returning to Italy for I feel you have found Manhattan and the queen world to be a toxic condition of the soul the same as I have[1] and you will be vastly relieved when you have struck roots elsewhere, particularly in a place like Rome or Sicily. We are leaving in May and have our reservations on the Ile de France which sails about the 20th. If I am not too exhausted by that time, I may take a little excursion into Scandinavia – Copenhagen and Stockholm to explore the glacial beauties and the blue Fjords . . . and to take the steambaths and the punishment of switches for my misdoings!

Although the first draft of my play (which is really the second or third) is rather a mess, I am pleased with the way I think it is going to be and I am hoping that it will be possible to procure Magnani for the lead. I cannot think of anyone else. The lead is a Sicilian-American widow with terrific emotions! Decidedly not neurotic unless being passionate is. The cast also includes a black goat and I am sure that I shall have to fight for it. Title: "The Rose Tattoo" – or "Right or Wrong, It is Done!" Which do you prefer?

I would advise you not to bother about a magazine at this point, particularly an English magazine published in Italy, by someone as mysterious-sounding as Bunny Adler. Is it the elevated shoes family or the theatrical one? I feel that your book, properly handled, will surely make a bigger

1. Another transference. He had become a habitué of the Blue Parrot, and the other East Side gay bars known as the bird circuit, whenever he was in Manhattan. I hadn't graduated from the service-men bars around Times Square.

splash than Buechner's[1] and that you will not want to be troubled with a resumption of editorial duties. Your book is the best of the season. Put that in your pipe and smoke it! And it has been a very brilliant season, but I feel that your and Paul's[2] books are the only ones so far that belong to "permanent literature" and Elder and Doubleday must have sense enough to give it the works.

Vidal has departed. The queens took a dim view of him, which doesn't matter, but so did the trade, which does. Vidal will have trouble until he learns that boys he goes to bed with are not "pussy cats". He is now in New Orleans. I miss him, for it is comforting to know somebody who gets along worse with people than I do, and I still believe that he has a heart of gold.

You must come here either before or after the visit to your Mother, for it has been so long since we have really spent any time together that we are almost like strangers, and I feel absolutely no doubt that you would adore Key West. I may be in New York next week and we can plan for it then.

Bigelow wrote a card saying he was "full of scurrilous gossip to give me" but apparently the amount was so great that it choked him. I have not heard a word since! He shepherded Bill Inge from the sanitarium to Wilmington, Delaware, where his play opened and all I heard about that was a wire from Audrey saying "Inge incapacitated", which I think is the most economical comment the lady has yet delivered on any known situation! What about "You Touched Me"? I have requested information from her. Has she flown into Cloud Cuckoo Land?[3] With Inge and Bigelow

1. "A Long Day's Dying" by Frederick Buechner.
2. "The Sheltering Sky" by Paul Bowles.
3. This request, repeated from the last letter, for information from me about the sale of the film rights to "You Touched Me" – which were entirely in Audrey Wood's and Tennessee's control, and which I could learn about only from Clift – lay the groundwork for the uneasiness I felt throughout the next year.

as attendant squires? Liebling went to Australia. You will not believe this! He is advising them how to produce "Streetcar". Grandfather says he will probably come back with a pair of boxing kangaroos, suitable for receptionists or road-companies as the Loman boys.

Love,

10.

P.S. Donald Van Wart who played the piano every summer at the Flagship in Provincetown is now here. Today came out on the beach in a bikini and a very bad humor as he had been hit over the head with a bottle last night and could not remember by whom or why, and his friend, who looks like a vamp of the silent movies, was equally mystified by the whole thing!

Ted Shawn is doing a solo recital tonight at local high school!

LETTER 132

Strange as it may seem, this letter upset and depressed me. Its perfection contrasted too greatly with the events going on. It was even physically too smooth. Rare among Tennessee's letters to me, it doesn't resemble one of his battered, self-typed manuscripts but the good copy of a script prepared by a professional typist – without a mistake or correction. He seemed to me to have joined Audrey in Cloud Cuckoo Land. In the state I was in,[1] I was ready to receive any public recognition, but a little surfeited with private assurances of my too-good-for-the-world-of-commerce purity. I hadn't solved the "dull problem". One straightforward word about the "You Touched Me" film option would have been easier to answer than a whole page of letter-perfect quotations from T. S. Eliot. Tennessee doesn't mention it, and almost simultaneously the contract arrives, "insanely mysterious",[2] followed by a letter from Jane Lawrence congratulating me on having the "You Touched Me" film riches: "We are all thrilled! Money for our sweetheart! Glory road!" Then I received my share of the advance on the option – all I would ever get – $387.60, followed by word from Clift that with the restrictions and complications he feared that the package deal would be too expensive and would almost certainly peter out – as it did.

1. From my journal, May 3, 1950: "Letter from Sandy yesterday telling of Bigelow's reading aloud the close of 'T.D.S.' for Tenn, and containing no other news of the book, unreasonably depressed me, or brought to a climax my unreasonable depression. Yet I cannot help fearing that slowly, quietly, all is going wrong with the reception of the book and soon I shall realize that nothing has happened and that it is all over."

2. See page 267, footnote 1.

Sherry-Netherland Hotel, [New York, N. Y.]
May 7, 1950

Dear Donnie:

I am happy to see that this really good notice of your book has come out in the Sunday *Times*.[2] I am sure Sandy has sent or will send you a copy of it, but I will enclose one, too. One cannot have too many copies of any good notice except a rave for Arthur Miller.

Late last night I finished reading the book again and it left me with a feeling of pure exhilaration. I doubt that there has been any book in our time put together with such subtle congruity of all its parts, and I think the exhilaration comes from the sheer perfection of it as a completely and perfectly realized work of art. A kind of catharsis, not the usual kind that comes from being deeply moved by the tragedy of a character. I did not feel very sorry for Blackie. He was not made pitiable. He was too austere for that and the writing was too pure, but the very quality of sorrow, of desolation, becomes a palpable, almost solid, four-dimensional thing in the book, not for the character but through him as though the quality and not the character was what existed. For the first time in a work of fiction I was unable to pity the character in the way that I am unable to pity myself, because of not seeing from the outside. His world and the desolation of it becomes an absolute reality, penetrated to almost abstract terms. It is closer to plastic art than any writing of prose that I have read. Everything that is seen or touched becomes vivid and true, the only [things] that remain dim and mysterious are the hearts and impulses of the people which is exactly

1. To Taormina.

2. *Adolescent, Doomed,* by Hubert Creekmore, *New York Times Book Review,* May 7, 1950.

right for Blackie who could only come close to one person whom he could worship and whom he had lost. I think Creekmore has shown a remarkable perception of the theme of the book, which is woven in and out so delicately that many reviewers might miss it. I like all of the book but perhaps the part that thrilled me most was the description of the sky and city just before the death of Blackie and the rain. It is the final coming out of a thing held in wonderful suspension throughout the story, like a chord which a whole composition has led up to. It was at this point that my absorption suddenly turned into a sense of exhilaration. If it had been less pure, less distilled by its very rightness and beauty, I would have cried, but I am not sure that a pure work of art brings tears unless you cry for perfection or unless you are sitting among a crowd of emotional people as in a theatre, but in a theatre I don't think art can ever be pure; that makes it easier to cry but much harder to feel washed clean and exhilarated.

I am very anxious to hear what you feel about Sicily and Taormina. I shall have to go there this summer as my new play "The Rose Tattoo" is about Sicilians only as I know them through Frankie and I want to get the Italian dialogue translated into good Sicilian dialect if I can. All of the passages, and there are a good many, where verbal meanings are not necessary are written in my very bad dictionary Italian supplemented by Frankie's phonetic spelling of Sicilian of which he doesn't seem to have learned very much. This summer I must take a sort of rest-cure at a place where there is good swimming. We are sailing May 20th on the same boat as Janie [Lawrence], taking the car with us. I expect Frankie will drive on down to Rome but I may begin with a week or so in Spain to see the bull-fights. I believe you once said something about having Raffaello's address. I'd like to have it if you still have it with you.

Our last meeting in New York, the night of the dinner at your place, had a rather sad and baffled air about it. I guess this is always true of meetings when the continuity, the day-by-day association of a friendship has been broken. You don't accept the division, the changes, and that makes a strain. There is a wonderful allusion to this in Eliot's[1] "Cocktail Party". ("Ah, but we die to each other daily. What we know of other people Is only our memory of the moments During which we knew them. And they have changed since then. To pretend that they and we are the same Is a useful and convenient social convention Which must sometimes be broken. We must also remember That at every meeting we are meeting a stranger.") – It is much better to meet without expectations of the automatic resumption of feelings that grew out of a continuity, when that continuity has been broken for a long time. The sadness and strain come out of the unreasonable demands that we make of old friends at new meetings, and so it is better and far more comfortable and wise not to expect anything at all at these meetings except the few imperishable qualities in the person we have always known were there and sometimes we are not even sure what those imperishable qualities are in ourselves or in others or what mutations they may have gone through since we last knew them. With people like Gore – in fact with almost everybody, now – I don't make the old pathetic effort to pretend that the new meeting is a simple and pleasant continuation of the ones before. Joyous outcries and embraces cannot ring true after really long separations although the thing that existed in the past is just as real as ever, and perhaps the changes visible in ourselves do not make the fatal estrangement which we are so much afraid of.

With love

TENN.

1. T. S. Eliot, one of Tennessee's phobias before his success, became one of his favorites afterward.

It was about this time, ten years ago, that you and Butch and I were moving into that lovely apartment on E. 37th Street. I am so glad you dedicated the book to Butch. No other dedication was right or possible.

The following letter and its tailpiece, simple in themselves, could stand a volume of commentary. When I recently reread the first letter, I wondered what could have occasioned it. It seemed unlikely that I should be complaining at this late date to Tennessee about the quote for "The Dog Star"; but I remembered no newer incident that might have elicited from me such a protest as he seemed to be answering; and I looked among my journals, and my letters to Sandy, to see what I could find.

As Tennessee says, I had not answered his previous epistle, ten months earlier; but the real event that drew a "heavy chalk line" across our relationship that year is not mentioned in that letter, or in this one, or indeed anywhere in our correspondence.

The year before Tennessee had finished, and in September published, his novel "The Roman Spring of Mrs Stone". It has little resemblance to his early short stories that I admire, but it is a fascinating book – his first fictionalized self-portrait after his success – and it displays a hair-raising degree of self-knowledge. More to the point, it sprang from the short story mentioned in letter 121, supposedly about a mutual acquaintance of ours. Nothing of her remains in it, but Tennessee has borrowed the name of her Italian lover, as well as the facts of a financial speculation he had been involved in, and echoed details from her unpublished stories that he and I had read – quite enough in ordinary circumstances to trouble his conscience and to make him, with his customary transference, attribute hostile thoughts to me. The circumstances, however, were not ordinary. I had gone from Taormina to Venice that summer. The friend from whom he had borrowed this material had arrived in Venice after the publication of "Roman Spring", fleeing Rome, and had given me her Roman apartment, where I had spent the fall. As the year ended, I was not thinking about Tennessee's vicissitudes; and I was certainly in no position to cast stones at anyone who based his fictional characters on real people. As far as I was concerned, the causes of our mutual silence were nearly a year old. But when I started home in January, I uncovered signs that for the last months he had been covertly transferring to me his own doubts.

My first hint of this came when I reached London and saw Maria Britneva. "Have you and Tennessee had a spat?" she asked. I said not that I knew of. "But he writes you endless letters and you refuse ever to answer." I admitted to not having answered one; and she insisted that, in any case, he was very upset and I should reassure him.

When I arrived in New York, I found that Tennessee's desires to see me and not to see me were counterbalanced. I could not get beyond Frankie when I telephoned. But almost every day some friend telephoned to say that Tennessee had asked her to invite me to dinner with him. I would accept, then in the afternoon the date would be postponed. Finally, Tennessee called and offered me a ticket to the newly-opened "Rose Tattoo". When I arrived at the theatre, there was no ticket in my name. I ran into him on the sidewalk outside as I was leaving. Apologizing profusely, he slipped me in to sit in a box, then disconcertingly sat beside me and watched my face as I watched the show.

While Tennessee was out of town for a week, I heard from several people that he was upset because I was "needling" him about his work. He returned the eighth of March for a screening of the film of "Streetcar". That morning, Oliver Evans came to see me and said that Tennessee had written and invited him to the screening but hadn't yet gotten in touch with him to tell him where it would be. In the afternoon Tennessee called me, asked for Oliver's telephone number, and added that he would be in town until Sunday and hoped to see me. A couple of hours later, Jo Healy rang up and said Tennessee wanted me to meet them at Warners and go to the screening. He hadn't asked me earlier because there hadn't been sufficient transportation to East Orange, where the preview was to be. Oliver would pick me up. He was late. When we reached the Warners office, no one was there.

The next morning, after Oliver told me that Tennessee was furious we had not arrived promptly, it seemed to me that time had come for matters to be cleared up. I sat down and wrote Tennessee a note, apologizing for not having answered his letter of the previous spring and trying to explain why. After lunch, I walked to Buffie Johnson's, where he was staying, and slipped my note under the door.

The following letter is his answer. There is no doubt that the emotions he expresses in it are sincere. If he had been worrying for months that certain of his acts were wrong, it must have been a great relief for him to receive a letter from his conscience that did not mention them, as though they didn't exist. And the entire weight of his psyche must have urged him to believe that the misunderstandings my note did mention were so petty and false they could only come from a hostile conscience that they discredited altogether. It is a heartfelt letter; and it might have smoothed over the roughness dividing us if, between the time he wrote it and I received it, there had not intervened a day of farcical events that in their turn discredited his probably no-more-than-usual dramatization of his social situation to such a degree that he must have felt again that he could not face me.

The day began with Jo Healy's telephoning and inviting me to dinner with Tennessee. I accepted. At six, Jo called again. She had spoken to Tennessee and been told that, yes, he remembered her invitation, but that as no one had bothered to confirm it, he preferred at that late date to make other arrangements for the evening. To calm Jo, who was in tears, I suggested that we go to the ballet, as I could get free tickets. On my way, I stopped at Hamburger Heaven. There I encountered a girl who had worked at View. "What a coincidence to see you!" she cried. "Last evening at Prince Obolensky's I ran into Tennessee and asked how you are. He acted as though I'd made a faux pas and said he hadn't seen you in five years." At the theatre, as Jo and I entered, we suddenly came face to face with Tennessee and Gore, both in tuxedos. From then on, diabolically, the four of us ran into each other at every intermission. At the second, in the crowded bar across the street from the theatre, where Tennessee couldn't *reach the bartender in the crush, I bought him a drink and told him the girl's remark. "I categorically deny the statement," he cried gaily; "where is my lawyer!" The next morning – before I received his letter – I reacted to the absurdity of the evening by sending him an Easter Bunnygram: "What's this I hear – you haven't been behaving too well? Hmm! Remember, I'm the one who brings the eggs and candy on Easter morn. Signed, Peter Rabbit."*

A few days later, no longer thinking the situation so funny, I sent him a small box of candy Easter eggs to Key West, to make up for the Bunnygram.

Here is his answer to my note. Followed by his thanks for the candy.

.133.
[235 E. 58th St., New York N. Y.]
[*March 12, 1951*]

Dear Donnie:

I am deeply touched and moved by your letter and I am glad that you wrote me, at long last, so frankly about the various things that had troubled you and estranged us. In the old days, how we would have laughed together at the Kafka-like complications of misunderstanding that have brought about that estrangement! Donnie, I haven't changed. Not essentially. Gotten older, yes, less fun to be with,[1] not as strong, not as well, but I am as honest and honorable a person as I hope you used to know me to be. What troubles *me* is that you attribute such petty motives or designs to me now, as if I were a cheap sort of person, not the sort at all that you could ever have liked or admired. The worst of all is your idea that I could have dictated a letter to you and sent you a carbon copy of it, especially a letter dealing with your

1. For once, I think he is transferring what he feels about *me* to my opinion of him.

book.[1] I remember that letter so clearly. I had sat up all night reading the book. I remember the pure elation I felt when I finished reading it and the immediate, irresistible impulse to sit down and tell you about it. And doing so before I slept that night. How could you feel it was insincere? Why, for what purpose! I have never wavered in my profound admiration of your work, an admiration that I have felt for the work of no other living writer [*added later*] except Carson. I have been, at times, a little envious, perhaps because my work is in a form where such purity is not possible. Do I still love you as a friend? I don't know. The more important thing is that I loved you as a friend and that that fact exists inviolably. When there has been such a mass of misunderstandings, present feelings toward each other are bound to be strained and confused. Perhaps it's wise not to do anything about it right now. But I will try to answer some of the things you hold against me. The whole business about the quote! I simply said in a few words what I thought was true and still believe is true. I have no recollection of the paraphrase you mention. How little, how terribly, terribly little and *false* I would be if I had made the quote in such a spirit![2] Then you think I have always *pretended* to like your work?! – What can I offer but what is called "a categorical denial"! which you may or may not accept. Probably not, since you think me such a small[3] person. How can you say that you like me when

1. Why this, which upset me because it seemed impersonal, should be "petty" and "cheap" and "worst of all", I don't understand.

2. Paranoiacally, perhaps, I had considered "finest young talent since Carson McCullers" to be another step in his attack on Truman and Gore a week earlier in his review of Paul Bowles' "The Sheltering Sky": "After several literary seasons given over, mostly, to the frisky antics of kids, precociously knowing and singularly charming, but not to be counted on for those gifts that arrive by no other way than the experience and contemplation of a truly adult mind . . ."

3. Together with "mean", "little", "false", the word "small" is not from my note, as the phrases he puts in quotation marks must be, but from his interpretation of it.

you think me capable of such meanness? "Bureaucratic statement" – "legally establish" – "insanely mysterious contract"[1] – all this is surely about two other people, not you and me! I haven't read this contract but I shall ask Audrey to show me a copy and try to see what you mean. – Now do I think that I am faultless in our relationship, that I have never been thoughtless or negligent? No. I know myself too well to make such a boast. The endless complications of my professional and social life during the very short periods that I am in New York don't need to be dwelt upon. You must know how it is, and also how little physical and nervous strength I have to fall back on. It's so easily exhausted. For instance, since I've been here this time. I had to see the play twice, make notes and have conferences. I had to meet and talk to and be friendly with all the actors, dine with the producer, with Audrey, with Mr. Feldman, see two previews, one public and one private of the screenplay of "Streetcar", confer with Kazan about it. Then I had a lot of work to do. I haven't even had time to cruise. It's always about like that in New York. I had hoped we would see each other in Italy or Sicily but you never answered my letters and I could only assume you didn't want to see me. I felt hurt, but not bitter

1. From my journal, June 1, 1950: "In the evening, contracts arrive for the movie option on 'Y.T.M.'. The joy I should feel distinctly shaded by a feeling of the necessity for attention. Maybe I should not be suspicious, but such strange things go on. Throughout, my name has been spelled three ways: Windham, Windam, and Windom; where I am to sign, 'Donald Windham, also known as Donald Windam'; and sometimes this phrase with the name spelled correctly *both* times. As this is entirely strange to me, I have crossed out all these and corrected the spellings of my name. I wish I had a lawyer or someone to ask about this, but common sense indicates that I should not sign contracts as 'Donald Windham also known as Donald Windam' when to my knowledge, legally or otherwise, I have never been known as this. Also, last week's cablegram becomes suspicious, for where it asks me to sign rather than initial the others have only initialed. I have complied and signed, but noted in my letter that this is with the understanding that it makes my position no different from those of Tennessee and Frieda Lawrence. I feel as though I am dealing with a Medusa head, each snake to be watched."

about it. Now what do I feel? A little shocked or stunned by the charges you brought against me, the suspicions that you seem to have entertained – but relieved that you've told me all this, completely uncertain about what ought to be done, if anything, to change your conception of me: able only to say you were wrong, you were mistaken, none of it is true! Face the facts about us both, Donnie. Remember my weaknesses and your own, but never think I am a treacherous person who does small, mean, petty and cheap things out of "politics", dishonesty,[1] Etc. I wish I were not so tired and depressed at the moment. Perhaps I could write you more eloquently, more persuasively, but I am at least writing you the truth as I see and feel it.

With love,

TENN.

.134.

[1431 Duncan St., Key West, Fla.]

[March 2?, 1951]

Dear Don –

Grandfather says "Thank you" for the Easter candy. He is the one that eats it. I can't afford to indulge in both candy and liquor. The choice is simple. Frank is in New York for a spectacularly brief visit, only three days. Then my sister, Rose, arrives with her nurse-companion, for a week's visit. Her most recent letter began "Sick as a dog, happy as a king!" A good title for almost any thing!

Love –

TENN.

---

1. Once again, "dishonesty" is not my word; I expected all these to-me-honest misunderstandings to vanish into thin air, as I had expected Sara Melton to a decade before.

Tennessee no longer got in touch with me when he arrived in New York – although he sometimes did just before leaving. He was, nevertheless, fairly continually in my thoughts: I had started "The Hero Continues".[1] And I always knew when he was in town. The newspapers announced it and mutual acquaintances invariably telephoned and asked me where he was staying.

.135.

Robert Clay Hotel, Miami, Fla.

4/21/52

Dear Donnie:

It was a great joy to receive a letter from you again and did a lot to relieve the depression of ending another season in Key West and separating from Grandfather at least for the summer. Frank flew ahead to New York, some very bad news from his family [. . .].

I've been seeing a lot of Gilbert, indeed a bit more than desirable. He visited us in Key West. Frank flew at once to Havana and Grandfather endured the visit with little of his customary grace. Gilbert always drank a good deal, but now

1. As an example of my feeling about Tennessee at the time I was beginning "The Hero Continues", this description of the protagonist from my journal, April 23, 1952: "But it is the story of an individual with an extraordinarily complex resource of human and warm emotions. No single reaction of his is simple or cold. None abstract. He can be cruel, but he is cruel like a vengeful child. Or like a selfish lover. Never like a person of insufficient feeling. He suffers from a persecution complex – but never from self-pity, an important distinction. He resorts to hysterical surface movement for inner calm – never merely to excite himself emotionally, but to bring his emotional excitement to a climax from which calm will follow. His character is always rich, never meager, like those of almost all the characters in my last story. So much richer than my own that I shall have to strain to reflect it. I tend to equate one and one. To each scene he brings a myriad reflection."

269

he gets maudlinly drunk at almost every social occasion. He has written a novel, I'm afraid not a very good one but one that had considerable success in the lending libraries and he is now at work on another which I fear is no better but should have even greater success to judge from the passages that he read me aloud. He makes a pretty good living here in Miami conducting what he calls "creative study groups". That is, he has groups of amateur and would-be writers who turn out things called "short-shorts" and whisk them over to Gilbert who reads them for a couple of fast bucks and pronounces them brilliant and suggests the proper place for them to be exposed to the world. The groups meet from time to time and Gilbert reads aloud to them, usually from his own works in progress. They are mostly middle-aged ladies who are going through or have recently survived the menstrual cessation, and they adore Gilbert and they get along wonderfully. He took me to a meeting. He was deep in his cups and had some difficulty in remaining upright in his chair and was reading them a "long-long" by Albert Halper. It was in a Jewish lady's apartment on Miami Beach and all the faithful were assembled. There was also a big old Tom cat that kept frisking and hopping about among the cute bits of terra-cotta. All at once Gilbert slammed the book down and shrieked: "SILENCE! I will have you remember that this is a *creative study group*!" – There was a stunned silence and then the hostess said timidly: "Gilbert, that was just the cat." – "Well," said Gilbert, "that goes for your fucking cat, too!" – A meeting also occurred between Gilbert and Bigelow when Paul came down this Spring to help me prepare a film-script, but the meeting was an extremely cool one, at least on Paul's side and particularly when Gilbert said: "Polly, what is your official age this season?" – But I enjoy Gilbert a great deal, in small doses. Of course he rarely comes in anything but large ones.

I've just finished building a studio on the lot beside my house in Key West. It is a completely separate living unit and will be awfully nice for guests. I do hope next year you and Sandy or at least you, if Sandy is in a show, will pay us a visit. I'll be in the South with Grandfather for several weeks before I get back to New York. How was Truman's play?[1] Most people loved it who tell us about it but think it was badly directed.

                    With love,
                                          TENN.

.136.

[*Telegram*]
New York, N. Y.
June 7, 1952

DEAR DONNIE OVERWHELMED WITH WORK WAS TOO EXHAUSTED TO SEE ANYBODY TILL NOW WE ARE SAILING THIS WEDNESDAY IF YOU WILL FORGIVE ME. PLEASE CALL MURRAY HILL 86744 LOVE

                                    TENNESSEE

.137.

[1431 Duncan St., Key West, Fla.]
Dec. 31, 1952

Dear Don & Sandy:

I was very, very happy over the book.[2] I love documentary writings they are so full of fresh idioms. We did very little

1. From my journal, March 28, 1952: "Last night to the opening of Truman's play, 'The Grass Harp'. I hope it is a hit, from my liking for him rather than for the play. Before the opening, at the Martin Beck, he was on the sidewalk across the street, together with the bummier spectators, delightedly watching the celebrities enter, and pointed them out to us after he saw us and called us over to him. 'Oh, there's the Countess so-and-so, etc.' "

2. "Lay My Burden Down: A Folk History of Slavery" edited by B. A. Botkin.

about Christmas as we had our hands full down here, what with Mother and Grandfather and all of us together under one roof and Dakin expected on leave. He hasn't come yet. We're going to have a little post-holiday celebration when we get back to New York. It is downright hot here today. I just had to take off my shirt, although all the jalousies in my studio are open to the winds. The studio is simply heaven. I want you and Sandy to occupy it sometimes when Frank and I are abroad. It would be comfortable in summer, as there is a ventilator in the roof and air from all sides through the jalousies. It has a complete bath-shower and female sockets for electric grills, Etc. so it could make a complete living unit. We're going to put in a double brass bed soon as we find one. The walls are covered with brilliant posters, there's a long work-table and a sky-light above it and I have a gorgeous Chinese lantern with wind-chimes suspended from it. Now that "Camino" is really finished, I am doing some painting out here. It is a good retreat from the house which is frequently rent by the protests of contending "house-wives", Mother, Frank, Grandfather and the maid Leoncie all trying to take command, and Mr. Moon putting in his two cents' worth whenever there is a hassle. He is looking more and more like a small Hippo. But still wets the floor immediately before going outside in the morning, a curious sort of convention that he has established for himself – so we can't put the rugs down.

We'll be back in N. Y. very soon after this reaches you. Happy New Year and love!

10.

*Tennessee had been in New York in November about the pro-
duction of "Camino Real" and had read my play "The Starless
Air". Before he went away, he recommended it to Bigelow, who
had become the play reader for the Theatre Guild. The last person I
wanted to be involved with was Bigelow; but I had been showing the
play around for months, without success, and in December I submitted
it to the Theatre Guild. When Tennessee returned at the end of January
for the "Camino Real" rehearsals, Bigelow had had "The Starless
Air" for two months, professing great interest but refusing to pro-
ceed further – with the mysterious phrase, "Time is of the essence."
In my efforts to get the play either optioned by the Theatre Guild
or someone else, I secured an agent, Phyllis Anderson, and sent a
copy to Joanna Albus at her theatre in Texas. When Tennessee,
complaining to me of Kazan, said that he wished he could direct his
own plays, I asked if he would like to experiment by directing "The
Starless Air" in Houston. He embraced the suggestion enthusiasti-
cally. As soon as the Theatre Guild learned that Joanna wanted to do
the play, they optioned it for a summer production in Westport.
Tennessee agreed to direct the play both places; after the opening
of "Camino", he went off to Key West to rest.*

.138.
[*Telegram*]
Key West, Fla.
April 1, 1953

CAN NOT FIND YOUR PLAY AMONG PAPERS HERE
PLEASE MAIL ME ANOTHER COPY SO I CAN PLAN
HOUSTON STAGING ALSO PLEASE CALL ME COL-

LECT 2-5717 SOON AS POSSIBLE MANY THINGS
TO DISCUSS HAVE NOT BEEN WELL LOVE

TENNESSEE

.139.[1]
[*Telegram*]
Key West, Fla.
April 5, 1953

READ PLAY AGAIN LAST NIGHT WONDERFUL
SHAPE EXCEPT BEDROOM SCENE A LITTLE DIF-
FUSE HAVE A FEW SUGGESTIONS LANGNER
CALLED ME BOTH HE AND JOANNA WISH TO
PRODUCE ON BROADWAY SUGGEST YOU COME
HERE ANYTIME AFTER APRIL 10TH[2] BE JOYFUL
CHRIST HAS RISEN LOVE

TENNESSEE

.140.
1431 Duncan St. [Key West, Fla.]
April 6, 1953

Dear Don:

I talked to Joanna and Langner both since our phone
conversation. Joanna said she would call you at once in
Atlanta so I didn't call you again. She said April 22nd or
May 5th were the open dates, that she would arrive in Miami
April 12th and stay through the 17th and that we should
return to Houston with her. Then Langner called me a couple

1. To Atlanta, where I was visiting my mother.
2. Postponing the date of my invitation to Key West.

274

of days ago about the Westport production. I told him, again, that I had a booking on the United States for June 5th and so I could hardly participate in that production. He said he would make a later booking for me just in case I wanted to stay over – that is, an alternate booking. I saw no harm in letting him do it so I presume he did. It appears that they both want to have options for Broadway productions. This is a good situation, and I'm sure it will all work out to your ultimate advantage. Two simultaneous interests always help! So the first important object has been achieved: a PRODUC-TION!

Phyllis sent me another copy of play and I read it over again, very carefully. I really like it better each time, even though each time I discover more problems from a produc-tion standpoint. At first I had thought it might be possible to give it a non-realistic staging but I see now that that wouldn't really work out. There is too much important very realistic business going on, the preparation of the dinner and all that. I think it must be done realistically with just whatever poetic under and overtones we can put into it, but most of all, simply and truly. All the kitchen scenes are fine, and the family conference is one of the finest scenes I know in modern theatre. I am worried about the bedroom scenes involving Sara and Bobby and Lois. In fact the whole Sara-Mel sub-theme is still a bit weak. I don't think Sara's pique over his past affair is made important or significant enough, and my idea is that Mel might have lied to her about it, or simply not told her, and that the revelation came to her through some anonymous letter or something of the sort [added later] which he admits, under pressure, is true (drama!). I think it is the horrible *mendacity* of the men, their sly dishonesties and hypoc-racies, that the girl would revolt against. If the boy, Mel, had made a clean, honest confession to her of his past, then I think she would not have been so disturbed, to the point of wanting to break the engagement in spite of her love for him, but if he had exhibited the same cheap, lying, mendacious pattern that she despised in the lives of the other middle-aged men and couples in the family – then I think that if the girl had, above everything else, an ideal of honesty between people – then her stand would be dramatically understandable. As it now stands, the disclosure seems a little trite or meaningless. As for the bedroom scenes, I think once that central theme – revolt against lying! – has been established, the scenes in the bedroom can be built effectively around it – it makes a firm and powerful sub-structure as a thematic element of play. I love Lois's long speech about her married life, the sort of soliloquy by the trunk, but the rest of the bedroom stuff is comparatively ineffectual and would be terribly hard to hold an audience with. If you read them over you'll see what I mean. Ordinary "stage drunk" comedy will not do the trick with Bobby, the pathos of his character and situation have to be developed a little more clearly and tellingly. Potentially these bedroom scenes can be so touching, so lovely, and that's why I'm making a point of this. I know you don't intend to do much work on the script before Houston, but if you just made a start along those lines, concentrating only on the bedroom, I think the problem would solve itself, at least by the time the play is ready for New York production.

It would be nice if there could be a scene between Sara and Mel toward the very end, the audience will be waiting for it. But you may have a sound prejudice against such a scene so I merely say that I think it might be nice. I thought he might bring her dinner up to her instead of Ivy and sitting on the edge of the bed and not much dialogue, one of those delicate, almost wordless, little scenes with a poignant fade out, children rushing through the hall with new toys, snow falling outside, Etc. – while Lois and Hannah face the dissolution of the home-place. But I am thinking in terms of audience-appeal and that may be wrong.

I needed two or three weeks of absolute rest but now I'm feeling okay, and I think I can face the world again now with some composure. Come down whenever you feel like it. The guest room is waiting, and sun-room with writing table. I would have said come at once but I had to be quite alone for a little while, as you doubtless understand.

Love,

TENN.

Tennessee was an inspired director. But there were "morbidly sensitive" feelings from the beginning. I had hoped that from his experience as an author he would be particularly considerate of me. The first thing he did was to bar me from rehearsals, saying that my presence would make him nervous. After several days I slipped in and watched a scene and found that he was writing and inserting speeches about mendacity that belonged in a play of his and not of mine. (They turn up, almost word for word, in "Cat on a Hot Tin Roof".) Foreseeing the same fate for this play as for "You Touched Me" if I remained silent, I spoke out. A compromise was reached that allowed the script to be improved but kept it in my control. The results pleased everyone. After the opening, Audrey Wood and Phyllis Anderson took me aside and told me that I owed it to Tennessee to have him guaranteed as the director of the Theatre Guild's Broadway-bound production. There had been half-a-dozen times during the preparation and rehearsals of the Houston production when I was sure that Tennessee would have left if leaving had not been more difficult than staying; and I told Audrey and Phyllis that, as much as I would like it, I did not believe he would go through with directing the play again. My objection was overridden and the agreement was made. Tennessee left for Europe. Langner's option, for a June production, was extended for three months, without any additional payment beyond his original $100. And he began telling me changes to make in the script.

.141.

United States Lines, [Le Havre, France]
June 8, 1953

Dear Don:

We're lying alongside the docks at Havre about ready to disembark. Frank has gone up to let Mr. Moon out of the kennels. Moon blames me entirely for his confinement and has stopped speaking to me though he still lavishes attentions on Frank. He associates me with all unpleasant alterations in ways of living and may not ever forgive me. He will be down here in a minute and we'll go ashore so this must be a quickie.

I've read over Lawrence's [Langner] notes. I guess some of them are good but I do think it is dreadfully dangerous to make specific suggestions to an artist. To a hack writer, yes, but not to an artist, especially when they come from a producer who presumably is in a position to impose his taste unless the author has a strong mind. However I don't think Lawrence is going to take that sort of attitude. The play *does* need work before Broadway. That was apparent in Houston but I think you will have to feel your own way through it. My own suggestions would be quite general. Such as: a little more dramatic intensity in the Mel-Sara story, it comes through as something a little bit thin and commonplace. Some way of avoiding the two long duo-logues (Lois-brother & Lois-Mel) coming right together, head to tail, in the beginning of Act Three. They are both strong scenes but should be spaced further apart. Shorter time-lapse between Bobby's fall and entering kitchen with maids.

Practically all the bits you've done so far are good, especially bringing Bobby into scene one, but I don't feel just inserting new passages, especially just dialogue, will solve the problem. Scenes three and five ought to be re-written from scratch. That doesn't mean you can't keep the good stuff in them, but what they really need is a different attack, in my opinion. Mind you, I say "my opinion". Naturally you should follow your own. But do try to work more with dramatic situation and less with mere speeches about it.

Of course I'd be happy to direct it again if everybody's still sure they want me to. There are two things that might prevent: my health or nervous condition, both of which are badly deteriorated right now – and the possibility of my having a play of my own ready for production next season. But of course those two contingencies are already understood, and about the latter one I could be fairly certain by the first of August. Anyway even if something ruled me out, you'd probably be safer and feel safer with any one of a number of far more experienced directors, for this is not really a difficult play and will be much less so when you've finished your work on it, and the fact we're old friends, morbidly sensitive to each other's reactions, is an added complication rather than otherwise. I like the play as much as ever, or more. It has great warmth and truth in it, and it has one priceless advantage, a formal unity and straight story line: cohesion. Don't worry about it. Don't rush it, it's bound to work out.

Can't tell you what pleasure Frank and I both got out of that book about India.[1] We actually quarrelled over it. He'd stay awake nights to read it after I put it down, and vice versa. It's a real discovery, I'd never heard of it.

Have a good summer and "play it cool" as they say . . .

With love,

TENN.

.142.

11 via Firenze, Rome [Italy]
7/28/53

Dear Don:

"The dog star rose with the sun and the day was hot as soon as it was light."[2] In other words, it is getting very hot here. I took flight to Spain which was cooler (at least

1. "Hindoo Holiday" by J. R. Ackerley.
2. The opening sentence of "The Dog Star".

Barcelona was) but in all other respects less tolerable. The food made me ill and I had to spend half the visit in bed. Then Paul Bowles passed through on his way to Rome. He has been engaged to do a film for Visconti, the English dialogue, and I returned with him here. He has two Arabs with him, his lover [—] (stolen but now relinquished by Libby Holman) and a chauffeur and we all live on the same floor of this apartment building, a top floor which has only a trickle of water for us to divide among us. The Arabs smoke kif and eat "majum", which is some sort of drug that tastes like date-preserves, and Paul sweats and fumes over constant anxieties and discomforts which I find rather endearing as I do the same thing. He has some liver trouble and is down to 115 pounds. I can be sick as a dog and lose not an ounce, which is very provoking indeed. I wired Maria to join me in Spain. Then I wired her not to join me. Now I've written her that we may go to Portofino. Truman Capote and Jack Dunphy are there and have extended an invitation (Quite surprising!) but it does not include Mr. Moon as they have a female bull. So if we go we'll put up at a hotel. The heat and water-failure make some departure almost mandatory. And Mr. Moon stinks so! I never knew any animal could smell so strong, he simply waddles in a cloud of stink, his head hanging so low that it barely clears the floor, looking up at us with great sorrowful eyes, huffing, puffing, and stinking wherever he goes, rolling like an old sailor almost too drunk to move. Frank gives him chlorophyll tablets and turns the hose on him when there is any water but the smell is totally intransigent. He did not have it in the States and we don't know whether it's the summer heat or something constitutional that has come with maturity in him.

Have you worked on the play? I've been thinking about it and it seems to me that the bad scenes (S[ara] & B[obby] in Three and parts of Two) are simply too "On Beat". There are two kinds of writing, on beat and off beat. Some very good writers are always on beat, such as Irwin Shaw and most of Steinbeck and a host of other, mostly successful writers, nearly all female writers except the southern ones. They do good onbeat writing. But [*Page ends and next page begins:*]

I got such a sweet letter from Phyllis, whom I am terribly fond of, and I have bought her an aerial photograph of Rome, quite a large one. It has to be sent in a tube and Frank has not yet got around to doing this, but let her know it is coming. I also heard from Joanna, who harbors hurt feelings that you never write her, and who said there is money for you from the production. I find it strange that you haven't gotten it yet, though perhaps by this time it has come.[1]

In retrospect it seems to me that we had a good and productive experience there, although we did have those quarrels. They were quite inevitable, I suppose, I with my exhausted nerves and you with your very natural tension about the impact of another personality on your work, and the difficulties of sitting together with those elements between us.

Later – Maria has wired that she is coming to Rome, and we are all moving into an apartment in Monte Parioli which we are sub-leasing from an American actor going on a vacation. There will be three bedrooms and a servant's room so it ought to contain us fairly comfortably if we all get along together. [—] is torturing Paul by not sleeping with him. It seems that Libby [said] that such relations were very evil and the opinions of a lady with thirty million dollars cannot be taken lightly by a young Arab whose family live in one room. Paul looks haggard and is almost too disturbed to do a good job on the film. "They call it love-

1. It arrived that month: $308.97

282

hatred and it hails from the pit" is one of the best lines Strindberg ever wrote.

I hope that things are going well with you and Sandy and that you've gotten out of the city, now and then, this summer.

Oliver wrote that he had seen you in New Orleans, stopped the car to talk to you and that you had replied with an indifferent shrug and gone right by. But sometimes things seem to take place in Oliver's mind which never happened.

I have a feeling that Grandfather and I will be in New Orleans next year a good deal of the time. I have never felt so much at home anyplace else, and the social atmospheres of New York and Key West have become less and less tolerable to me. We are taking a furnished apartment in Johnny Nicholson's building in New York but that crowd has always upset me. Unless I have work there I don't think I could take it.

Let me hear from you, care of American Express, Rome.

Love –

10.

·143·
[Rome, Italy]
August ?, 1953

Dear Donnie:

I still think the changes you showed me before I left the States are good, in the right direction, but I am disappointed to see that you didn't carry them further, especially the fact that Scene Three is substantially the same as it was. But what really threw me was the new ending. I guess it has what the Hollywood boys call "an up-beat" but it does all seem a bit sudden and contradictory and even a bit Pollyanna, all this sudden revolution of character and in-

283

spired reform with a petrol pump for a crucifix at the head of the procession. If this is what you want, then you must keep it, but it isn't for me, I would never be able to handle it, since I couldn't believe it and since it seems to me to invalidate all the preceding characterization of the shiftless brothers. If they just carried Bobby in, in the chair, and set him down in the bedroom when it started to snow, forgot him and rushed out hunting, leaving the girls to carry him on into the next room, as they have to carry everything else – why, then I could see it, visually and dramatically and it would do no violence to the mood of the play or its (to me) meaning. But anyway it is your play and I don't have sufficient confidence in my own taste and judgement anymore to try to dictate a different one to you. I have no confidence at all and nothing has happened lately to restore any to me. Like you, I just keep working at a play and wonder if I'm making it better or worse. Under the circumstances I think you ought to explore the possibility of another director, and there are several reasons for this. You want to start the production early. As I told you, I can't leave Europe till early in November, as I have this date the end of October in Helsinki, the drama festival and speech to university. Then I can't honestly agree with the course the play has taken nor feel able to stage it successfully on Broadway when it now appeals to me less than it did in Houston. I'm sure you must see this and not blame me for it. But this you must remember: it is only my own reaction and what you have done may be right. My advantages as a director are fairly ephemeral and their loss should not dishearten anybody concerned.

Maria is here and so are Paul and his Arabs and it takes two Jaguars to get us around together. Maria always wants to go to the most expensive restaurant, Paul always wants to go to the cheapest. I've found a nice private pool but rarely have energy to swim ten lengths – perhaps I'll feel better after a week or two on the sea. Maria and I are trying to decide on a place – maybe Sicily, maybe Rapallo, maybe Positano . . .

I feel a bit listless, and having to write you this letter, which I know may disappoint you somewhat, does not lighten my spirit. I'm only writing about the play to you since I don't want my reaction to possibly affect anyone else's but of course you may show the letter to Phyllis if you like, and please give her my affectionate greetings.

With love,

P.S. The Bobby bit in scene one is lovely but I saw that in New York before sailing. I would use that as a springboard and give him a totally different treatment in scenes two and three, avoiding the burlesque "Captain Rockley" bit with the bottle, and scene three – Well, like I told you in my last letter, it is an "on beat" piece of writing. It could be so lovely if you gave Bobby and Sara the same fresh sort of feeling and observation that you gave Blackie and Mabel and Pearl and the Mother in "Dog Star", which was a fine work of art for the simple reason that it never once (well, maybe except for one or two over-stretchings of the mythical parallel) descended to "on beat" writing. Too much of my own recent work has been "on beat" and I know the difference. You stated it yourself very precisely in your last letter. When will or volition takes over where the mysterious animation should be and once was and somehow ceases to be.

Adio, mio caro . . . (Sob!)

P.S. Maria just this moment came from Amexco with your letter and Langner's. I think you will be grateful for this breathing space. I find no connection between his comments and mine. Sending you this anyway but I shall not say anything to L.L. (D.D.) unless you want me to. MARIA SENDS "MOLTI BACCI". We are now going to eat at the most expensive restaurant she can think of.[1]

.144.

Amexco, Rome [Italy]

9/4/53

Dear Donnie:

I did not misunderstand your motives in the re-writing you have done, I realized that you were trying to please tastes outside your own, but you did apparently misunderstand my letter about the new script. I did not mention the many little improvements, definite but slight, that you have made in the script, because I thought it more important, practically, to deal with the big one, the new ending, which may be theoretically justifiable but still comes across as a Pollyanna ending. You will see if you read my letter over that I said that knowing you and your work I knew this ending couldn't suit you any better than it did me, at least the way it is handled.

I don't think it's necessary to go on and on with these comments since really it all boils down to my feeling that the script is now at the awkward stage that a script always passes

1. From my journal, August 30, 1953: "Tenn's letter came ten days ago. I haven't felt like recording it here before now. I gave it to Phyllis. Yesterday I finally answered it, as was necessary, explaining what he must know anyway. The gist of his letter, which mentions only the Langner-suggested last scene, is: 'If this is what you want . . .' Anyway, I wrote, explaining that these are the best maneuvers I have been able to make, having to please Langner, never sure who is to direct, but fortified (with what diminishing faintest hopes) by the idea of having him on my side, and agreeing to his objections to the last scene. I did say that the body of the play is now the way I want it and gave him a full out by insisting that I want him as director only if he does like the play and isn't doing this wholly to please me."

through when there is a change of conception. I know that it will all fall into line according to your plan if you don't rush it, if you take your time and keep your balance about it. How could I possibly say at this point that I will direct it this coming season when I know how long it takes even a writer who works as fast as I do to get a script over the hump, when drastic changes have been made in the meaning. I say the meaning because what you say was the meaning, that the loss of the homeplace was a blessing, was never apparent in the play as it was and there was no way to make that meaning come across, even if I wanted to, I mean was able to feel it, without it being indicated in the script in a palpable way. This is a new play that you are talking about, a good deal more original since it bears less resemblance thematically to the "Cherry Orchard", and yet I must say, sadly, that I liked the old one better. It seems to me that the loss of dear things is always a terrible loss and I can't see, personally, how it makes things better. Oh, theoretically, yes, like it's better to give up drink or part from a beautiful lover who drives you mad, but – people after reform always seem sort of dull and commonplace to me, even if they are socially more adjusted. I didn't think the parallel to the Chekhov play was damaging since it was so different in treatment and quality, since the humor was so delightful and it was really so terribly poignantly true. I did love the old ending, it made me cry whenever I listened to it. Have you thought more about having the brothers carry Bobby as far as Lois's room and then run out leaving him there when the fall of snow calls them out hunting? How charmingly characteristic that would be. I also love the idea of the filling-station, it's really such a delightful thing that you could play with, but not as a symbol of a regeneration that no perceptive audience could believe in. I love Henry and Stuart, lazy, goodlooking, worthless, selfish brothers, always reclining on something with their legs falling apart and hitching at their belts and thinking about good times, these are the elements in the play that tickle and delight, and the laborious working out of a theme that you, no more than I, from our rather similar experiences and backgrounds, could truly believe in, will only weigh it under and make it something that only Eric Bentley would care for.

Is this any plainer than what I said before? You mustn't think me indifferent to the economic angle as it affects you, I know all about that and how hard it is and I wish I knew how to solve it, but I can't help thinking more about the purity of your work, in the face of which I have always felt happily humble.

We'll be back soon, meanwhile I am only writing about the play to you and to Phyllis. If I write Lawrence I will only say that I think the play is going through a period of re-adjustment or something as vague as that. And only if you advise me.[1]

Fondly,

TENN.

---

1. From my journal, September 17, 1953: "Langner *intends* to keep the option but wants to give me one hundred dollars rather than the five hundred the contract calls for." September 25: "Langner refuses to renew his option, says he can't do anything until Tenn returns." October 1: "Langner says he will keep option, month by month." October 5: "Langner wants to pay two hundred and 'wait until Tennessee comes back'. Says 'without Tennessee it will be hard to get backing for this play'." October 7: "Langner agrees to do the play without Tennessee if Phyllis gets him a co-producer with the backing and a star. As Phyllis is to be seeking a co-producer, he won't pay me any option money." November 2: "I read in the *Times* that Tenn arrives today, with Paul Bowles." November 12: "Last night Tenn telephoned but didn't mention 'The Starless Air'. He talked only of my story *Rome*, in *The Paris Review*. 'I loved the part about D.'s cruising,' he said; 'you don't suppose that's why he's been barred from Italy, do you?' I told him that D.'s trouble had been political. 'Well, I guess it was political, too,' he said. And having scored this point he abruptly ended the conversation." December 22: "Cadmus saw Frankie at a party. Frankie said, 'Tennessee tries so hard to help Donnie but Donnie won't allow himself to be helped.' "

[1431 Duncan St., Key West, Fla.]
[*January 3, 1954*]

Waiting for the "sunshine of your smile".

Love

TENNESSEE[1]

.146.
[1431 Duncan St., Key West, Fla.]
Feb. 20, 1954

Dear Donnie:

It was good to get your letter as I was afraid that you were cross with me, as Frank said you'd asked for your script back and gave him the impression you thought I had sort of let you down in your relations with the Guild. I really don't think so. I only wrote you about your re-write of the play, nobody else, and the one time I talked to Langner after I got back from Europe he showed as much interest in the play as ever and I repeated my own very earnest endorsement of it. It seemed, however, that it was no longer under option and Bigelow told me that Phyllis and you had taken it away from the Guild because of a disagreement over option terms.[2] The solution of the problems in this play are so very easily in your power that I think it is just as well that you have this chance to work them out all by yourself, without influence or pressure, as an artist should do.

As for me, I could never in this world have directed a play last Fall. If we'd seen each other you'd have understood why.

1. On a card accompanying a two-inch-high, fetuslike celluloid dog, standing on its hind legs and holding an umbrella.
2. The terms as summarized: he was willing to keep the option indefinitely, but refused to pay any money after his $100 of March, 1953.

You remember my condition last Spring, but Europe failed to improve it, this time, and I was pretty much of a wreck. I managed to hang together till I got to New Orleans but there I went into a hospital. I'm trying to put myself back together down here but, if I can, it's a slow process, very slow, and the beach and the movies are about all I'm good for. I know how you feel about people who continually proclaim their dissolution, immediate or impending, real or imaginary, so I will say no more in this morbid vein.

I liked your trenchant letter to the *Times* about the Goetz play.[1] David Stewart wrote me about it, saying it was "dull, unimaginative", so I'm not surprised at your reaction. But I'd like to see it for the performances, and I do hope I'll get back while Eliot's play[2] is still running. I have a feeling the critics must have missed the point of it. I am longing to see the book. Eliot and Dr. Kinsey are the two nicest men that I've ever met. They radiated a similar kind of honesty and warmth.

Do you know that Jane and Tony have a baby? It's a girl they've named Clare Lanier, born in Nürnberg where they're now living. We saw Janie and Tony in Rome last summer when she was very pregnant and they were travelling about southern Europe in third-class, staying in cheap pensiones, and eating in trattorias, and Tony was taking her, pregnant as she was and exhausted, to various architectural and esthetic shrines. – Apparently she survived it. – They're pretty wonderful, both of them. – I'm not sure that always being unselfish is the only good way to love. It may be the least natural.

Remember me in thy orisons! I hope to be better when I see you again.

Love –

10.

1. "The Immoralist" an adaptation by Ruth and Augustus Goetz of the Gide novel, reversing its meaning in my opinion.
2. "The Confidential Clerk".

Our contacts during the next years all short-circuited. The main one I remember before the following letters was during the Philadelphia tryout of "Cat on a Hot Tin Roof". It was the story of "Roman Spring" and "Rose Tattoo" all over again. Tennessee had been rewriting "Cat" for Kazan. "Don't tell me what you think of the play," he called at intermission; "I don't want to hear it now." I didn't; and before I saw him again I heard that I was "needling" him about his work. Depressed, I felt that in my role as his conscience I was ceasing to exist for him as a person. Both of us needed our friendship, and both of us made attempts to keep it going; but circumstances, aided sometimes by one, sometimes the other, no longer allowed them to succeed. The short-circuitings took on a pattern: I would approach Tennessee and be rebuffed, then I would hear that he was very fond of me and distressed that I wouldn't see him.[1]

.147.

[*Telegram*]
New York, N. Y.
April 1, 1955

THANK YOU FOR GIVING ME YOUR VERY BEAU-
TIFUL STORY BOOK[2] WHICH I ENJOYED MOTHER
WILL BE RECEIVING IN THE LIBRARY OF THE ST
REGIS HOTEL AT FIVE PM SUNDAY IF YOU AND

1. For how far my faith in Tennessee had metamorphosed by this period into a need to understand him, see the appendix.
2. "Servants With Torches", printed in a limited edition with an original serigraph illustration by Paul Cadmus, which I had left him as a peace offering.

.148.

[1431 Duncan St., Key West, Fla.]
Jan. 5, 1957

Dear Sandy:

Purdy himself had sent me a copy of "63: Dream Palace",
saying that you had suggested he let me see it.[2] I think it's
just about the freshest new writing since "Dog Star". And
I wrote him a letter about it, expressing this opinion. I was
glad to get another copy, and it was sweet of you to send it.

Tell me something about him, what's he like? When I go
North again I would love to meet him. I would also love
to see you and Donnie again. Sufficient time has passed for
us all to get over our various hurt feelings and remember the
more important thing, which is that we were friends.[3] The
difficulty is that when I am in New York I am under almost
unbearable pressure and I can't be the better part of myself
anymore. I am planning to start analysis soon as I return the
end of this month, and then continue it in Zurich, as I am
tired of living with myself as I am.

With love to you both,

TENN.

1. Not only Mrs Williams but, seated on the same couch with her, Marilyn
Monroe, looking demure, and Carson McCullers, looking down the declivity
of Marilyn's breasts, received us and a hundred other guests.

2. From my journal, December 18, 1956: "James Purdy came by for a drink
last night. Van Vechten, who had him send us his books, said 'Firbank writes
as though every sentence has a double meaning. Purdy writes as though every
ninth sentence has.' "

3. From my journal, January 26, 1957: "At breakfast this morning a telephone
call from Gilbert Maxwell in Miami, informing me that my lack of friendship
has caused Tennessee more unhappiness than anything else in his life, that he
needs friendship so badly now, with all his troubles with Frankie, his mother,
his sister, and will I telephone him in Key West and go to see him . . ."

Hotel Comodoro, Havana, Cuba
June 13, 1957

Dear Sandy:

I answered your strange letter[1] before I left New York but left it unmailed there. Of course I haven't any clear idea of what you are talking about in your reference to the Mike Wallace broadcast. I was completely knocked out, drunk, and all but unconscious. It was the evening of the day that *The New Yorker* came out with that devastating notice of "Orpheus" and also the evening of the day of my father's death, and although my father and I had not seen each other for over ten years, he was still my father, and there was an emotional shock, more than I would have thought for. As for my relations with you and Donnie, I thought that I had explained all that the night that we played the truth game at Tallulah's in Coconut Grove. I didn't try to excuse it, but I did think I explained it.[2] You will naturally do as you please about seeing me or not seeing me. I think the old tensions between us have worn themselves out, and I, at least I, could see you both again without discomfort, and perhaps with pleasure.[3] I will

1. Something Tennessee had said on the Mike Wallace television program had drawn a letter of protest from Sandy.

2. This explanation, developed over the years, became another fable in Tennessee's "Bulfinch's anthology": that he and I were close only when we neither had lovers and were cruising together, which was for a period of four months in the winter of 1942-43.

3. From my journal, August 22, 1957: "Sailaway, Bridgehampton. Out here to visit Truman. Two nights ago Tennessee, a companion, John Myers, Herbert Machiz, Sam Barber, Chuck Turner, were to dinner. Denunciations of Bankhead. Tennessee: 'She has given up and only cares about making money now.' Also he made the remark: 'She likes me. I know. She has never said but one unkind thing about me in print.' Jack Dunphy, on phoning and hearing about the evening, only wanted to know one thing: How did Don and Tennessee get on? I don't know. Sandy and I were walking on the beach when he arrived. He rushed into the kitchen, saying: 'Give me a drink. I'm frightened

be at the Riggs Institute, in Stockbridge, Mass., for the summer, beginning a course of analysis or psychotherapy, entering there June 18th. I would be happy to see you if you'd like to visit me, and it's a lovely part of the country in summer, I hear. If you just want me to sign some books, send them there and I will sign them and return them with love.

TENN.

.150.

[124 East 65th St., New York, N. Y.]
1/3/58

Dear Donnie:

I want to thank you for your phone-call about the play.[1] It makes me realize that you have always been sincere and unprejudiced about my work and so it clears up a lot of past resentments which no doubt came out of my "mild paranoia" or "walking lunacy", as it may be.

Love to Sandy, too. I am going immediately to the airport from the theatre, opening night, to rest and recuperate in a sweet, sweet place, the little house in Key West with Horse[2] and dog. When I get back, don't forget I am right around the corner from you all now! Let's see more of each other: analysis has helped me![3]

Much love,

TENN.

to death of those two bitches.' This is the biggest step forward our relation has taken for years. From this it might progress somewhere. But it never would from: 'I love Donnie so much but he won't see me.' "

1. "Suddenly Last Summer", which I had seen at a preview and thought his best work since "Summer and Smoke".

2. Tennessee's nickname for Frank.

3. From my journal, February 11, 1958: "Incidentally, it is interesting to learn that right after Tennessee wrote me saying he hoped we would see each other when he returned to town, the day on which he said he was departing, he gave a large party in his apartment 'right around the corner'."

.151.

The Towers, Miami, Fla.
December 2?, 1958

A Happy New Year!

—10.

.152.

[Hotel Nacional de Cuba, Havana, Cuba]
4/6/59

Dear Donnie:

The movie producers of "Orpheus Descending" are dissatisfied with that title which they regard as too literary and
have been bugging me to dig up another. I have offered a
number, none of which is quite pleasing to them. So I finally
thought of a wonderful title that you once used for a short-
story that came out in the New Directions Annual. *Flesh
Farewell.* It would be a wonderful title for "Orpheus": – they
also think so.[1] Of course it won't be used without your consent. Martin Jurow will call you about it. I told him you
should be compensated financially for the use of the title, if
you allow us to use it, and I think there should also be some
film-credit or public announcement giving you credit for its
original use. I should think they would be willing to pay a
sum for it that would make it worth while for you, and in the

1. Perhaps they thought having it would be like knocking on wood. The
year before, Capote had succeeded with a title of mine: "Breakfast at Tiffany's".
My book was stories about sex during the war, from incidents told me by
Lincoln Kirstein and others. In the title story, a civilian picked up a handsome
marine who was remarkably agreeable in bed. Come morning, when asked if
there was anything he would like to do, the marine replied, "Let's have breakfast at Tiffany's." It was the 1950's and I abandoned the book as unpublishable.
Truman asked if I would give him the title. I did, and later he complained
that Tiffany's had never rewarded him for it.

long run it might draw attention to that very beautiful story which I remember so vividly even after so long.

Also you would be helping me with a work that I know you have always admired very much: "Battle of Angels" – "Orpheus". Magnani, Brando, Joanne Woodward and probably Maureen Stapleton are going to star in it, and it's going to be shot in Mississippi and on Long Island this summer. I will be back there, stay in the States this summer to supervise the filming and continue work on the script. I hope we'll see more of each other. I was in New York, of course, for the rehearsals of "Sweet Bird" but was under such constant strain and tension that I couldn't see anyone but people involved in the production and Frank and my sister. Also you must realize that I am still feeling guilty and embarrassed about the long lapse in our friendship, which is the most unfortunate thing, in some ways, that has ever happened to me. Believe me, I've always loved you as a dear friend and always will, no matter how odd my behavior. [*Added later*] (And sometimes yours!)

Ever,

TENN.

Ask them for 5 grand or at least 25 hundred. I think they'll buy it![1]

1. In a few days, both Tennessee and his producers were in town. From my journal, April 16, 1959: "A voice on the telephone demands, 'Tennessee Williams.' When I say he isn't here, the voice demands to know who I am. When told, it becomes a little less announcerlike. 'Oh, this is Marty Jurow,' it says. 'I thought Tennessee was there. I'll call him at home.' And that's that. He hangs up." And that was that. No one ever again mentioned to me buying the title.

At the end of March, 1960, I sent Tennessee "The Hero Continues". It was published a month later in England, and in August in the United States.

.153.[1]
1431 Duncan St., Key West, Fla.
4/4/60

Dear Donnie:

A book of such subtlety as "The Hero Continues" should be read at least twice before one attempts to say much about it. I have just finished reading it once, and I am sure that I will read it again since I read "The Dog Star" three times with increasing appreciation. But with apologies for the immaturity of my comments, here they are for what little they are probably worth. I am not a good novel-reader. Kazan says I can't even judge a play or a movie-script and he's probably right about it, but then I would say that he can't either sometimes.

To begin with, I was touched by the book's effort to understand and penetrate with sympathy the opaque and twisted nature of the continuing hero. I must admit I had expected, if it was, as I had been warned, what Bigelow calls a *roman à clef*, to find myself (that is, if it *was* myself) dealt with less mercifully. What the book catches most truly is the solitude of Denis, a sort of self-imposed sentence to solitary confinement. A refusal to believe in almost any love or affection for himself, related, most likely, to a profound sense of guilt,

---

1. To Madison Avenue. I sailed in May for Greece, on a Guggenheim Foundation fellowship, which I had finally been granted on the nth try.

shame, inadequacy, impotence,[1] which is most likely the result of an incredible kind and degree of bullying to which he was subjected, first by his father, and then by all the father-substitutes such as the toughs of the neighborhood who called him a sissy, the fraternity brothers who made him the favorite butt of their ridicule and their paddles, the bosses and straw-bosses he slaved under for three years in the great depression for sixty-five dollars a month, Etc., Etc., so that out of sheer surfeit of being beaten down, he gathered out of his father's fierce blood the power to rise somehow. And how could the rise be gentle?

But hardly had the rise been accomplished when a less tangible bully with a more terrible fist began to beat down again the continuing hero, and let's put the hero in ironical quotes as he should be, and as he rightly is in the book.[2] I will enclose with this letter a copy made on my duplicating machine of a letter that I wrote Kenneth Tynan in the summer of '55. He sent me a copy of it recently because he wanted to print it in a forthcoming volume about the theatre of the Fifties. When you read it you will see why I couldn't give him permission to use it. I send it to you because I think you would use it as an artist some day in an effort to understand the continuing "hero" with that depth of understanding which is inescapably compassionate. Spring 1946. That, more than anything else, even more than the disaster of success, made the "hero" the zombie you have depicted, because in his sense of being a man infected with creeping death,[3] he

1. From here on, this paragraph is about autobiographical elements of Tennessee's life, ones that do not exist in my novel.

2. The hero is not treated ironically. From my journal: "A hero, not a man one worships, but by whose example one learns."

3. Someone who hasn't read the novel will hardly guess that the hero is *not* portrayed as a zombie and *is* portrayed as believing that he is infected with creeping death.

felt himself excused from emotional participation with anything but the people he could create in his work, who were nearly all projections of various interpretations of his own terrors, despairs, ferocities of resentment and distrust and longings for someone, almost anyone, to break through his crustacean armament to what really used to be and potentially still was a great capacity for responding understanding, sympathy, and affection.

I think we must wait till sometime under the influence of liquor or an hypnotic tablet I can talk to you, vis-à-vis, about what the book still lacks in depth of perception. At present it is best described in a quotation from Crane that you use: "As silent as a mirror is believed, realities plunge in silence by." That is the artistic key-note of the book, which is a work of art but still a little manqué: not yet completed. It is worthwhile for me to make this personal comment on it because I know you will publish it some day in the States, and that you will have a chance to supply what is not yet complete in it, and then I think it will rank with "The Dog Star" as one of the finest American novels of the century, one of the very few finest.

Right now I have put aside new work to re-write a play already produced and finished on Broadway and limping about the country on tour, "Sweet Bird of Youth". It violated an essential rule: the rule of the straight line, the rule of poetic unity of singleness and wholeness, because when I first wrote it, crisis after crisis, of nervous and physical and mental nature, had castrated me nearly. Now I am cutting it down to size: keeping it on the two protagonists with, in Act Two, only one or two suitable elements beside the joined deaths of the male and female heros so that instead of being an over-length play it will be under length (conventionally) and the first act and third act will not be disastrously interrupted by so many non-integrated, barely even peripheral, concerns with a social background already made clearly implicit, not needing to be explicit.

Donnie, if it is me, you have made in the book one shatteringly wrong surmise about my kind of behavior and feeling. A cablegram telling me that a friend was mortally ill and needed financial help from me would not elicit from me a suspicion of a hoax being played on me. I would have called America at once to check on the report, if I thought it untrue, and though I would not have flown to his bedside, I would certainly never, never have failed or even delayed to give the needed assistance. My record of this kind of material assistance is not as bad as you seem to believe, despite my feeling that this kind of assistance is a source of estrangement and resentment between friends. And also, of course, despite a nearly blinding preoccupation with an effort to outrun time in the completion of what I hoped would turn into a major body of work, if I gave all of myself to it.

I write you all this hoping that you will return to the book as I am returning to my last produced play, not to make the "hero" more sympathetic but less of a shadow, beautifully projected but still a shadow.[1] Of course if you are trying to say that to each of us the other one is a shadow, then you have achieved your aim with perfection. The book is perfectly formed and a true work of art: I'm only saying it is somewhat premature in comparison to its potentials.

With love, (and hommage)

TENN.

P.S. Unable duplicate Tynan's duplication of my '55 letter on my duplicator so will have to have it typed for you.

---

1. This letter reassured me, on the contrary, that I had portrayed the hero accurately and solidly.

Dear Ken:

This is a somewhat drunken letter. To write it, that is, to get the uninhibited state that would make writing it possible, I had to wash down a seconal with a double dry martini. (Probably would have done it anyway, this being my drunken summer.)

I am flattered as hell that you want to do this piece about me but the more I think about it the more it alarms me. I think we know each other pretty well, now, despite so little actual contact. I want the piece to be very truthful, very candid, with no attempt at flattery, but I don't want it to kill me professionally in the States, for despite my nihilistic attitude this summer, I think I may still want to have plays done on Broadway, and we are at the mercy, more or less, of our columnists and our detractors such as *Time* magazine, *Confidential,* Etc.

I think it would be fitting for you to give the true date of my birth, March 26, 1911, not 1914 as it is given out in biographical matter other places. I am bored with this silly dissimulation about my age. I once looked much younger than my age, in fact when I was 28 they would sometimes still refuse to serve me in bars because I appeared under-age, but now I think I look my true age, and anyway, if there is ever any posthumous interest in me, my birthdate is recorded in Columbus, Miss., so the truth would out. I am now 44. I went to college in 1929, the year of the Wall Street crash and was taken out by my father during the depression and put to work in the shoe-business, as I told you, where I stayed three years – for which I am now very grateful. I learned about people's lives in the little white collar job class. I used to have a terrific crush on the female members of my family, mother, sister, grandmother, and hated my father, a typical pattern for homosexuals. I've stopped hating my father and I do hope you won't put in any hurtful things about him. He was not a man capable of examining his behavior toward his family, or not capable of changing it. My mother devoted herself to us three kids and developed an hostility toward him, which he took out on me, the first male to replace him. He thought me, which I certainly was, a terrible sissy, and used to call me "Miss Nancy", and things such as that. Because I wouldn't play baseball with the other boys and preferred girl play-mates. Off and on he would make abortive efforts to show affection, would ask me to go downtown to the movies with him. I would go but would be frozen stiff with fear of him and being defeated repeatedly, he gave up. But he was very nice, always, to my younger brother and he treated my unfortunate older sister, Rose, not with understanding, not with much attention, but with civility, and she was the only one of us children to whom he gave an allowance, though a small one. He came from one of the most distinguished families of the South, being directly descended from two colonial governors and countless notable figures in southern history, but he grew up under rough circumstances after the family fortune had been entirely dissipated and without a mother. (She died soon after his birth.) I find him a tragic figure, now, not one that I dislike any longer. So if you mention my family, please don't attack him.

About the operation and the "shadow of death" that hung over me from 1946 till –

My recent history dates from that occasion. You may wisely decide to make no reference to it, but if you do use it, I think I had better tell you more about it. I used to think I would reserve this whole story, the big one of my life, till sometime when I felt able to write it myself, calling

302

it "Spring 1946", but I doubt now that I would ever get around to it and I think it has an interesting bearing on all my work since then, romantic pessimism, preoccupation with mortality, Etc. Of course it only became explicit, something I finally dared to deal with directly, in "Big Daddy" in "Cat". Here's a very rough outline of the experience.

In the early spring of 1946 I left New Orleans for Taos, New Mexico (where a friend awaited me) by way of home, Saint Louis. I'd felt more or less ill for months, and debilitated, strengthless, work going badly. I'd purchased a second-hand car, a very old Packard coupe that looked charming still but had no oil-pressure and many other disabilities which were manifested enroute. It got me to Saint Louis. One night a week later William Inge and I went to fun-fare, as you call it, on Grand Avenue. When I came home I had an attack of cramps. Evacuated: afterwards discovered I had a cutting pain in my abdomen when I walked. Was naturally alarmed but didn't mention it as I was desperately anxious to continue my trip. The pain was slightly better in the morning and I left as planned. By the time I got (going West) to a town near the Kansas border the pain had moved around to my left or right side, I don't remember which, and it was so severe that I called a doctor to my hotel that night. He took a light view of it, said it was a touch of chronic appendicitis, not acute, and recommended a dose of mineral oil and some bella donna. I went on. Pains resumed in Oklahoma and at just the same time, the bearings in the old jalopy burned out and it stalled outside the ugliest, dullest place I've ever been, a town called Alva, Oklahoma. Car was towed into a Ford agency-garage, operated by the beastliest crook I've ever known. He literally confiscated the car, promising to repair but never even opening the hood, and forcing me to remain there for about five days, with the most cynical assurances that he'd ordered new bearings, which he hadn't. All this time my abdominal pains continued and got worse, had now changed to shooting pains down the urethra, knife-like, whenever I took a step. I went to a local doctor who was a nice guy but admitted he was mystified by the symptoms, though he thought they might come from a kidney stone and who sent me to a hospital in nearby Wichita, Kansas. There I had a fearful experience under a sadistic doctor and nurse who conducted a probing examination of urethra and kidney with a long wire that had a flash-light on the end of it, sticking it up my prick all the way to the kidney. They gave me no drug to relieve the incredible pain and even refused to let me smoke a cigarette while I endured it. There was no kidney stone. They then said I must go to the hospital and have further tests and examinations as it was probably an acutely infected appendix, in an unusual position, pressing on the nerve of the urethra. I did, went through various X-rays, Etc. Their report was so deliberately vague and ambiguous that I became panicky and wired my friend, waiting in Taos, to come at once. He did. He talked to the doctors and I also felt that he was deceiving me about the report. They only advised me to rest a few days, and then go on wherever I wanted. After three days my friend and I continued by bus to Taos, New Mexico. The bella donna had reduced the acute pains to occasional twinges but by the time we reached Taos, the knife-like pains struck again. Fortunately there were some friends in Taos, Frieda Lawrence and Brett and Mrs. Luhan, and also a pair of surprisingly good young doctors and a very up-to-date little hospital endowed by Mrs. Luhan and I went there the day after my arrival. They diagnosed my pains and my very high blood-count as a ruptured appendix with incipient peritonitis. An operation was imperative at once. Since I'd had a bad heart since childhood (result of diphtheria with severe complications) I thought my goose was cooked. I made out a will and the operation was performed that evening. Soon as they put the ether mask on my face I began to fight the nuns (it was a catholic hospital) and scream, "I'm dying!" – claustrophobia, feeling of suffocation, are my greatest dreads. The operation, I was told, lasted four hours, because as soon as they cut into the abdomen, they discovered an acutely infected diverticulum of the small intestine which they had to consult about before proceeding further. The appendix was likewise infected. The thing that made me think I was doomed occurred the next morning, shortly after I had come out of the ether. One of the catholic sisters (whom I later discovered to be the staff pathologist or laboratician) was bustling cheerily about my room. She remarked to me, "Well, you're all right now. Of course you're probably going to get something like this again in a few years, but we all have to go sometime, or other, don't we?" – I suppose she was used to talking to Taos Indians and other stolid types and did not anticipate my penetrating interpretation of her remarks. An hour later the doctors came to call and said they had found that the diverticulum, which they said was congenital, something called a maecles diverticulum, had been found to contain "aberrant pancreatic tissue" which would have dissolved the intestinal wall (digested it!) if it had broken in me. So, as I told you I put two and two together and the sum was cancer, pancreatic cancer, which had transplanted to the intestine. I chewed this over for an hour or two and demanded the doctors come back. I told them the conclusion at which I'd arrived, and the good sister's jolly revelations as I was coming out of ether. Apparently they gave her hell, for a little while later she flew into my room, while I was still critically ill, taking plasma, and hissed at me: "I don't know what you got and I don't care what you got, it's nothing to me, I didn't give it to you, Etc." It is this experience, more than their fairly consistent black-listing of my plays, which has given me some anti-catholic bias, but to be fair, I know that catholic sisters are usually good and compassionate nurses. I simply discovered that their order does not preclude inhumanity, and I certainly have never encountered that sort of thing in a non-religious hospital out of the many I've been in and out of over the years. I think this is enough of the story at least for now.[1] This was where the desperate time started, and how it started, which was to produce my best work, "Streetcar", and later, "Cat", perhaps all the ones I've written since '46. Following that: a singular series of providential accidents which revived and comforted my spirit, at least two great friendships, Carson McCullers and my Good Man Friday, Frank Merlo, who has been with me, now, seven years, as if God dropped him into my hands out of pity for my lost state, just at the time when "Summer and Smoke" failed, in the Fall of 1948. Carson came to me earlier, in the summer of 1946 at the height of my imaginary dying, she came to Nantucket Island which I had chosen to die on, and the moment she came down the gang-plank of the ship from the mainland, in her baseball cap with that enchantingly radiant, crooked-toothed grin of hers, something very light happened in me, I dropped my preoccupation with the thought I was doomed, and from then on, with various setbacks, of course, there was a process of adjustment to the new situation, and by the late fall of 1947 I was able to release all the emotional content of the long crisis in "Streetcar". In my case, I think my work is good in exact ratio to the degree of emotional tension which is released in it. In a sense, writing of this kind (lyric?) is a losing game, for steadily life takes away from you, bit by bit, step by step, the quality of fresh involvement, new, startling reactions to experience, the emotional reservoir is only rarely replenished, by some such crisis as I've described to you at such length,

1. His immediate version of this story is given in letter 93.

and most of the time you are just "paying out", draining off. To offset this, to some degree, usually not enough, is the accumulation of insight and "sophistication". Sometimes the heart dies deliberately, to avoid further pain. Long ago, in 1940, I had a talk with Margaret Webster when she was with me in Mississippi, to get the atmospheric background for "Battle of Angels" which she was about to direct and she was concerned about how I would feel if the play failed, and I said, "I've begun to develop a sort of insulation about my feelings so I won't suffer too much." She said, "That's a dangerous thing for a writer." A very perceptive remark! Once the heart is thoroughly insulated, it's also dead. At least for my kind of writer. My problem is to live with it, and to keep it alive. I've lost a lot of friends since 1946. Some of them have become shockingly hostile because they don't know or understand why I have narrowed down my life, socially, emotionally, to its present limits. Because I had to, I felt, concentrate all I had left on the one big thing which was work, and foolishly expected them to understand this necessity.[1] I suspect that you have something of the same sort of drive, you seem like a driven person, and you will understand this better. There are lots of things we could have talked about that we didn't, but that's life for you!

Fondly,

TENN.

1. In his 1949 review of Paul Bowles' "The Sheltering Sky" he was aware of and pointed out – transferring himself to "they" – the danger of this "necessity" and what he feared from it. "In America the career almost invariably becomes an obsession. The 'get-ahead' principle, carried to such extreme, inspires our writers to enormous efforts. A new book must come out every year. Otherwise they get panicky, and the first thing you know they belong to Alcoholics Anonymous or have embraced religion or plunged headlong into some political activity with nothing but an inchoate emotionalism to bring to it or be derived from it. I think that this stems from a misconception of what it means to be a writer or any kind of creative artist. They feel it is something to adopt *in the place of* actual living, without understanding that art is a by-product of existence."

[1431 Duncan St., Key West, Fla.]

[*June 20, 1960*]

Dear Donnie:

When I got back a few days ago from the West Coast where I took Mother instead of Europe, a compromise that turned out to be a wise one, I found this letter from your new American publishers,[2] and I thought you should see it before I answer it, because I am not sure that you would want me to comply with the request for a quote for the book's promotion because under the circumstances it might be in bad taste on both our parts if I did so.

Perhaps in England they didn't recognize the novel as a "roman à clef", Denis Freeman as Donnie's conception of T. Williams, but here it is pretty certain they will, what with the inscription[3] and the various quotes and paraphrases from my writings like the trail of bread-crumbs that Hansel and Gretel scattered behind them in the forest, on their way to the ginger-bread house of the witch and her cages and oven.

There's one quote I'll always give you, baby, however little you need it. "Donald Windham lives and grows as an artist the way one should live and should grow, steadily, strongly, and bravely. Angels, watch over him waking and sleeping. Amen."

When I returned from the Coast I wanted to find the book and read it over again, for time number three, but it had disappeared from the house. I suspect that Frankie has hidden it with the mistaken idea that it is a thorn in my not-so-thick hide. It isn't. I love the book because it's as beautiful

1. Sent to Athens, forwarded to Mykonos.

2. A stupid letter from the promotion department of Crowell, which says, "We think this startling, behind-the-scenes novel of the Broadway theatre may be of particular interest to you . . ."

3. The book is dedicated to Tennessee.

and terrible as life. I did resent the bit about Denis declining to believe that an old, dear friend was dying of leukemia in order to avoid the hospital expense, but then I thought, Well, maybe the factual untruth of such an implication is artistically defensible, just as Sebastian's being eaten up by those whom he had eaten was the poetic abstraction of a truth which is truer than any factual one.

I got your "fond farewell"[1] via my answering service in New York, but I dare to hope that, now that you've gotten this book off your chest, and now that I, too, have purged myself of vain resentments, distrusts, wounds of ego, Etc., we can remember the old friendship between us, I think the deepest I ever felt however oddly manifested at times, and put aside paranoia in favor of understanding affection and recollection.

Last night a boy next door, one of the crazy, wonderful "Conchs" that make up our social life here, smashed up everything in his house while his mother was out on her night job, caring for a pair of bed-ridden ancient spinsters. Sat on the front porch with a kitchen knife, swinging in the swing and defying neighbors and police to enter or approach. And they respected the warning, just stood outside the fence, in the dark road, whispering, head-shaking, and clucking, till Frank and another wild young Conch that we were entertaining for dinner, went over there and took him to our house. Presently his mother arrived, with cousins, uncles, Etc. Frankie conferred with them outside, on the dark road, and persuaded them to leave the boy with us, which they did, and after four Miltowns and several whiskies, he went quietly home to bed in the totally demolished interior of the house.

That is life for us, baby!

Afterwards Frankie and I made love, and that is life for us, too.

1. When I left for Greece.

309

Do you get the message? Hell, yes, you do, you've been writing it almost as long as I have.

So don't give me anymore of that fond farewell shit via the answering service!

Love,

10.

We met again in Italy the following April. Tennessee was in Rome for a few days with Marion Vaccaro. We sat together on Via Veneto; it was fun to see him surrounded by the paparazzi; but it was a little unreal, as though we were on the set of a Fellini movie. Casually, bringing up the subject himself, he said that I seemed to like Rome so much that I ought to sell one of the manuscripts he had given me of his plays and use the money to live in Rome with. In the fall, when I was briefly back in New York, I decided to act on his suggestion.

·155·
[*Postcard*]
Taormina, Sicily
April 26, 1961

Dear D & S

Aspects of eternity, ice cold water, but very stimulating for the old circulation. Return through Rome in a few days. Will call you and Sandy.

Love –

TENN.

·156·
[1431 Duncan St.,] Key West [Fla.]
Sept. 26, 1961

Dear Donnie:

I'm glad you've decided to move on the MS. sales. If it's true that the original copies of "Streetcar" and "Menagerie"[1]

1. In addition to these, Tennessee had given me the original mss. of "Battle of Angels", "Stairs to the Roof", and of the story from which "Menagerie" came, *Portrait of a Girl in Glass.*

311

are worth what my new lawyer told me, or even anything like it, it would help you to live in Rome while you finish your Italian novel. I think you dig Italy more than any where since Atlanta so you would do well to work there, in my opinion. Also I hope to spend a few months there myself soon after the next play[1] opens.

Would you like me to write out some sort of affidavit as to the authenticity of these first drafts?

While riding my bike to the beach with my hands off the handle-bars and going full speed, I hit a thick palm branch lying across the road and suffered a slight concussion, as well as many abrasions. Came to struggling for breath and people were clustered about me, jabbering excitedly. Call an ambulance. Pick him up, put him in my car, I'll take him to the hospital. All I could do was wave my hand in a gesture of rejection of these proposals. I finally caught my breath, got back on the bike and rode on out to my swim, but I think I was in a state of shock which I am just coming out of completely.

Frank came back today which is a big relief, I don't seem to function very well on my own.

Jamaica has the finest summer climate I've found in this hemisphere. Hot, dry days with almost constant trade winds and such chilly nights you need a blanket. Fabulous swimming at Ocho Rios. Marion and I stayed at the Silver Seas Hotel there. I hope to go back while the play is doing part of its break-in run in Chicago. That is, unless we are in such trouble I have to stay on hand.

"Cousin" went back to Savannah. I took him to the Reverend Sidney Lanier's office one morning and told the Reverend that, as he very well knew, I lived a Bohemian life in a Bohemian world and I didn't think that either I or my life was a good influence for this innocent "cousin". Just

1. "The Night of the Iguana".

before I left for Jamaica I heard he was on his way back to New York, but this news did not delay my departure, although he did have some moments of considerable charm.

I'll be back in New York about the end of the first week in October and will get in touch.

Love,

TENN.

.157.[1]

Chicago [Ill.]

Nov. 29, '61

Dear Don:

Sandy called me yesterday about the affidavit of the "Menagerie" Ms. and I have accordingly made out the enclosed. Along with the letter from Key West, it should fully establish your right to sell the Ms. I am mailing it to you in Rome as I failed to get your New York address from Sandy.

How I envy your being in Rome, even though it is winter! Give my regards to the Via Veneto, say hello to Trastevere, and tell all the boys in the Villa Borghese that I'll be back ere long!

WRITE ME! SUBITO! 124 E. 65th till Xmas. Then I cut out for somewhere.[2]

Love,

TENN.

1. To Rome, where I had returned.

2. Unfortunately, even this friendly gesture turned out badly. Tennessee hadn't told me that it was legally necessary for one of his manuscripts to be sold in order to establish a market price, so his lawyer could deduct from his income taxes the value of the papers he was giving to the University of Texas. The manuscript of "The Glass Menagerie", auctioned at Parke-Bernet, the best way I knew to sell it, went for $6,000 – considerably less than the $10,000 he expected – and I was soon hearing that I had sold it the wrong way and cost him a great deal of money.

313

*I had more or less given up writing Tennessee. Both these letters
are responses to his having been sent a book by my publisher.*

.158.

Silver Seas Hotel, Ocho Rios, Jamaica
January [13,] 1964

Dear Donnie:

Scribner's sent me a copy of your new collection of stories[1]
and I'm reading them down here where I've gone to recover
as best I can from my latest professional disaster.[2] The place
is dull, God knows, but the faggot in charge of entertainment
has finally stopped bugging me to play games and take trips
and socialize with the guests. I creep about as privately as
one of the lizards of which there are an infinite number.
In the pamphlet for new guests there is a reference to them
that says, Don't kill the lizards, they are friends of man.

The stories have a marvelous delicacy and control, never
splash over, they make me think of Picasso's finest line-draw-
ings. I divide my time between swimming and reading your
book.[3]

I was hurt that you never called or wrote me a note when
Frank died last September. I was sure you knew that next

1. "Emblems of Conduct".

2. The second Broadway production of "The Milk Train Doesn't Stop Here
Anymore", with Tallulah Bankhead.

3. He is trying to please but, in his difficulties, seems unaware of my book.
Its unmentioned title is the title of one of his favorite Crane poems, from
which he took "Summer and Smoke", and it is not stories but autobiography.
Yet there is no doubt that he is writing, particularly in his version of "Don't
kill the lizards" in the next paragraph, with the hope of hearing me refute
his transferred self-judgement, which I am afraid I did not do.

to my work, Frankie was my life. We were very close to each other the last nine months of his life, closer than we'd been any period in the last five years together. I think that his illness had been coming on much longer than the fool doctor in Key West knew. It showed itself mostly in his attitude toward me, which became so humiliating, at last, that I had to cut out. We immediately came together again when I learned of his hopeless illness. Well, I suppose you feel that I'm someone who cares for no one. What awful mistakes we make about each other in this crazy life!

I am here trying to figure out my next move. So far all I have figured out about it is that it will probably be alone, and to some place on the sea, probably Athens or Rhodes, as soon as the Aegean sea starts to warm up a bit. Not much. I love cool water.

Are you and Sandy coming abroad? I would love to see you somewhere outside the mad-house of Manhattan.

Love,

10.

Good luck with yr. book!
Don't remember yr. address.
[*Sent c/o Scribner's*]

·159·

145 West 55th Street, [New York, N. Y.]

2/5/65

Dear Donnie:

Coward-McCann called to ask me if they could send me a copy of your new novel[1] and of course I was delighted to get it. I've finished it, now, and I agree with the publisher that it's your best book. It made me terribly home-sick for

1. "Two People".

Rome and I've just about made up my mind to go back there as soon as possible, and stay there. I think you must be the first "white anglo-saxon protestant" who has ever understood the Italian (and Sicilian) nature and portrayed it so authentically in a novel.

I am caught right now in a very strange and nerve-wracking professional situation. I have two short plays that are supposed to go into rehearsal on Monday next. Everything is ready, director, cast, designer, costumer, composer, but the producer, Bowden, has not yet raised the money. The dilemma is very hard on my nerves, which were already close to the point of collapse. Almost any solution seems better than the present suspense.[1]

As soon as I'm off this hook, I'll call you.

Last night was a fantastic occasion. Edward Albee had invited me to a late supper he was giving for a group of Russians in the theatre. I had decided not to go, didn't feel up to it, so I went out to dinner with my cousin Jim, both of us wearing tie-less sport-shirts. After dinner which included several martinis, Jim persuaded me to go to the party. It was in the Village so I didn't imagine our informal appearance would matter, but Albee's house turned out to be very grand and everyone was very meticulously dressed. Of course after a few drinks I didn't mind so much. The Russians were expected after the play ("Tiny Alice") but they didn't show and it was finally announced that they had all caught colds and gone home to bed. And all that caviar . . . The cold war dropped several degrees below zero.

Love,

10.

---

1. "Gnädiges Fräulein" and "The Mutilated". Charles Bowden presented them a year later under the title "Slapstick Tragedy".

Several times in the late sixties, I wrote Tennessee, asking for help on some autobiographical pieces about my early days in New York. He didn't answer. I heard, however, from the inevitable mutual acquaintances, that he said I wrote him only when I wanted something. The accusation was now true. But I wrote once more, saying that if he felt that way I would not write again. I was sure this would bring forth a response of some kind. It didn't. And our correspondence ended.

Epilogue

"Here I sit alone this chilly September morning, with the rain just beginning to rattle on the roof, and the writing of his name has sent my heart back to the happy hopeful past when one was capable of everything because one had not yet tried anything. The years have taught me some sharp and some sweet lessons – none wiser than this, to keep the old friends. Every year adds its value to a friendship as to a tree, with no effort and no merit of ours. The lichens upon the bark, which the dandyfiers of Nature would scrape away, even the dead limbs here and there, are dear and sacred to us. Every year adds its compound interest of association and enlarges the circle of shelter and of shade. It is good to plant them early, for we have not the faith to do it when we are old. I write it sadly and with tears in my eyes. Later friends drink our lees, but the old ones drank the clear wine at the brim of our cups. Who knew us when we were witty? who when we were wise? who when we were *green*?"

J. R. Lowell

APPENDIX

I

From my journal, December 28, 1955: "In Sartre's book on Baudelaire, he says that Baudelaire did not challenge good, he did not transcend it, he simply found it unsatisfying. The possibility of another world with other standards, which lay behind the world he knew, didn't exist for him. But by accepting his non-satisfaction and dreaming of impossible escapes, he asserted his supreme value. There was no solution and he didn't seek one; he simply became intoxicated by the certainty that he was worth more than the infinite world because he was dissatisfied with it. Everything that was had to be. Man dreamt of the unattainable and the contradictory. Those were his claims to nobility.

"Does a similar attitude explain Tennessee's appearance of complacency and self-satisfaction that I cannot reconcile with everything else? Certainly 'Camino Real' seems an examination of Baudelaire's viewpoint and the conclusion that only poets and madmen and the pure of heart can escape – but perhaps Tennessee does not include himself in any of these categories now. Anyway, 'Cat' says: 'You can be young without money but you cannot be old without it.' It is also pertinent that of the three characters who escape, or at least attempt to escape in 'Camino', only one is a character portrayed in the play; only Kilroy; the two other merely enter, make a speech, and go off. Kilroy is Tennessee as he was, but as I do not think he believes himself capable of being any longer. Still, he is a sympathetic character, caught in a trap of circumstances, and not unpleasant, as are all the characters in 'Cat', who seem to suffer from their own defects rather than from fate, which is the opposite of classic tragedy, toward which Tony says Tennessee's work is moving in

'Cat' with its continuous action and single setting. Kilroy's character and the best scenes of 'Camino' were written, however, before 1948, before 'Roman Spring' or even 'Rose Tattoo'. The earlier plays were always about sympathetic characters caught in inescapable situations, all three in 'Menagerie', in 'Streetcar', in 'Summer', and more or less in 'Tattoo'. Is it my prejudice that sees nothing sympathetic enough in the characters in 'Cat' to give them dimension and perspective? Isn't it true that each one is trapped only in his own character, not in a dramatic situation, and that except for the scene between the father and son in the second act the situation is described rather than dramatized, the dramatic elements dragged in through clichés which bring to mind other plays rather than life? In rewriting, all the unpleasant characters in 'Camino' were enlarged and yet not made understandable: this world with its standards is the only one that exists. The few extravagant exceptions, the few martyrs, are gone in 'Cat'. Or is Big Daddy, or Brick, or Maggie one and I do not see it? I no longer trust my objective judgement. I think that I want to see the opposite of what I see and that the facts are overwhelmingly against my desire. But perhaps I desire to see what I see and cannot face *that* fact, and the truth of the play escapes me.

"Brick complains of mendacity, of lies ruining his life. But when lies have produced events that harm you, it is the events that you hate and complain of, not the lies of other people. Tennessee suffers from believing that he has done wrong and benefited by it; the guilt he feels is for his actions, not their results, which he could have accepted happily if they had come about by other means. It is because he cannot face his own actions that he denounces lying and mendacity in others. He has to blame the world (as Brick does), and present it as a place in which you cannot live without money (as Maggie does), in order to cancel his guilt and to prove that he is worth, if not more, at least not less than the infinite world. His portrait of Brick is a distorted act of self-justification. Mendacity is offered as the theme of the play; but when the story comes out, it is not lying, by himself or anyone else, that is destroying Brick; it is his refusal to face what he has done. Tennessee has used circumstantial and narrative explanations to twist the simple facts, which could have been dramatized. Yet he knows! The truth does come out in the play – in one single speech by Big Daddy to Brick at the end of the second act. It might even truthfully be said to be the point of the play; but the presentation has been distorted to conceal it. Mendacity is not what upsets Tennessee; it is a smokescreen. The red herrings and the artificial fireworks of the staging darken everything which should be light, obscure everything which should be clear. Yet I still cannot be sure that my impression is anything but prejudice.

"Up until 'Camino', Tennessee's work (and life?) seems to me self-dramatization. From 'Camino' on, it seems self-justification. The change occurs between the two versions of 'Camino'."

II

From my journal, November 3, 1958: "Last night's performance of Molière's 'Don Juan' made me think that the Don Juans of our time are the Don Juans of friendship rather than of love, people who, like Tennessee, find their flattering mirrors in companions of enthusiasm rather than of the bed. For the triumphs of friendship are rarer now than those of sex – the difficult goal to obtain is now the mind (and heart?), not the body. And in Vilar's performance it was made clear that it is for the reassuring view of himself, which he sees in them while he is winning them, and which the relinquishing of their virtue is the utmost test of, that inspires Don Juan's physical conquests, not any desirability of the bodies themselves. Molière points this out in the other actions by which he shows Don Juan striving to see himself thought well of, in his otherwise inexplicable hastening to the defense of Don Carlos, in his finally giving the louis d'or to the poor man. And the problems which today meet these people who tell others what the others want to hear, rather than what they think, are the same. Their method, like Don Juan's, requires the aid of a 'servant' who has no illusions but who sticks it out for his 'wages'. It requires an outlet of contempt and rudeness to old and unavoidable connections, and to dropped 'lovers' like Dona Elvira. It also ends, inevitably, with calculated hypocrisy when the accumulation of disillusioned lovers becomes too large for their unflattering reflections any longer to be successfully avoided. Just as Don Juan decides that he will no longer admit his true feelings with new conquests, as he has with the old when he was caught out, but will continue to dissimulate and lay to admirable reasons his changed attitude, so these affable people finally decide to pretend and rely upon their own avowed emotions (rather than those believed in by others) for their good opinions of themselves. And if this parallel holds good, then alcohol, drugs, and insanity are the Commander's statue that at last drags them away from a world where there is no longer any chance of their avoiding what they cannot bear to see, where it is no longer possible for them to believe, without support, in their own desired image of themselves. For it is with an admirable desire to be better than possible that this deception begins, a desire not to hurt others, which loses its virtue only when the desire not to hurt becomes the desire *not to witness pain*, not to be present when the blow falls, the desire, as Baudelaire puts it, to be generous at a bargain – which makes them blind to the fact that although insincere praise to those who do not need it may be harmless, to those who do it is a counterfeit coin given to a hungry man, to put off his despair while he is in their sight, regardless of how much greater that despair will be when, having dropped his guard, he finds himself humiliated and denounced as he tries to buy food."

INDEX

References are to pages. Where a reference occurs only in the footnote, the page number is followed by an n.

Melton, Sara (Sally), 26, 30, 36n, 38, 40, 55, 204, 268n
Melville, Herman, 138, 184n, 185, 186
"Member of the Wedding, The" (McCullers), 247
"Memoirs" (Williams) XIV, XV, 32n, 33n, 88n, 171n, 184n, 190
Merlo, Frank, XIII, 226, 228, 229, 231, 232, 233, 234, 235, 236, 238, 239, 240, 241, 242, 243, 244, 246, 249, 250, 252, 259, 263, 268, 269, 272, 278, 279, 280, 281, 282, 288n, 289, 292n, 294n, 296, 306, 308, 309, 312, 314, 315
Merrick, David, 35
Metro-Goldwyn-Mayer, 62, 65, 66, 69, 70, 71, 72, 73, 74, 75, 76, 78, 79, 81, 82, 83, 85, 89, 91, 94, 97, 99, 106, 109
Metropolitan Museum, 133
"Mexican Mural" (Naya), 3n, 52n
Michelangelo, 207, 215
Mielziner, Jo, 164, 175, 208
"Milk Train Doesn't Stop Here Anymore, The" (Williams), 314
Millay, Edna St. Vincent, 144
Miller, Arthur, 232, 258
Miller, Henry, 123, 136
Mills, Carley, 27, 29, 33, 36, 42, 49
Mills, Clark, 61
"Miracle of the Rose" (Genet), 233
Miranda, Carmen, 179
Mitchell, Thomas, 81
"Moby Dick" (Melville), 25, 144
Moctezuma, 18
Molière, 321, 322
Monogram Pictures, 116
Monroe, Marilyn, 292n
"Moony's Kid Don't Cry" (Williams), 16n
Moor, Paul, 144, 149
Moore, Marianne, 144
Moorehead, Agnes, 101
Morgan, Henry, 101
"Morning Star, The" (Emlyn Williams), 51
Movie Called "La Terra Trema", A (Williams), 209

"Mrs. Miniver" (film), 51
Munsell, Warren, 179
Murder Inc., 164n
Museum of Modern Art, 85, 138
"Mutilated, The" (Williams), 316
Myers, John, 293n
"My Life" (Chekhov), 130

Nathan, George Jean, 154, 226
National Institute of Arts and Letters, 133
Naya, Ramon, 3n, 52n, 162
Neblett, Walter, 32, 40
New Amsterdam Roof, 192n
New Directions, 55, 77
"New Directions Anthology 10", 199n, 295
New Dominoes (Windham), 130
New School for Social Research, 3, 24, 27n, 29, 121
New Yorker, The, 35, 110, 293
Nicholson, Johnny, 283
Nicholson, Kenyon, 22
Night (Windham), 110, 115, 116, 119
"Night of the Iguana, The" (Williams), 312
Nijinsky, Waslaw, 134n
Nims, John Frederick, 163
Novarro, Ramon, 75

Obolensky, Serge, 264
O'Brien, Margaret, 85
"Oklahoma!" (Rodgers & Hammerstein), 103
"Old Ladies, The" (Ackland), 137, 151
Old Vic, 241
Olivier, Laurence, 239, 240, 241
One Arm, (Williams), 27, 175, 176
"Only the Heart" (Foote), 82, 83, 167
"Orpheus Descending" (Williams), 19n, 293, 295, 296
"Ox-Bow Incident, The" (film), 91, 101

Pale Horse, Pale Rider (Porter), 36
Paramount Pictures, 65, 67

Smith, Tony (Tone), 103, 104, 123, 192n, 198n, 205, 226, 242, 246, 250, 251, 253, 290, 319
"Southern Exposure" (Crump), 250n
"Spinning Song, The" (Williams), 109
"Stairs to the Roof" (Williams), 16, 35, 61, 311n
Stapleton, Maureen, 296
"Starless Air, The" (Windham play), 273, 274, 275, 276, 277, 278, 279, 280, 281, 282, 283, 284, 285, 286, 287, 288, 289
Starless Air, The (Windham story), 195, 196, 197, 198
Stein, Gertrude, 144
Steinbeck, John, 282
Stevens, Ashton, 163
Stevens, Onslow, 112
Stewart, David J., 290
Stewart, Marianne, 174n
"Strangest Kind of Romance, The" (Williams), 144n
"Streetcar Named Desire, A" (Williams), 184, 192, 198, 201, 203n, 205, 229, 240, 249, 256, 263, 267, 306, 311, 320
Strindberg, August, 283
"Suddenly Last Summer" (Williams), 294
"Summer and Smoke" (Williams), 131n, 171n, 202, 208, 211, 221, 225, 230, 234, 235, 249, 294n, 306, 314n, 320
"Summer Belvedere, The" (Williams), 68n
"Sun Is My Undoing, The" (Steen), 62, 65
Sur, 127
"Sweet Bird of Youth" (Williams), 296, 299, 300

Taglioni, Maria, 146n
Tandy, Jessica, 203, 240n, 253
Tarkington, Booth, 81, 86
Taylor, Laurette, 154, 155, 156, 157, 159, 160, 161, 163, 164
Tchelitchew, Pavel, 85n, 140, 143, 150

"Tempest, The", 162
Temple, Shirley, 85
"Ten Blocks on the Camino Real" (Williams), 184, 189
Tennant, H. M., 220
Theatre Arts, 192n
Theatre Guild, 4, 13, 15n, 21, 22, 24, 41, 50, 169, 273, 278, 289
Thery, Jacques, 83, 86
"This Gun for Hire" (film), 30
"This Property Is Condemned" (Williams), 16n, 27n
Thompson, Helen, 167
Thompson, Howard, 246n
Tiffany's, 158, 223, 295n
Time, 301
"Time of Your Life, The" (Saroyan), 12n
Times, New York, 8, 15n, 35, 143, 169, 213, 246n, 258, 288n, 290
"Tiny Alice" (Albee), 316
To Europe (Capote), 224n
Togliatti, Palmiro, 223
Truman, Harry S., 214, 238
Turner, Charles, 293n
Turner, Lana, 63, 65, 66, 67, 68, 69, 72, 73, 77, 82
"27 Wagons Full of Cotton" (Williams), 144n, 182
"Two People" (Windham), 312, 315
Tyler, Parker, 140
Tynan, Kenneth, 190, 298, 300, 301
Tyner, Don, 32
"Un bel dì", 75
"Uncle Vanya" (Chekhov), 84
United States Engineer Office (War Dep't), 44, 47, 52
University of Tennessee, 172
University of Texas, 99n, 250n, 313n

Vaccaro, Marion, 19n, 311, 312
Valentine, Sherman, 135, 140, 144
Vanderbilt, Gloria, 245
Van Eyck, Peter, 89, 93, 94, 95, 96, 111
Van Gogh, Vincent, 62
Van Vechten, Carl, 292n
Vázques, Pepe Luis, 174n

1. The exclamation point was added to the title of "You Touched Me" before the Broadway production but was never used by Tennessee and me.